Gender,
Families,
and Close
Relationships

CURRENT ISSUES IN THE FAMILY SERIES

Series Editor
Timothy H. Brubaker, *Miami University*

The pace of change in contemporary society has had an enormous impact on the workings of its most important institution, the family. This series of volumes explores the various dimensions of societal change and how the family is changing with them. Each edited volume contains the latest theory and research from leading scholars in the family field on a topic of contemporary concern. Special attention is paid to the impact of this research on the work being done by family therapists, family life educators, and family policymakers.

Volumes in this Series

Other series volumes are in preparation.

Gender, Families, and Close Relationships

Feminist Research Journeys

EDITED BY

Donna L. Sollie
Leigh A. Leslie

2 Current
Issues
in
the
volume **Family**

SAGE Publications

International Educational and Professional Publisher
Thousand Oaks   London   New Delhi

Copyright ©1994 by Sage Publications, Inc.

For information address:

SAGE Publications, Inc.
2455 Teller Road
Thousand Oaks, California 91320

SAGE Publications Ltd.
6 Bonhill Street
London EC2A 4PU
United Kingdom

SAGE Publications India Pvt. Ltd.
M-32 Market
Greater Kailash I
New Delhi 110 048 India

Printed in the United States of America

Library of Congress Cataloging-in-Publication Data

Gender, families, and close relationships: feminist research
    journeys / edited by Donna L. Sollie, Leigh A. Leslie.
        p.   cm. — (Current issues in the family; v. 2)
    Includes bibliographical references and index.
    ISBN 0-8039-5207-4 (cloth). — ISBN 0-8039-5208-2 (pbk.)
    1. Family.   2. Interpersonal relations.   3. Feminist theory.
  I. Sollie, Donna L.   II. Leslie, Leigh A.   III. Series.
  HQ518.F45   1994
  306.85—dc20   94-17098

FTW
AHR9634

94 95 96 97 98 10 9 8 7 6 5 4 3 2 1

Sage Production Editor: Diana E. Axelsen

Contents

To our sons, Ethan and Evan

Acknowledgments

Through working together on this project, we truly have lived the meaning of the word *cooperation*. The ease with which we worked together during the last 3 years and shifted the load as needed to be responsive to the demands in each of our lives was a rare experience. It is unfortunate that there is required to be a first and second author designation because this has been a collaborative effort in every sense of the word. Therefore, we determined the ordering of the names by the flip of a coin.

Despite our rewarding working relationship, the two of us never could have produced this book alone. It is a result of the efforts of many people. Certainly we are appreciative to the contributors for their fine work. The contributions of others, however, are less obvious. A special thanks goes to Trish Barnes, at Auburn University, for her administrative assistance throughout the project; her attention to details made everything run smoothly. We want to thank Mitch Allen, at Sage Publications, for his support of the project and for his guidance through the various stages of book production. Thanks also go to Diana Axelsen and Linda Poderski for their fine editorial work. Very special thanks go to our husbands, Chuck Hill and Fred Curdts, whose support has nourished us for many years.

We also would like to acknowledge the important role of two groups in our lives. The Feminism and Family Studies Section of the National Council on Family Relations has provided us a professional home in which to integrate our discipline and our feminism. The friends and colleagues from that section have greatly enriched our professional and personal lives. Finally, a debt of gratitude goes to our students—past, present, and future—who challenge us and accompany us on the journey.

Foreword

I am honored to write the foreword for this book about feminist research on families and other close relationships. The authors weave together discussion of feminism as social commitment, their personal voices as researchers, the tension between the discipline of family studies and feminism, and research process as feminist practice. This unique book brings these themes together and at long last, provides a context for feminist research and, for many of us, a sense of "coming home."

The chapters in this book tell stories of lives and of work in progress. For the authors, both feminism and scholarship are lifelong journeys. All of the authors revise themselves, their feminism, and their research as they go along. The intermingling of commitment, incompleteness, and change makes me feel free. The notion fills me with hope for myself, for my work, and for feminism. I can feel the authors grow stronger as they tell their stories, rethink past work, and move on to the future. As I read the chapter, the authors' accomplishments made me smile. I have known some of the authors for many years. Others are new friends and colleagues; and there are a few whom I do not know but dearly wish I did. When I am discouraged, I will read a chapter or two of this book. The authors give me courage to commit myself anew.

As a reader, I felt liberated by the lessons in this book. Lesson 1: There are many sources of knowledge. The authors talk about research and scholarship as sources of knowledge, but they also talk about novels, news-papers, students, activists, clinicians, family members, and each other as sources of knowledge. Lesson 2: There is no dogma that we have to fol-low to justify our feminism. Every feminist can start where she—or he—is. The chapters abound with stories of generous-spirited, caring col-leagues who make feminist practice possible. We need to help each other grow, not criticize one another for not being far enough along. Lesson 3: It is dangerous to expect too much of ourselves. Many of the authors note that as hard as we try, it is not possible to live up to the all of the ideals of feminism. It may not be possible, for example, to attend to all diversity, to combat every form of domination, to sustain a truly collaborative re-search team, and to preserve the full subjectivity of our participants. We must not be discouraged. Feminism should free us, not constrain us.

Readers can learn much from this book. There is something here for everyone—scholarly ideas, practical considerations, and heartfelt emo-tions. The authors provide an inviting overview of how feminism has enriched the study of families and close relationships. The ideas set off fireworks in the reader's mind. The authors also chronicle their everyday struggles and successes as academicians and researchers. This knowledge is often hidden from others—details about the demands, doubts, dilem-mas, decisions, compromises, and accomplishments that clutter our days as we go about our work. Both feminists and nonfeminists will learn about research process, as an everyday and lifelong endeavor, from the chapters in this book. Finally, the authors tell passionate and powerful stories of how they came to feminism and how feminism informs their work. Each author's voice comes through strong and clear.

All of the authors in this book were trained, as I was, to be conventional researchers in traditional disciplines. We want to remain part of those disciplines while also doing the feminist work we feel passionate about. Part of learning from each other's practice of research is learning to man-age this tension and to work collectively to ensure that our discipline makes a place for us and for our work. This book signifies the coming-of-age of feminism in family studies. Read and savor it.

—Linda Thompson

1

Why a Book on
Feminist Relationship Research?

LEIGH A. LESLIE
DONNA L. SOLLIE

One of the struggles, and indeed one of the sources of intellectual excite-
ment in women's studies, is the critical dialogue that feminist scholars create within the various traditional disciplines. These dialogues are not
debates between outsiders and insiders; they are, rather, critical confrontations among those who have been educated and trained within particular
disciplines. The feminist debate arises because some of those insiders, who
are women, are outsiders. When women realize that we are simultaneously
immersed in and estranged from both our own particular discipline and the
Western intellectual tradition generally, a personal tension develops that
informs the critical dialogue. This tension, rooted in the contradiction of
women's belonging and not belonging, provides the basis for knowing
deeply and personally that which we criticize. A personally experienced,
culturally based contradiction means that in some fundamental way we as
critics also oppose ourselves, or at least that part of us that continues to
sustain the very basis of our own estrangement. Hence, the personal struggle of being both insider and outsider is not only a source of knowledge
and insight, but also a source of self-criticism.

Westkott, 1979, p. 422

With these words from her oft-cited feminist critique of social science,
Marcia Westkott eloquently captures the tension that motivated us
(Donna Sollie and Leigh Leslie) to compile this book. We have felt, and

1

continue to feel, a strong identification with our discipline of family studies, and we believe in the importance and relevance of the substantive areas addressed by the field. Yet as feminists, we have been frustrated as we have seen women's experiences in families and relationships ignored or pathologized in some of the research generated in our field. We have felt hampered by research dicta that seem to put a premium on uncontaminated data but that lose sight of the respondent and the researcher as people. Yet we remain insiders. But we are engaged in a struggle to find a way to let our position as both insiders and outsiders inform our work.

Our struggle, like the struggle of many of our friends and colleagues, often takes the form of questions. Just what does it mean to be a feminist researcher studying relationships and families? How should our commitment to improve the status of women shape our empirical work? Can one be both a feminist and an empiricist? Must we discard all of the lessons learned as graduate students and beginning scholars and start over? Are there guidelines or models that would facilitate our evolution as feminist researchers? And perhaps most dauntingly, what is the ultimate standard by which we can determine whether our work as feminists and family scholars is "good enough"?

Clearly many relationship and family scholars are asking similar questions and, as a result, rethinking and revising their programs of research. Yet no book exists that brings together this feminist-inspired research. Because the work is dispersed throughout numerous sources, it is difficult to ascertain fully the impact of feminist thought on the knowledge currently being generated in the family and close relationships fields. Additionally the publication of much of the work in traditional journal article format makes it difficult to assess how researchers are grappling with the challenges presented by feminist theory. We decided what was needed was a volume that attempts both to exemplify the links being forged between feminist theory and relationship research and to articulate the process by which scholars are building and modifying their programs of research to reflect feminist principles.

This book is intended for all those who are struggling with questions such as ours. Like us, many faculty members in departments of family studies, psychology, sociology, history, communications, and other fields concerned with close relationships were not exposed to the feminist critique of science during their graduate training. Although feminism may have influenced our politics for a long time, many of us are only now learning together how to be feminist scholars. Fortunately many of us also are learning along with our students. The struggle, though different, is just as real for graduate students. Feminism challenges them to question and critique the very disciplines of which they are working so hard to become a part. This book is for all of us. We hope it will provide a glimpse into how scholars are letting the tension in their positions as both insiders and outsiders shape their work. In addition we hope it will illuminate the diversity of feminist scholarship in the area of family and close relationships.

The goal of this book is twofold. First, we want to present the development and current status of the work of several feminist relationship researchers. Second, we want to consider their personal process and struggles as they have attempted to conduct feminist research. Toward this end, we asked contributors to address two major areas in their chapters. Contributors were asked to give an overview of the work in a substantive area, focusing particularly on their own research. In addition, they were asked to provide a reflective view of their own process as they modified and built their programs of research to reflect feminist principles. In keeping with the evolving nature of feminist thought within the study of family and close relationships, these bodies of work differ significantly in areas such as (a) the point at which feminism began to influence the course of the research, (b) the methods used, and (c) the issues or problems raised by attempting to integrate a feminist perspective. Despite these differences, we hope that integrating the histories, values, struggles, and choices of each researcher into the telling of the research story will not only illuminate the impact of feminist thought on current empirical knowledge but also serve as a guide for those attempting to conduct feminist research. Perhaps even more importantly, we hope the addition of this perspective will highlight how inseparable the person of the researcher is from the research process.

Clearly no one book can cover comprehensively all of the major programs of research in family and close relationships being conducted from a feminist perspective. Regrettably, many excellent models of feminist research could not be included. The selection of contributed chapters was based on several criteria. Our first criterion was that the researchers themselves identify their work as being influenced by a feminist perspective. Although this criterion might not meet some of the more stringent standards in the literature for feminist methods, we were delighted to see Shulamit Reinharz (1992) take a similar stance in her recent book *Feminist Methods in Social Research*. She, too, used an inductive approach and identified as "feminist" any research conducted by self-identified feminists and/or found in feminist publications.

The second criterion for selecting authors was that the final combination of contributed chapters reflect both feminist reconsideration of established topics of study in family and close relationships and the evolution of new topics of study growing out of a feminist perspective. For example, although the topics of relationship development and sexuality have long been the focus of research in family studies, the work has had a decidedly masculine and heterosexist bias. Letitia Anne Peplau, in her chapter on women's and men's love relationships, and Kristine Baber, in her chapter on sexuality, revisit these topics, illustrating how their work has been influenced by their recognition of the social construction of gender. On the other hand, wife abuse and division of domestic labor are topics that for many years received little attention by family scholars. The feminist call for study of issues relevant and important to women led to the emergence of research on these topics. Thus chapters such as those by Kersti Yllö on wife abuse and by Maureen Perry-Jenkins on division of labor summarize feminist-inspired work on relatively new topics in the family and close relationships fields.

The third criterion we used for selecting chapters was that the final mix of chapters represent a balance of the diversity of points at which feminism can influence the research process. Some chapters, such as Peplau's and Rosemary Blieszner's, address established programs of research that did not originally employ feminism as a theoretical foundation but that have evolved to incorporate a feminist perspective as the author has grown in her own feminism. Others chapters, such as Katherine Allen's, are reflections through feminist eyes on completed work that initially was not conducted from a feminist perspective. Finally, some of the chapters report on research that was based on a feminist perspective from the inception, such as the work by Beth Emery and Sally Lloyd on women who use violence in heterosexual dating relationships.

As a result of the diversity in both the histories of the programs of research covered in this book and the personal development as feminists of each of the contributors, there is a variety of formats among the chapters. Each contributor approached our questions thoroughly and thoughtfully, yet each integrated the personal and the scholarly in a way appropriate for her or his own story. Beyond presenting the organizing questions, we as editors did not want to impose a blueprint of how the chapter should be structured. The result, we believe, is an exciting medley that allows both scholarship and people to be revealed.

Setting the Foundation:
An Overview of Feminist Methodology

Although the intent of this book is to teach through example, it is possible that many readers will not be familiar with the basic elements of the ongoing discourse on feminist theory and methodology. Thus the purpose of this chapter is to provide an overview of the fundamental tenets of feminist research, particularly as they apply to the study of families and relationships.

The characteristics of feminist scholarship have been, and are being, articulated, debated, and revised both for science in general and for specific diverse disciplines. Fonow and Cook (1991) point out that any examination of feminist discourse and methods will be dynamic and will capture the discourse only at that "moment in time." Thus, although the fullness of this dialectical process is beyond the scope of this chapter, a synthesis of the present discourse suggests at least three critical elements in feminist scholarship (see Cancian, 1992; Cook & Fonow, 1986; Fonow & Cook, 1991). First, gender as a socially constructed variable is a focal point of analysis and empirical work. Second, scholarship is based on a belief that women continue to be devalued and oppressed and, as a result, their experiences have been neglected and/or distorted in science. Third, the scholarship is characterized by an activist orientation that challenges the status quo. Empowering women and other disenfranchised or marginalized groups is at the heart of feminist research.

For our purposes the relevant question is: How does such a perspective influence the empirical methodology used to study families and relationships? In her efforts to answer this question, Thompson (1992) identified the components of research methodology as *agenda, epistemology,* and *ethics.* She then discussed the implications of each of these areas for feminist research methods. Although the lines of demarcation between these three components are not always distinct, we think it is helpful to address the impact of a feminist perspective on research methodology by examining separately each of these components. We will, however, adapt her framework to include a separate discussion of the issue of methods.

Agenda

Agenda refers to the focus of our work—what we choose to study. Although women sometimes have been the object of scientific inquiry, particularly in the family and relationship fields, this work often does not capture women's experience. Instead it frequently has reflected the perspective of the researcher and/or society at large.

A feminist research agenda is concerned with empowering women. Although a focus on empowerment requires corrective action such as challenging sexism in current thinking on women and filling in gaps in our knowledge on women, it also requires research that liberates women and enhances their lives (Thompson, 1992). This requirement often is referred to by feminists as doing research "for" women, as opposed to "on" women (e.g., Allen & Baber, 1992; Stanley & Wise, 1983), and implies study of topics vital to women's lives that give voice to their experience and that provide guidance on changing the status quo. For example, recent work on incest and date rape has not only validated the experience of women who for so long have silently accepted responsibility for the crimes committed against them but has also awakened public awareness to the breadth of the problem. Yllö's work, summarized in this book, also has been in the forefront of efforts to challenge the prevailing ideology around wife abuse and the patriarchy that spawns violence against women. Also in this book, the work of Alexis Walker on caretaking relationships between adult daughters and their elderly mothers and of Perry-Jenkins on division of labor in the home serve a feminist agenda by making public the ignored work that women do for their families.

Epistemology

Perhaps no other question has so captured the attention of feminist scholars as the question of the origin and nature of knowledge (e.g., Gergen, 1988a, 1988b; Harding, 1986, 1987; Stanley, 1990). Feminism challenges the basic tenet/assumption of positivistic science, which is that the research process (including the researcher) is objective and value-free. Hubbard (1988) notes that the discovery of scientific "facts" is not a solitary endeavor that occurs in a vacuum, but instead is a social enterprise. The implicit rules of scientific practice control who is allowed to produce scientific facts, how one gains membership in this group, and what behavior is expected by group members. Thus, she points out, "science is made, by and large, by a self-perpetuating, self-reflexive group" (p. 3) that historically has been upper- and upper-middle-class white Western males (Hubbard, 1988). In this book, Yllö provides an excellent example of how "facts" can only be made by the designated group when she discusses how domestic violence researchers often discount the knowledge of shelter workers as impressionistic and nonscientific.

The composition of the scientific community and of the patriarchal system in which it exists has led to an androcentric bias in science, which previously was thought to be neutral "fact." For example, androcentric science has given us an emphasis on dualities such as public versus private, mind versus body, and reason versus emotion, that constrains what we see as "truth" (Harding, 1986, 1987). In the study of relationships, the influence of this dualistic framework is amply evident in writings on the bifurcated worlds of women and men: one private, characterized by connections and nurturance, the other public, characterized by autonomy and reason.

Further, Gergen (1988a) notes that facts do not exist independently of their producer's linguistic code and that our language favors a male perspective. Examples of this linguistic bias abound in the fields of family studies and close relationships. The prevalence of the term *domestic violence* instead of *wife abuse* makes invisible the gender of the perpetrator and the victim. Likewise the term *demand-withdrawal,* used in communication research, although implying reciprocal interaction, suggests that the cycle begins with the partner who is requesting change, often the woman.

In contrast to this assumed neutrality in research, feminist scholars reject the notion of value-free research and strive to make explicit the values guiding our own work. Quoting Gergen (1988a):

> Rather than deny or deceive oneself or others about value questions, feminist methodologists would interrogate themselves regarding the dominant evaluative dimensions of the project in question. Instead of trying to destroy the influence of values, the feminist social scientist would respect the political and social aims inherent in their work. (p. 49)

With feminism's rejection of an objective truth, a critical epistemological question becomes, What is a feminist stance on the nature of knowledge? Three answers to the question were outlined by Harding in 1986 and have been used and elaborated by feminist scholars (e.g., Allen & Baber, 1992; Hawkesworth, 1989; Riger, 1992) in the ongoing dialogue. These approaches are feminist empiricism, feminist standpoint epistemologies, and feminist postmodernism.

Feminist empiricism maintains that the bias found in knowledge is not inherent in the scientific process. The philosophical foundation of science (knowledge can be gained separately from the characteristics of the knower) and the basic tenets of the practice of science are accepted as sound (Hawkesworth, 1989). Although feminist empiricism acknowledges the androcentric and exclusionary biases and uses of science, corrective efforts are needed to identify and eliminate this bias. As Allen and Baber (1992) point out, such corrective action would require that the context and constraints of any research be acknowledged and that the resulting potential for bias be identified.

Critics of this approach maintain that values are an inherent part of the research process, just as the research process is part of (is structured by and reflects) the larger culture. From the construction of theories to the selection of research problem to the choice of methods, both the values of the culture and the values of the researcher are present (Hubbard, 1988). For example, Clyde Hendrick, a well-known researcher on love, pointed out in 1992 at a meeting of the International Society for the Study of Personal Relationships that the use of sound scientific principles has contributed to the reification of the idea of men's and women's styles of loving, with men being seen as involved in more ludic or "gamelike" styles of loving simply because they fairly consistently score half a point higher on the scale than women. Even with every attempt to be bias-free, the nature of scientific method encourages this bifurcation based on group means, even when the love experiences may vary widely among both men and women.

Feminist standpoint epistemology maintains that what we know depends on the "knower's historical locus and his or her position in the social hierarchy" (Maracek, 1989, p. 372). Thus women's knowledge of the world is different from men's, and even among women, knowledge varies as a function of class, race, age, and countless other characteristics. This approach requires relinquishing the "master theory" belief that one explanatory theory can reflect knowledge of all people (Harding, 1987).

The term *subjugated knowledge* refers to the knowledge or experience of individuals who are not part of the dominant group. This knowledge is considered more nearly complete because members of subordinate groups must be attuned not only to their own experiences and perspectives but also to those of the dominant group if they are to survive (Nielsen, 1990).

The major criticism of this perspective is that, as Riger (1992) puts it, "carried to an extreme this position seems to dissolve science into autobiography" (p. 734). The challenge is to respect diversity yet identify commonalities in the experience of subjugated groups.

Feminist postmodernism is based on the postmodernist assumption that science does not reflect reality, but instead creates it. The relationship between power, gender, and truth is of critical importance in light of the postmodernist claim that position and power allow some to define truth or reality and that the definition of reality then benefits or serves the interests of those in power (Riger, 1992). The challenge is to deconstruct existing knowledge and to identify the values it perpetuates or the ends it serves. For example, the term *family standard of living* implies that all members of a family unit experience similar economic and/or material well-being. Use of this term conceals the fact that in many parts of the world women do not have the same access to food as their husbands or children or that in the United States women, even those who manage the family budget, may have less discretionary income than their husbands. Thus a focus on material inequity within families can be diverted by something as simple as the wording of a concept.

In its place, feminist postmodernism offers a reconstructed knowledge that "places women in the center of the analysis" (Allen & Baber, 1992, p. 5). Attention to the social construction of knowledge, however, leads to a recognition that this knowledge is evolving continuously.

Critics point out that the stance that all truth is constructed reduces quickly to the stance that there is no truth and all knowledge is relative. Harding (1987) cautions that relativism is a "solution to a problem, only from the perspective of the dominating groups" (p. 295). From a feminist perspective, the relativistic stance is problematic because it has the potential to undermine feminism's call to social action on the basis of the "truth" of women's oppression (Allen & Baber, 1992).

One of the struggles evident in almost all of the chapters in this book is the contributor's stance on the epistemological question. Certainly all were trained in an empiricist (nonfeminist) tradition. Although many moved through periods of practicing feminist empiricism, most now seem to employ a standpoint frame of reference, acknowledging that the scientific process cannot be cleansed of values and that their own work is constrained by their experiences and perspective. Still they grapple with the questions raised by postmodernism. For example, Allen basically deconstructs her own earlier work and reconstructs new knowledge by using the original data. She shows the evolving nature of knowledge based on the person she was at that time and the person she is now.

Ethics

Feminists are concerned with the place of the research participant in the research process and with the relationship of researcher to participant.

In an effort to make research nonoppressive, Thompson (1992) points out that the emphasis is on empowering, rather than exploiting, women. This emphasis requires that participants' voices be heard and that they be viewed as collaborators in the discovery of knowledge. This also requires demystifying the scientific process for research participants and minimizing the hierarchical arrangements that make the researcher the expert on interpreting participants' lives.

Although such an ethical stance toward participants is laudable, many feminists have pointed out that it is also extremely difficult to achieve. Acker, Barry, and Esseveld (1983) note that emancipatory intent is not the same as emancipatory outcome and that researchers cannot always control the purposes for which their data will be used. Further, problems arise when efforts to reduce hierarchy themselves become exploitative. Acker and her colleagues (1983) and Stacey (1988) examined this potential in their own work as each attempted to minimize the interpersonal distance from participants. Yet they were left with a realization that these relationships could never be reciprocal and were in danger of being manipulative because the power inherent in the position of the researcher, though it can be minimized, can never be completely eliminated.

Moreover, efforts to give participants a voice and to avoid forcing the researcher's interpretation onto the participants' lives are complicated by values. Engaging participants in a collaborative process of interpretation is a step in the right direction, but Acker and her colleagues (1983) point out the tendency to give priority to the perspectives of those participants who shared their worldview. Ultimately it is the researcher who must provide some framework for understanding the stories and voices of participants. Collaboration and consultation with participants cannot negate the fact that the final responsibility for analysis lies with the researcher (Risman, 1990). Without analytic guidance or interpretation by the researcher, participants and readers alike are left to impose their own explanations or interpretations. Sprague and Zimmerman (1989) remind us that much of this interpretation will not be based on women's perspective, but on the patriarchal ideology that structures current thought for *both* men and women.

Many of the contributors write about this struggle to respect participants' experience and voices but not to abdicate the responsibility for analysis. For example, Stephen Marks, in his chapter on coworker intimacy, considers the ethical implications of a male researcher bringing back into the public domain the conversations of the women in the Relay Assembly Room of the Western Electric Hawthorne plant. Some 60 years ago, when the data in this well-known study were collected, women were not all that pleased at having their daily routine and shared intimacies recorded by male observers.

Methods

Methods refers to the actual empirical procedures used by researchers. As noted previously, feminist scholars have been critical of methods based on an assumption of scientific impartiality and independence of the researcher. In contrast to a positivistic stance, which attempts to deny or minimize the relationship between researcher and participant, feminism encourages the use and development of methods that acknowledge the larger social reality of research. It is important to note here that there are no "feminist methods" in the sense that feminist researchers have developed an entire new genre of research methods (although Reinharz [1992] does identify the development or "rediscovery" of several unique methodological approaches by feminist scholars). However, there are "feminist methods" in the sense that some existing methods of scientific study are more consistent with the tenets of feminist theory.

Flowing from the previous discussion of agenda, ethics, and epistemology, feminist methods have at least two necessary features. First, the interdependence between researcher and research participant is acknowledged and potentially used. This acknowledgment may range from a researcher's recognition of how her own social position affects how she makes sense of her data, to incorporating research participants' involvement in the construction of explanatory analyses. Second, efforts are made to preserve the context of the phenomenon under investigation, be it physical, social, or historical. Decontexualization of phenomena (i.e., experimental design) has been glorified in the social sciences as the finest in research design, yet as Gergen (1988b) points out, "the notion of context-free circumstances [is] .... nonsensical thinking" (p. 49). For example, laboratory studies of husband/wife communication that do not allow for the daily demands on each partner to be considered (e.g., ringing phones, crying children, project deadlines) not only give a distorted picture of how spouses talk to one another but also tend to favor a personal trait (or gender trait) explanation over a social or contextual explanation.

In light of these issues, we do want to address specifically one question in the debate over feminist methods. Unfortunately discussions of appropriate methods frequently degenerate to a question of whether only qualitative methods are "feminist." This reductionist focus is unfortunate because the implications of a feminist perspective are much more complex than simply attending to whether qualitative or quantitative methods are employed.

Qualitative methods—ethnography in particular—have been promoted by some as being inherently more feminist because they minimize the detachment of researcher from participant, enhance appreciation of contextual issues versus imposing dualisms, recognize diversity, and potentially elevate the participant's voice and role in constructing analytic frameworks. However, as both Peplau and Conrad (1989) and Sprague and Zimmerman (1989) point out, any method can be based on sexist assumptions or used for sexist purposes. The critical issues are the theoretical foundation and value system undergirding the work. Increasingly, feminists are recognizing that methods are simply tools and that different tools are appropriate for different problems (e.g., Allen & Baber, 1992). Whereas qualitative methods may diminish objectification and the asymmetrical relationships between researcher and participant (Thompson, 1992), quantitative methods allow for discourse on a more public level (Sprague & Zimmerman, 1989). The key, it seems, is in realizing that no one source of knowledge provides a complete picture. Although one's view of a picture may be constrained by one's method, the entire picture is most likely to be revealed when multiple views or methods are incorporated.

Contributors to this book have all wrestled with the question of appropriate method. Clearly the recognition of the compatibility of qualitative methods with feminist theory and the unique insights offered through such methods have led almost all of the contributors to incorporate some ethnographic methods into their research. Yet most have chosen to continue to use quantitative methods—some because quantitative methods are valuable in illuminating questions in need of further study, some because these methods seem to provide a valuable perspective on a specific topic and, yes, some because these are the types of methods that often must be used for professional survival. Such is the reality—the tension—that Westkott (1979) refers to of being both an insider and an outsider as a feminist researcher.

Final Thoughts

The idea for this book came into being during what seemed like an endless midsummer ride from Oxford to York, England, in a train car without air conditioning. We had just attended the International Conference on Personal Relationships, which was characterized, as usual, by interesting paper presentations on a diversity of topics about close relationships. We left the conference to begin a relaxing tour of England and Scotland, yet even after five days of conference-related activities and discussions, we found that we could not leave the conference behind us in Oxford. We were struck by what we considered to be a major omission on the conference program: the lack of attention to a feminist perspective on close relationships. This gap was all the more obvious because feminist perspectives had become much more visible in the major disciplines of the conference participants, including communications, family studies, psychology, and sociology.

As we talked, we became focused on how a feminist perspective was challenging us to rethink much of what we thought we knew about families and relationships. We talked about our own research and how our increasing feminist awareness was causing us to reevaluate our own work, to question the importance and relevance of research efforts to which we had devoted significant energy in the past. We saw ourselves moving in new and sometimes unfamiliar and controversial directions as researchers and as teachers. We also talked of how exciting it was to have students who were energized by feminism but also of our concern about how vulnerable these students were without the protection of the rank and tenure we enjoyed. If we needed help and guidance in trying to live with the insider/outsider tension, they needed it much more. It became clear to us that we wanted to showcase how feminism was influencing not only the method and focus of research in our disciplines but also how the researchers themselves were struggling with, managing, and sometimes even flourishing in that tension. We arrived in York, wilted from the heat but excited about the prospect of this book.

As we began this process, we were uncertain what the weaving of scholarship and personal journeys would produce. We believed, however, that as feminists we had to recognize the researcher along with the empirical findings. We could not be more pleased with the outcome. We offer sincere thanks to the contributors, who shared not only their research but also themselves. We know it took courage to break with the traditional mode of summarizing one's work in our academic disciplines—for some more than others. Although most contributors have long academic careers and rank that allows them the freedom to reflect openly, others still grapple with the professional costs of challenging the status quo. No matter how much lip service is given to the acceptance of feminist perspectives in academia, those who truly try to integrate their personal and professional selves know a price still may exist for being "a feminist." A caring colleague advised Donna Sollie, one of the editors, to go up for promotion to full professor before this book was published because editing such a volume might be viewed negatively by university administrators.

Almost to the person, each contributor told us this was one of the most exciting and difficult things he or she had ever written. To honestly put oneself in the middle of one's research is a challenge few scholars undertake. We thank you for your struggle, your openness, your investment in this project, and for making this book even more than we envisioned on that long, sweltering train ride.

References

Acker, J., Barry, K., & Esseveld, J. (1983). Objectivity and truth: Problems in doing feminist research. *Women's Studies International Forum, 6*(4), 423-435.

Allen, K. R., & Baber, K. M. (1992). Ethical and epistemological tensions in applying a postmodern perspective to feminist research. *Psychology of Women Quarterly, 16,* 1-15.

Cancian, F. M. (1992). Feminist science: Methodologies that challenge inequality. *Gender & Society, 6*(4), 623-642.

Cook, J. A., & Fonow, M. M. (1986). Knowledge and women's interests: Issues of epistemology and methodology in feminist sociological research. *Sociological Inquiry, 56,* 2-29.

Fonow, M. M., & Cook, J. A. (1991). Back to the future: A look at the second wave of feminist epistemology and methodology. In M. M. Fonow & J. A. Cook (Eds.), *Beyond methodology* (pp. 1-15). Bloomington: Indiana University Press.

Gergen, M. M. (1988a). Building a feminist methodology. *Contemporary Social Psychology, 13*(2), 47-53.

Gergen, M. M. (1988b). *Feminist thought and the structure of knowledge.* New York: New York University Press.

Harding, S. (1986). *The science question in feminism.* Ithaca, NY: Cornell University Press.

Harding, S. (1987). The instability of the analytical categories of feminist theory. In S. Harding & J. F. O'Barr (Eds.), *Sex and scientific inquiry* (pp. 283-302). Chicago: University of Chicago Press.

Hawkesworth, M. E. (1989). Knowers, knowing, known: Feminist theory and claims of truth. *Signs, 14*(3), 533-557.

Hubbard, R. (1988). Some thoughts about the masculinity of the natural sciences. In M. M. Gergen (Ed.), *Feminist thought and the structure of knowledge* (pp. 1-15). New York: New York University Press.

Maracek, J. (1989). Introduction: Theory and method in feminist psychology. *Psychology of Women Quarterly, 13,* 367-377.

Nielsen, J. M. (1990). Introduction. In J. M. Nielsen (Ed.), *Feminist research methods: Exemplary readings in the social sciences* (pp. 1-37). Boulder, CO: Westview.

Peplau, L. A., & Conrad, E. (1989). Beyond nonsexist research: The perils of feminist methods in psychology. *Psychology of Women Quarterly, 13,* 379-400.

Reinharz, S. (1992). *Feminist methods in social research.* New York: Oxford University Press.

Riger, S. (1992). Epistemological debates, feminist voices: Science, social values, and the study of women. *American Psychologist, 47*(6), 730-740.

Risman, B. (1990). *Methodological implications of feminist scholarship.* Paper presented at the Annual Meeting of the National Conference on Family Relations, Seattle.

Sprague, J., & Zimmerman, M. K. (1989, Spring). Quality and quantity: Reconstructing feminist methodology. *The American Sociologist, 20*(1), pp. 71-86.

Stacey, J. (1988). Can there be a feminist ethnography? *Women's Studies International Forum, 11*(1), 21-27.

Stanley, L. (1990). *Feminist praxis: Research, theory, and epistemology in feminist sociology.* London: Routledge.

Stanley, L., & Wise, S. (1983). *Breaking out: Feminist consciousness and feminist research.* London: Routledge & Kegan Paul.

Thompson, L. (1992). Feminist methodology for family studies. *Journal of Marriage and the Family, 54*(1), 3-18.

Westkott, M. (1979). Feminist criticism of the social sciences. *Harvard Educational Review, 49*(4), 422-430.

PART I

Intimacy in Close Relationships

2

Men and Women in Love

LETITIA ANNE PEPLAU

There are two perspectives on love. Lovers focus on the uniqueness of their feelings for each other and on their joy at having found one special person. Researchers trying to understand men and women in love seek common themes and general principles that apply to many relationships. In this chapter I chronicle my efforts, now spanning more than 20 years, to understand some of the many ways that gender affects romantic relationships.

I have approached this topic as a feminist social psychologist. Shulamit Reinharz (1992) aptly characterizes feminist social scientists as working at the intersection of two different worlds, each with its own values and conventions—the world of their discipline and the world of feminist scholarship. For me social psychology has provided a particularly congenial disciplinary home. Social psychologists are trained to look for social influences on human experience and have long valued research on social issues. Both of these emphases are compatible with a feminist perspective on social life. My involvement in the world of feminism has changed over time, as the women's liberation movement of the 1960s led to the rich feminist scholarship of the 1990s.

In 1968 I entered an interdisciplinary doctoral program in social relations at Harvard University to study social psychology. Many talented women were among my cohorts, a very recent change from the long his-

AUTHOR'S NOTE: I am very grateful for thoughtful comments on drafts of this chapter provided by the editors and by Susan Campbell, Susan Cochran, Steve Gordon, Charles Hill, Zick Rubin, Carol Tavris, and Heidi Wayment.

19

tory of discrimination against women in graduate education. In the late 1800s, for instance, a lone woman, Mary Calkins, was permitted to attend graduate psychology courses at Harvard, but only if she sat behind a curtain. Despite such obstacles, Mary completed a doctoral dissertation and in 1905 was elected president of the American Psychological Association. Regardless of her distinguished work, Harvard University denied Mary Calkins a Ph.D. because of her gender (Scarborough & Furumoto, 1987). My own experiences as a graduate student were mercifully different and included financial support from fellowships and intellectual support from progressive male professors in social psychology.

As I began graduate school, the Vietnam War, civil rights struggles at home, and sexual freedom were topics of the day, as was the emerging women's liberation movement. Among my friends, conversations often turned to the latest feminist speaker on campus or to a provocative new book. We were interested in "consciousness raising," which meant looking at our life experiences in new ways. I was part of a generation of middle-class girls who were taught in school to be traditional homemakers. In junior high we learned to cook and sew and spent months on our "Dream Home" report. In high school we were required to take part in the national Betty Crocker "Homemaker of the Future" contest, testing our knowledge about correct wash temperatures and baking techniques. (In fairness I should add that the test also included an essay on a controversial new topic: mothers with paying jobs outside the home.) In college I learned the finer points of pouring afternoon tea as part of Gracious Living and had my posture checked during Freshman Fundamentals, a physical education course for women in which we also learned the proper way to lift vacuum cleaners. But as a graduate student the feminist insight that "the personal is political" urged a reexamination of the meaning of such seemingly mundane activities as washing dishes or shaving legs. Male-female relationships were an important topic for feminist analysis. In *Sexual Politics,* for example, Kate Millett (1970) argued that the ideology of romantic love hides the reality of women's subordination and economic dependence on men. Society, she suggested, uses "love" as a means of emotional manipulation that justifies household drudgery and women's deference to men.

As a graduate teaching associate at Harvard, I had the opportunity to develop an interdisciplinary seminar on sex roles. In 1970 a dozen bright Harvard undergraduates and I spent an exciting year reading and debating all of the materials on gender we could find from anthropology, psychology, and sociology. Because my own education predated the creation of women's studies, I learned alongside my students as we worked together to separate fact from fiction about women's lives and to find useful analytic frameworks. Two years later I was invited to write a chapter on sex roles for an introductory psychology textbook produced by *Psychology Today* (Peplau, 1972). Also during this time, Matina Horner arrived at Harvard as the first woman faculty member in psychology. She already had gained national visibility for her research on women's "fear of success." Matina's presence and her graduate seminar on the psychology of women gave further intellectual legitimacy to the study of women's issues.

My research interest in close relationships developed largely by chance. About the time I began graduate school, a new assistant professor named Zick Rubin was hired at Harvard. Zick was part of a gutsy group of social psychologists who recently had begun to study love and romance. In the early 1960s, Ellen Berscheid, Elaine Hatfield, and others used the creative experimental approaches of the day to study interpersonal attraction (Berscheid, 1992). At the University of Michigan, Zick Rubin (1969) had conducted an innovative doctoral project designed to put love on a 9-point scale—that is, to assess romantic love systematically and to distinguish love from liking. At Harvard, Zick created new courses on interpersonal attraction that piqued my research interest in relationships—a topic that never had been part of my undergraduate training in experimental psychology. When Zick asked me to work with him on a study of dating couples, I readily agreed.

The Boston Couples Study was designed to follow a large sample of dating couples for a 2-year period to learn about the early stages of romantic attraction, the ways relationships develop over time, and the factors that lead some couples to stay together and others to end their relationship. With funding to Zick from the National Science Foundation, the study was to combine use of extensive questionnaires with laboratory experiments and intensive interviews. My involvement in the Boston Couples Study began an unusually congenial and productive collaboration with Zick and a fellow graduate student, Charles T. (Chuck) Hill, that has continued ever since.

For me the Boston Couples Study offered an opportunity to combine my growing interests in women's issues and in close relationships. For all of us the research provided an empirical look at issues of importance in our personal lives: love, power, commitment, and other facets of male-female relationships. At the time we were all in our late 20s, not really so much older than the college students we learned from. And we were all in love: Zick and Chuck were recently married, and I was dating a class-mate. Feminist scholarship was in its infancy, as was the social psychological study of close relationships.

In this chapter I describe the Boston Couples Study in some detail, highlighting findings most pertinent to gender. Then I present subsequent studies of the relationships of lesbians and gay men. Finally I discuss a 15-year follow-up of the participants in the Boston Couples Study. Throughout I consider ways in which feminist values have influenced my work on close relationships.

The Boston Couples Study

When the Boston Couples Study began in 1972, our investigation of gender focused on three broad issues. First, we were interested in comparing systematically the experiences of men and women in dating relationships. At the time, psychological research was being justly criticized for relying on biased samples that underrepresented women. Family studies sometimes showed an opposite tendency, relying on descriptions of marriages provided by wives rather than husbands. We wanted to give equal emphasis to men's and women's experiences in relationships. Jessie Bernard (1972) had argued persuasively that in every male-female relationship there are at least two relationships: "his" and "hers." We were eager to describe both men's and women's experiences. Because relatively little was known about dating couples, we often found ourselves testing the accuracy of cultural stereotypes about men and women in love relationships.

Second, we were interested in contrasting traditional male-female relations with newly emerging patterns. In the 1970s a beginning men's movement (Pleck & Sawyer, 1974) urged men to be more emotionally expressive. Advocates of sexual freedom discussed cohabitation as an alternative to marriage, as well as open marriage and group sex. Young couples were exposed to many contradictory messages about male-female relations, and we wanted to know how they reconciled conventional norms with newer ideas.

Third, we wanted to understand the role of gender ideology in shaping dating relationships. As social psychologists we cast this issue in terms of individual differences in sex role attitudes. Because standardized measures of sex role attitudes were not available at the time, we created our own 10-item Sex-Role Traditionalism Scale (Peplau, Hill, & Rubin,

1993). The measure asked respondents to indicate the extent of their agreement or disagreement with such statements as "When a couple is going somewhere by car, it's better for the man to do most of the driving" and "If both husband and wife work full-time, her career should be just as important as his in determining where the family lives."

The young adults we studied varied considerably in their attitudes. Some endorsed traditional rules for male-female relationships, viewing men as the primary decision makers and breadwinners, and women as the primary homemakers and childrearers. Paul and Peggy were a traditional college couple. Both lived at home with their parents. When they went out, Paul usually picked up Peggy, suggested the evening's activity, and unless he was broke, paid for both of them. "I feel it's my place to pay if I have the money," he explained. Although both had cars, Paul did virtually all of the driving. Both envisioned marriage in traditional terms. After graduation Peggy would teach for a while and then devote herself full-time to raising children. Paul wanted to put off marriage until he had a good job, but he looked forward to starting a family. He hoped his first child would be a boy because he "can't wait to get a baseball glove on my own kid."

Other participants had more egalitarian views, believing that men and women should share equally in all decisions and that women's careers should be just as important as men's. About 15% of women were members of a women's consciousness-raising or discussion group. Ross and Betsy were an egalitarian couple. They lived together and shared expenses as equally as possible. They believed it was essential to divide household chores in a fair and non-sex-typed way. Although they were strongly committed to their relationship, they planned to postpone marriage until they had launched professional careers—he as a microbiologist, and she as a lawyer. They believed that neither his job nor hers should take precedence in decisions about where to live or how to divide homemaking and childrearing.

In the sections that follow, I describe the participants in the Boston Couples Study and present some of our findings about gender issues as they apply to specific features of relationships, including love, self-disclosure, power, sexuality, and intellectual competition.

The Sample

The participants in the Boston Couples Study were members of 231 college-age dating couples. To maximize the potential diversity of the sample, we recruited from four colleges in Boston: a small "elite" private college, a large private university, a Catholic university, and a state college for commuter students. In the spring of 1972, we sent an initial recruiting letter to a random sample of 5,000 sophomores and juniors at these colleges; half were women, and half were men. The demographic background of participants reflected the student composition of Boston colleges at the time. Nearly half (44%) were Catholic, 26% were Protestant, and 25% were Jewish. Virtually all participants (97%) were white. The participants' socioeconomic origins were predominantly middle class, but they spanned the range of this broad category from working-class residents of Somerville and South Boston to affluent suburbanites. When the study began, the modal couple was a 20-year-old sophomore woman and a 21-year-old junior man who had been dating for 8 months. (Further details of sampling procedures and characteristics of the sample can be found in Hill, Rubin, Peplau, & Willard, 1979.)

In the spring of 1972, both members of each couple independently completed identical versions of a 38-page questionnaire about their background, attitudes, and dating relationships. Follow-up questionnaires were administered 6 months, 1 year, and 2 years later. A subset of couples participated in a series of experiments during the summer of 1972, and other couples participated in personal interviews. These repeated contacts with participants plus project newsletters helped foster a sense of identification with the research. Throughout the study we paid our participants for their help, at rates reflecting inflationary trends: $2 per person for the initial 2-hour questionnaire session and somewhat more for subsequent sessions.

Loving and Leaving

In popular lore women often are depicted as the more sentimental gender, the ones more likely to fall in love at first sight and to stick by their partners no matter what. Men are cast as the hard-hearted and rational gender, in control of their emotions and able to fall out of love quickly if a more desirable prospect comes along. Our research found that these cultural stereotypes were not only wrong but opposite to actual sex differences in romantic relationships (Hill, Rubin, & Peplau, 1976; Rubin, Peplau, & Hill, 1981).

Men in our sample scored higher than women on measures of romantic ideology, endorsing such beliefs as that love conquers all and that love overcomes barriers of religion and economics. Men also gave greater importance than did women to "the desire to fall in love" as a reason for entering their current relationship. The woman's feelings toward her boyfriend were better predictors of whether the couple would break up over a 2-year period then were the man's feelings. When a breakup was not mutual, it was more often the woman (51%) than the man (42%) whom both partners identified as the person more interested in ending the relationship. Perhaps our most interesting finding concerned links between who initiated the breakup and the relative involvement of partners in the relationship. The general tendency was for the partner who was least interested in continuing a relationship to initiate the breakup. But in a minority of cases, the more involved person, seeing that the relationship was not working out as hoped, precipitated a breakup. In these asymmetrical situations in which one's own love was not reciprocated, women were more likely than men to relinquish their love and to end the relationship. Finally, former dating partners were more likely to remain friends when the man had initiated the breakup. Women appeared better able than men to put aside feelings of rejection and to redefine their relationship as friendship.

We considered several possible explanations for these patterns. We suggested that women might be more skilled than men at managing their emotions—in this case, their feelings of romantic attraction and of hurt at the ending of a relationship. We also suggested that women's economic dependency on men might play a part. As family sociologist Willard Waller proposed in the 1930s, "There is this difference between men and women in the pattern of bourgeois family life. A man, when he marries, chooses a companion and perhaps a helpmate, but a woman chooses a companion and at the same time a standard of living. It is necessary for a woman to be mercenary" (1938, p. 243).

Self-Disclosure

We believed that young adults in the 1970s were confronted with two contrasting sets of social expectations about self-disclosure (Rubin, Hill, Peplau, & Dunkel-Schetter, 1980). Traditional norms dictated that men should be emotionally restrained and inexpressive, even in their closest love relationships. At the same time, there was an emerging norm of "full disclosure" in intimate relationships—an ethic of openness spawned by the counterculture of the 1960s, the encounter group movement, and new forms of therapy. Joseph Pleck (1976a) proposed that among middle-class Americans the traditional male role was being replaced by a "modern male" role that encouraged intimate disclosure so long as it was confined to a close heterosexual relationship.

We asked our subjects how much they had revealed to each other in 17 different topic areas such as "my religious views" and "my feelings about our sexual relationship." Most couples had engaged in full and equal disclosure. Ross explained that loving Betsy meant that "I'm never going to hide or hold things from you, that you are the person I'm going to be totally open with and I hope will be totally open with me." When disclosure was not equal, however, women usually revealed more. Gwen told us that Gil never talked about his worries concerning finding a job: "I guess he feels that he shouldn't have any worries or that if he doesn't talk about them, they won't be there." Couples such as Gwen and Gil followed the traditional norm of male emotional restraint. The tendency also was for men and women to reveal most about somewhat different topics. Women revealed more than men about their fears and feelings concerning their parents. Men revealed more about their political views and the things about which they were proudest. Sex role attitudes affected boyfriends' disclosure but not girlfriends'. Men with traditional sex role attitudes tended to disclose less than men with egalitarian attitudes, although half of the most traditional men reported full disclosure. Finally, to test a possible power explanation of sex differences in self-disclosure, we examined whether more powerful partners tended to receive more information than they gave in return. We found no support for this prediction.

The Balance of Power

In the early 1970s, young adults were confronted with contrasting ideologies about power. Many had grown up in what they perceived to be father-dominant households. A majority (53%) of our participants said their father had been more influential, 29% said their mother had been more influential, and only 18% said their parents shared equally in power. At the same time, young people also were exposed to newer ideas about equality in relationships. What type of power relationship would our young couples want? Fully 95% of women and 87% of men endorsed an equal-power ideal for their current dating relationship. In actuality, however, only about half of the students believed they had achieved equal power in their dating relationship. When relations were not equal, male dominance was the most common pattern (Peplau, 1979; Peplau, Rubin, & Hill, 1976).

We considered several factors that might tip the balance of power away from equality. First, we found, not surprisingly, that male dominance was more common among sex role traditionalists than among students with egalitarian beliefs. Second, we tested the "principle of least interest," the hypothesis that when one partner is less interested in continuing a relationship, he or she will have relatively more power (Waller, 1938). The possibility that lopsided love can set the stage for power inequality received strong support in our study. Third, drawing on social exchange theory, we found that a person who had more interpersonal assets than the partner tended to have greater influence. For instance, a person who was more physically attractive (as assessed from full-length color photos taken by our research team) than his or her partner tended to have greater say in the relationship.

The impact of women's educational and career goals on power was also of interest. We reasoned that women with high career aspirations would be relatively less dependent on a romantic relationship than other women and so might be better able to achieve power equality. We found that as women's educational plans increased, the likelihood of male dominance decreased significantly. In discussing these results, we emphasized the differing social expectations for men and women about paid employment and advanced education. Because all men are expected to work for pay, their own educational and career aspirations were not related to their degree of involvement in a dating relationship or to the balance of power. In contrast, paid employment for women still was seen as optional. Consequently those women who sought higher education and full-time careers tended to have nontraditional attitudes about sex roles, were somewhat less involved in their dating relationship, and were less likely to report male dominance.

A final issue was whether the balance of power affected the level of satisfaction and closeness in these young couples. We found that egalitarian and male-dominant relationships did not differ on measures of satisfaction, closeness, or breaking up over a 2-year period. Both men and women in relationships perceived as female-dominant, however, reported lower satisfaction.

Sexuality

Traditional sex roles prescribe that men should be the ones to initiate increasing sexual intimacy in dating and that women should set limits on a couple's progress toward intercourse. A study of premarital couples in the 1950s had documented this pattern (Ehrmann, 1959). Would a similar pattern emerge in the much more sexually permissive climate of the 1970s?

We found evidence of the persistence of traditional sexual roles (Peplau, Rubin, & Hill, 1977). When our study began, 42 couples had not had sexual intercourse with each other. Most of the men in these couples wanted to have sex and cited their girlfriend's desire not to have sex as a major reason for their abstinence. In contrast, most women said they were abstaining from intercourse for religious reasons or because it was too early in the relationship; only 11% cited their boyfriend's reluctance to have sex as a reason. Whether a couple eventually had intercourse was more closely linked to the woman's sexual attitudes and prior experience than to the man's. Abstinence was more likely when the woman was Catholic, had traditional sex role attitudes, and was a virgin.

Another indication of female limit-setting was the woman's role in determining the timing of first intercourse in a relationship. Many couples (41% of total sample) had intercourse within the first month after they started dating. Others waited until later. Characteristics of the woman (but not of the man) were significant predictors of when a couple had intercourse. Intercourse occurred later when women were more religious, had more traditional sex role attitudes, and had less previous sexual experience. Despite the sexual permissiveness of many couples, a traditional pattern of male initiation and female limit-setting was apparent. We speculated that the traditional pattern provides a familiar and well-rehearsed script that enables partners to interact comfortably. We suggested that women might be reluctant to violate this script for fear they would be seen by their partner as unfeminine, demanding, or "oversexed."

Intellectual Competition

In an early analysis of the family, sociologist Talcott Parsons (1954) argued that if husbands and wives both had paid jobs, competition for status might weaken the solidarity of their marriage. In 1969, when the administration at Wellesley College considered admitting men to the all-female school, several women students voiced similar concerns: "For many capable girls, a school primarily for women helps solve another big problem: how can a girl maintain her role as a woman when she is in intense academic competition with men, especially if she is excelling?" ("Must Wellesley," 1969, p. 3). For many young people in the 1970s, concerns about the impact of women's careers on dating and marriage were of intense personal interest.

At the time, one popular perspective on women's intellectual achievement was Horner's (1970) concept of fear of success. She proposed that many women are in conflict about intellectual and professional achievement. Success—especially in competitive settings—can be a mixed blessing for women. Although such success brings the attainment of a desired goal, it may also lead to negative outcomes such as social rejection or loss of femininity. As a result some bright women actually may have a motive to "avoid success." To test her ideas, Horner developed a projective measure assessing individual differences in fear of success. Many people found the idea of fear of success persuasive, but I was skeptical. I believed that intrapsychic conflict might be much less important in women's reactions to competition with a boyfriend than conformity to traditional sex role norms. In other words the impact of intellectual competition on women's achievement behavior might be influenced more strongly by individual differences in sex role attitudes than by fear of success.

To examine this issue, 91 couples from the Boston Couples Study participated in a two-part experiment (Peplau, 1976b). Although both partners took part, I focused on women's reactions to intellectual competition with a boyfriend. At a first session each person worked alone on a verbal task (unscrambling such words as KROC and NUDROG). Although the verbal tasks were described as measures of ability, they were strongly influenced by effort or motivation. Women's fear of success also was measured. At a later session partners worked individually on another verbal task in one of two conditions that varied the feedback they would receive. Half of the women were assigned to compete against their boyfriend and told they would learn whether they or their boyfriend did better on the intellectual test. Half were assigned to work cooperatively with their boyfriend as part of a "couple team" and told they would receive only a combined couple score. (In fact, students never received feedback on their performance.)

Our results were clear-cut. Scores on our measure of fear of success were unrelated to women's performance in the competitive achievement conditions. Nor was fear of success generally related to women's sex role attitudes, grades in college, career plans, or characteristics of their dating relationship (Peplau, 1976a). Whether because of conceptual or measurement problems, other researchers also have found the effects of fear of success to be elusive, and the concept is no longer prominent. In contrast, women's sex role attitudes did affect their performance. Women with traditional sex role attitudes did best in the cooperative condition; direct competition against a boyfriend impaired their performance. Egalitarian women showed an opposite pattern. They apparently were spurred by competition to high levels of performance and did less well in the cooperative couple team condition.

One feature of this research was that it involved a collaboration with Joseph Pleck, then a graduate school classmate. While I studied women's reactions to competition with a boyfriend, Joe studied men's reactions to competition with a girlfriend (Pleck, 1976b). Joe believed that men vary in the degree to which they are threatened by women's performance, and he developed a measure of "male threat from female competence." As predicted, Joe found that the men who scored highest on his measure—who were most "threatened by female competence"—appeared motivated to show that they were more skilled than their girlfriend. They also preferred to avoid future competitive interaction with their girlfriend. In contrast, men low in threat performed better in the cooperative condition.

Comments

The Boston Couples Study provided a comprehensive look at the dating relationships of young, middle-class white students in a time of considerable sex role change. The study was conducted at an early stage in the development of feminist scholarship. We used the analytic tools of the time, relying on the language of sex roles and sex role attitudes and such then-popular concepts as fear of success. From the vantage point of more recent feminist analyses of relationships (e.g., Ferree, 1990; Thompson, 1992), the Boston Couples Study looks somewhat old-fashioned. This is, of course, a healthy sign that feminist family studies have made progress in the last 20 years!

Although the Boston Couples Study was not conceived as a feminist project, several feminist themes were evident. We investigated topics consistent with the feminist agenda in social psychology in the 1970s. We sought to subject stereotypes about men's and women's dating experiences to systematic empirical scrutiny. When we identified significant sex differences, we sought explanations not only in the socialization experiences of men and women and in prevailing norms about gender but also in the power relations of the couple and the broader economic context of heterosexual dating and marriage. We studied issues of special relevance to young women in the 1970s, such as intellectual competition with boyfriends, the use of contraceptives (Hill, Peplau, & Rubin, 1983), and living together before marriage (Risman, Hill, Rubin, & Peplau, 1981). We put men and women on an equal footing in the study and sought to understand both "his" and "her" perspectives on their relationship (Hill, Peplau, & Rubin, 1981). We considered diversity among men and women, primarily in terms of adherence to traditional versus egalitarian sex role ideology.

Our work predated feminist discussions of research ethics, but we were deeply concerned about the impact of our research on the young people who participated. In 1976 Zick wrote what may be the first paper to discuss the ethics of couples research, raising questions about the extent to which our inquiries might have had unintended consequences (Rubin & Mitchell, 1976). Ethical issues also arose about the publication of our research. I was invited to write a book chapter about power in dating couples for an edited volume on feminist research (Peplau, 1979). When I submitted the paper—with Zick and Chuck Hill as coauthors—I was informed by the editor that it was not acceptable to have male coauthors for this anthology. Zick and Chuck graciously agreed not to be listed as coauthors, in deference to the importance of publication for me as an untenured assistant professor. In retrospect I think we should have withdrawn the paper, rather than deny the contribution of my male colleagues. More generally, I think there is much value in encouraging men to study gender issues and to embrace feminist perspectives.

From Boston to Los Angeles

After finishing graduate school, I moved to California to begin my first academic job as an assistant professor at UCLA. The job seemed tailor-made for me: UCLA wanted a social psychologist who could teach a course on the psychology of sex differences. What I could not know in advance was that UCLA would turn out to provide me with an unusually stimulating and supportive intellectual community.

Among my new colleagues in social psychology was Harold Kelley, a major contributor to social psychological analyses of personal relationships. I confess that I was not fully aware of the significance of Kelley's work when I accepted the UCLA position. At Harvard we had studied George Homans's work on social exchange, rather than John Thibaut and Harold Kelley's analysis of interdependence. So my first exposure to Kelley's keen intellect and his relentlessly dyadic perspective on relationships came at UCLA. Over the years I had the good fortune to collaborate with him and others on a book, *Close Relationships* (Kelley et al., 1983). I have also benefitted from my involvement with women's studies faculty and programs on campus and, perhaps most of all, from collaborations with many talented and energetic graduate students.

Like many new assistant professors, I was advised by senior colleagues to develop my own identity as a researcher and, in particular, to launch a program of research distinct from the Boston Couples Study. So although continuing to collaborate on the dating couples research, I also struck out in two new directions. One new line of inquiry concerned loneliness, the painful experience people have when their relationships are unsatisfying in some important way (e.g., Peplau & Perlman, 1982). Gender issues did not figure prominently in this work. The second program of research I began in the mid-1970s was an investigation of the intimate relationships of lesbians and gay men.

Relationships of Lesbians and Gay Men

In my large undergraduate course at UCLA, Psychology of Sex Differences, I lectured about research on heterosexual relationships, including the Boston Couples Study. Although heterosexual students found this research interesting, lesbian students expressed disappointment. They questioned why the course contained no information about homosexual relationships and asked what they could read to supplement course materials. I explained that I knew of no empirical research on lesbian relationships. Although I usually take every opportunity to urge students into the library stacks, I actively discouraged these bright-eyed young people from reading the psychological literature on homosexuality, which in the early 1970s consisted largely of biased and unsubstantiated ideas and theories. Instead I urged them to read Rita Mae Brown's fiction or to go to women's music concerts. Undeterred, the students finally proposed that because I was a relationship researcher, I should study lesbian couples. I decided to follow this suggestion.

My willingness to study lesbian and, later, gay male relationships had two main sources. First, as I have emphasized in formal descriptions of this research, I believe that studies of same-sex relationships among friends, lovers, coworkers, and others provide a valuable perspective on the workings of gender in social life. Second and more personally, I wanted to use my professional skills to help in some small way to combat homophobia.

In college and graduate school, I watched as faculty and friends suffered from bigotry. I had only one woman professor at Brown University in the 1960s, a woman I liked and greatly admired. After I graduated, she confided to me about the difficulties of her life as a token woman and a closeted lesbian in a male-dominated environment. She ultimately left teaching. At Harvard, a graduate student friend was grappling with what it meant for her to be lesbian. As a scientist, Ellen wanted to know what research had to say about homosexuality, but she was dismayed by both the lack of research and the biased and flawed nature of virtually all of the studies then available. Some of the most informative materials she found were in newsletters of the Daughters of Bilitis, a lesbian organization that conducted surveys of readers' experiences and that published first-person accounts. When Ellen and I took Matina Horner's graduate seminar, Psychology of Women, we both wrote term papers on homosexuality. At this point I learned about heterosexual privilege. As a heterosexual I felt "safe" writing a paper about lesbians; after all, couldn't researchers study anything of interest? In contrast, Ellen was extremely worried that if faculty learned about her paper, it might jeopardize her academic standing. To allay some of her fears, Ellen turned in the paper with a title ("A Lavender Herring") but without her name so that anyone who happened to see the paper would not associate it with her. To make matters worse, Ellen was also the target of persistent sexual advances from a senior male professor in her program. Ultimately Ellen dropped out of graduate school. I was very troubled by experiences such as these and by the awareness that psychology, the field I had chosen, and the academy, where I hoped to spend my professional life, could be so hostile to lesbians and gay men.

In 1976 I began a series of questionnaire studies of lesbian and gay male relationships. This research differed from the Boston Couples Study in several ways. First, the work was prompted by a request from lesbian students that I use my professional training to help illuminate their life experiences and especially their romantic relationships. Lesbians were involved actively in developing the questionnaire used in our research. Second, unlike for the Boston Couples Study, we did not seek outside funding. At the time, government agencies were advised not to fund "social" research, and we doubted that our project would be looked on with favor. I did, however, receive several years of support from the modest faculty research funds available at UCLA.

Another unconventional aspect of this research was my relationship to the women who participated in our first study. In recruiting volunteers from the Los Angeles community, I sometimes had to overcome justifiable mistrust about psychologists. (Remember that until 1975, the American Psychological Association endorsed the position that homosexuality is a form of mental disorder.) I did my best to convince women that our project, with a focus on relationships, was worthwhile and ultimately might benefit the lesbian community. To this end I met with groups of lesbians at community locations and in homes to discuss the goals of our research and to answer questions. Some women wanted to know why a heterosexual was conducting this study—a question never asked by students in the Boston Couples Study. I urged women who were uncertain about the research to read the questionnaire before volunteering, so that they could see the kinds of issues we were investigating. Much to my relief, the response to the study was usually one of enthusiastic support. After completing questionnaires, many women volunteered to help us recruit other participants.

This research would not have been possible without the collaboration of talented graduate students. In research meetings, we considered not only typical issues about writing questionnaires or analyzing data but also the politics of our work. For instance, we believed it was important to shift the agenda for psychological studies of lesbians away from such traditional topics as etiology and psychopathology and toward the study of intimate relationships. We debated the pros and cons of research designs that explicitly compare lesbian and heterosexual couples and decided that our initial publications should focus exclusively on lesbians. We thought carefully about where to publish our studies; for example, we avoided publishing in sexuality journals because we wanted to emphasize that there is more to lesbian relationships than sex.

Lesbian Relationships

One goal of our research was to counter stereotypes that lesbians have trouble establishing satisfying relationships and end up alone and lonely. We knew these images were false, but we wanted to use the scientific methods of psychology to demonstrate our point. In one study, for instance, Christine Padesky, Mykol Hamilton, and I surveyed 127 lesbians recruited from both UCLA and the larger lesbian community in Los Angeles (Peplau, Padesky, & Hamilton, 1982). The women ranged in age from 18 to 59, with a median age of 26 years. All but two women were white. A majority of women (61%) were currently in a "romantic/sexual relationship" with a woman, and the rest had been in at least one relationship in the past. Current relationships ranged in length from 1 month to 25 years. Consistent with the young age of many participants, the median length of the current relationship was 2.5 years. In response to questions about satisfaction and closeness in their relationship, most women described their relationships in very positive terms. On standardized measures such as Rubin's (1970) Love and Liking scales, most women reported high levels of love and liking for their partner. Although the women in this study were not representative of lesbians in general, they clearly demonstrated that lesbians are capable of establishing happy and enduring love relationships.

In another paper, Mayta Caldwell and I (1984) investigated the balance of power in lesbian relationships. In a sample of 77 lesbians currently in a relationship, a majority of women (61%) said their current relationship was equal in power. We explored two factors that might tip the balance of power away from equality. We found strong support for the principle of least interest—the prediction that when one person is more dependent, involved, or interested in continuing a relationship, that person is at a power disadvantage. We also investigated the impact of personal resources on power. In our sample both income and education were significantly related to imbalances of power, with greater power accruing to the lesbian partner who had more education and earned more money. In this sample of younger women with relatively feminist attitudes, unequal power was associated with lower levels of relationship satisfaction, closeness, and commitment.

Another goal was to find meaningful ways to characterize the diversity of women's experiences in lesbian relationships. Susan Cochran and I chose to study variations in women's values about relationships, and the impact of these values on their relationships. The available literature suggested that two value orientations might be especially important, value dimensions we called attachment and autonomy.

The theme of *attachment* concerns the relative emphasis a woman gives to establishing an emotionally close and relatively secure relationship. Heterosexual women often have been depicted as emphasizing closeness and security in marriage. Social scientists also had characterized lesbians in these terms (e.g., Gagnon & Simon, 1973). Attachment values include wanting to spend a significant amount of time with a partner, wanting a sexually exclusive relationship, and wanting the relationship to last for a long time.

The theme of *autonomy* concerns the extent to which a person values individual pursuits apart from an intimate relationship. Although some people want to immerse themselves entirely in a relationship to the exclusion of outside interests and activities, others prefer to maintain greater personal independence. Abbott and Love (1972) suggested that lesbians, unlike heterosexual women, are not afraid to develop qualities of independence, self-actualization, and strength. Cassell (1977) postulated that women who become lesbians "seek autonomy and independence, and define the self by activity rather than relationships" (p. 75). We suspected that an emphasis on autonomy also might lead women to emphasize equality in a relationship as a way of preserving their independence within the relationship.

To study these issues, we developed separate multi-item scales of Attachment and Autonomy (Peplau, Cochran, Rook, & Padesky, 1978). We found considerable variation in women's values. Some women gave great emphasis to togetherness and exclusivity; others did not. Some women strongly valued having their own friends and interests outside the relationship; others did not. Factor analyses suggested that rather than being opposite ends of a single continuum, attachment and autonomy are best conceptualized as two separate dimensions.

Lesbians who strongly valued attachment were more religious than other women but did not differ in age, education, income, or parental income. They were significantly more likely to endorse a romantic love-conquers-all view of love, had somewhat more traditional sex role attitudes, were less involved in feminist activities, and were less politically radical about lesbian concerns. Women who scored high on attachment reported seeing their current partner more often, feeling greater love and liking for her, and anticipating that the relationship would be long-lived. They expressed greater willingness to move to another city to preserve the relationship and worried less that personal independence would create problems in their relationship.

Lesbians who scored high on autonomy tended to be younger, better educated, and less religious than low scorers. They had a less romantic view of love, had more egalitarian sex role attitudes, and were more involved in feminist activities and in lesbian work collectives, publications, or women's centers. Women who scored high on autonomy were less likely to live with their partner or to see her daily and expressed less willingness to maintain the relationship at the expense of work or education. They were also more likely to have a sexually open (rather than exclusive) relationship. Of considerable importance, however, values of autonomy were not related to any measures of closeness, satisfaction, love, or liking for their partner. Women who valued autonomy were no more likely than women who de-emphasized autonomy to have close and loving relationships.

Gay Men's Relationships

In our first questionnaire study of gay men, a primary goal was to show that gay men can establish successful partnerships (Peplau & Cochran, 1981). We also investigated whether the dimensions of attachment and autonomy would characterize the values of gay men. We recruited a sample of 128 gay men both from UCLA and from the larger gay community in Los Angeles. The men ranged in age from 18 to 65, with a median of 25 years. At the time of the study, 41% of the men reported being in a "romantic/sexual relationship" with a man, and the rest had had at least one relationship in the past. About half of the men currently in a relationship were living with their partner. As in the lesbian samples, gay men reported high levels of closeness and satisfaction in their relationships and strong feelings of love and liking for their partner.

The value dimensions of attachment and autonomy also were identified in this sample of gay men, and considerable variation was found in men's values. Unlike in the lesbian sample, however, only the attachment dimension was related to characteristics of gay men's relationships. Men who scored high on the Attachment Scale were relatively more conservative in their attitudes and behaviors. They believed more strongly in a romantic conception of love and were less likely to frequent gay bars and baths. When high-attachment men first had sex with their current partner, they were more likely to have been friends and knew each other longer than low-attachment men. Men who valued attachment saw their partner more often, reported greater closeness and love, and expressed greater certainty that their relationship would continue in the future. High-attachment men also reported greater sexual satisfaction and were more likely to have a sexually exclusive relationship. In reflecting on past relationships, high-attachment men reported greater distress following breakups than did low-attachment men.

We were puzzled that autonomy values had no discernible impact on gay men's relationships. We speculated that all men in our culture learn that they should maintain an independent life and identity apart from a primary intimate relationship. If men assume that a high degree of independence is expected in love relationships, then individual differences in autonomy values may have little impact on the nature of their relationships (see Cochran & Peplau, 1985, for comparable analyses of heterosexuals).

Another finding from this study was that 54% of the gay men had had sex with someone other than their primary partner during the past 2 months. In 1980 David Blasband and I pursued the question of sexual exclusivity in a study of 40 gay male couples (Blasband & Peplau, 1985). (It is important to emphasize that this work was conducted before public awareness of the current AIDS crisis, which has affected so powerfully the lives of gay men.) In particular we wanted to test a model of the development of gay male relationships proposed by Harry and Lovely (1979). They hypothesized that in gay men's relationships, there is an initial "honeymoon" phase of sexual monogamy. Over time, there is a "transformation of relationships from sexually closed to open ones" (pp. 193-194). They went so far as to suggest that sexual openness may be necessary for the survival of a gay relationship over time.

We found little support for the generality of the two-stage model. Of the 40 couples, only 20% indicated their relationship was initially closed and later became sexually open. The majority of men reported other patterns: 30% said they always had been sexually exclusive, 20% said they always had been sexually open, and the rest showed more complicated patterns. Men's reasons for having an open or closed relationship were diverse. Men in open relationships emphasized the benefits of sexual variety and personal independence. One man wrote, "It gives us both freedom and variety. . . . He is *not* my property nor I, his." Men in closed relationships emphasized their personal beliefs that loving couples should be monogamous and their desire to avoid jealousy. They emphasized the benefits of "peace of mind" and a "sense of security." Men in open versus closed relationships did not differ in their feelings of love and liking for their partner or in their reports of satisfaction and commitment. Both styles of relating could be equally rewarding.

Comparative Studies

We did not initially design our research to compare the relationships of lesbians, gay men, and heterosexuals. Such an approach may seem to take heterosexuals as a "standard" against which all other relationships should be judged, and we rejected this idea. Over time, however, we recognized that comparisons of matched samples might prove especially effective in refuting negative stereotypes. Our approach drew on the pioneering work of Evelyn Hooker (1957), who had used a comparative design to debunk the idea that homosexuals are mentally disturbed. In the 1950s, psycho-therapists were using their clinical impressions of patients to support the view that gay men suffer from poor mental health and/or have distinctive personality patterns. Hooker's research took a more scientific approach, recruiting nonclinical samples of gay and heterosexual men matched on education and other background characteristics. All participants were given the best standardized tests of the day. The results showed no sig-nificant differences in the test scores of the homosexual and heterosex-ual men, nor were trained clinicians able to identify a man's sexual orientation on the basis of his test results. Hooker's study and others that followed ultimately contributed to removing homosexuality from the tax-onomy of mental disorders prepared by the American Psychiatric Asso-ciation.

In our relationship research, Susan Cochran and I selected from the database of our prior studies matched samples of 50 lesbians, 50 gay men, 50 heterosexual women, and 50 heterosexual men—all currently in-volved in a "romantic/sexual relationship" (Peplau & Cochran, 1980). Participants were matched on age, education, ethnicity, and length of re-lationship. Most participants rated their relationship as highly satisfying, and no significant differences were found among the four groups on mea-sures of love, liking, or satisfaction. We also had asked respondents to describe in their own words the "best things" and "worst things" about their relationships. Responses included such comments as "We like each other. We both seem to be getting what we want and need. We have won-derful sex together." and "My partner is too dependent emotionally." Sys-tematic content analyses (Cochran, 1978) found no significant differ-ences in the responses of lesbians, gay men, and heterosexuals—all of whom reported a similar range of joys and problems. To search for more subtle differences between groups than a coding scheme might capture, the "best things" and "worst things" statements were typed on cards in a standard format with information about gender and sexual orientation re-moved. Panels of student judges were asked to sort the cards, separating men from women or heterosexuals from homosexuals. The judges were unable to identify correctly the responses of the four groups.

In another paper, Toni Falbo and I (1980) used this same matched sam-ple to compare the power tactics that lesbians, gay men, and heterosexu-als reported using to influence a romantic partner. We also investigated links between the balance of power in the relationship and the choice of influence strategies. We found that gender affected power tactics but only among heterosexuals. Whereas heterosexual women were more likely to withdraw and express negative emotions to influence a partner, heterosexual men were more likely to use bargaining or reasoning. However, this sex difference did not emerge in comparisons of lesbians and gay men influencing a same-sex partner. We also found evidence that supported a dominance interpretation of the choice of influence tactics. Regardless of gender or sexual orientation, individuals who perceived themselves as relatively more powerful in the relationship tended to use persuasion and bargaining. In contrast, partners low in power tended to use withdrawal and emotion.

Comments

The originality of our lesbian and gay research was primarily in the topic of inquiry. Previously investigators interested in interpersonal attraction and close relationships focused exclusively on heterosexual relationships. Researchers studying homosexuals typically studied gay men and addressed questions of etiology and personal adjustment. Our goal was to introduce new research questions that emphasized the importance of relationships for lesbians and gay men, that could combat negative stereotypes, and that might provide useful information about homosexual partnerships. During the 1980s, research on gay and lesbian relationships increased dramatically, and we now have a much richer picture of life among same-sex couples (see reviews by Kurdek, in press; Peplau, 1991; Peplau & Cochran, 1990). In general, theories about relationships originally developed with heterosexuals in mind, such as interdependence theory, appear to be applicable to lesbian and gay relationships. I am encouraged that we may be able to construct general theories of relationships that are relevant to many types of close relationships. At the same time, as Kurdek (in press) notes, although abstract concepts such as rewards, investments, and alternatives may be useful in understanding all relationships, the specific content of these concepts may differ greatly among lesbians, gay men, and heterosexuals. In addition some psychologists now are suggesting that we may need to develop new paradigms that begin with the experiences of lesbians and gay men, rather than with the experiences of heterosexuals. Thus Laura Brown (1989) asks what it would mean for psychology "if the experiences of being lesbian and/or gay male . . . are taken as core and central to definitions of reality rather than as a special topic tangential to basic understandings of human . . . interaction" (pp. 445-446).

A question raised by research on lesbian and gay relationships concerns who can or should conduct certain types of research. When our studies began, there were advantages to my being a heterosexual studying lesbian relationships. My work could not be immediately discounted as "self-interested" or as designed to serve a "political agenda." In recent years a change has occurred as more researchers who are openly gay and lesbian are electing to study gay and lesbian issues. This is a valuable change, and one that is likely to alter the focus of research—just as increasing numbers of women researchers have changed the research agenda in other areas. Nonetheless I think we all have a stake in asserting that membership in a group is not a necessary criterion for studying that group. There is value in studying relationships from many perspectives. Relationship researchers have found repeatedly that partners can have different views of their relationship and that the couple's perspective may differ from that of an outside observer. I think feminist research benefits from encouraging multiple perspectives or starting points in our analyses.

Relationship research often has implications for public policy, and this is a potentially useful contribution of studies of lesbian and gay couples (Peplau, 1991). For example, legal cases may raise questions about gay and lesbian relationships. In one case a man in a long-term gay relationship was killed by a reckless driver. His surviving partner sued the driver for damages from the grief and psychological distress of losing a spouse-equivalent. The driver's lawyer countered that gay relationships bear little resemblance to heterosexual marriage and that it would be ridiculous to provide such payments. Research about the strength of love and attachment in gay couples is pertinent to reaching a reasonable decision in this case.

Other policy issues concern the implications of psychological research for the education and professional practice of psychotherapists. Combatting homophobia among psychologists is a goal now endorsed by the American Psychological Association (APA). I recently served on an APA task force that investigated possible bias in psychotherapy with lesbian and gay clients. Our task force surveyed a large sample of psychologists to identify ways in which psychotherapists sometimes provide biased and insensitive services to lesbian and gay clients (Garnets, Hancock, Cochran, Goodchilds, & Peplau, 1991). Among the many recommendations we made was the suggestion that therapists receive more adequate education about the nature and diversity of gay and lesbian relationships and consider the potential value of couples' therapy for some gay and lesbian clients.

The Boston Couples Revisited

Recently Chuck Hill and I conducted a 15-year follow-up of the women and men who had participated in the Boston Couples Study. We were eager to see what directions their lives had taken over the years. Our own lives have changed considerably. Zick and Carol Rubin now have two teenage sons, and Zick has added a law degree to his professional credentials. Chuck and Pam Hill also have two teenagers, and Chuck is chair of the Psychology Department at Whittier College. I am approaching my 20th anniversary of teaching at UCLA. My husband, Steve Gordon, is a sociologist who has written about love and other emotions. Our collaborations include our son David, now 11, and two coauthored papers on relationships (Peplau & Gordon, 1983, 1985).

In 1987 Chuck and I mailed a short questionnaire to former Boston Couples Study participants. The response rate was high (70%), suggesting that participants remembered us warmly and still were willing to contribute to our research. A key question we examined was how the sex role attitudes young adults held during college affected their lives 15 years later (Peplau, Hill, & Rubin, 1993). Did the feminists of the 1970s follow different life paths than the traditionalists? During college, sex role traditionalists and egalitarians held different attitudes about marriage and careers. Although most students expected eventually to marry, traditionalists were more confident they would marry, expected to marry at a younger age, felt more strongly that a wife should take her husband's name, preferred a traditional to a dual-earner marriage, and wanted to have a larger number of children.

By the time of the follow-up, three fourths of the participants currently were married, either to their college sweetheart or to someone else. But college sex role attitudes were not related to their marital histories. No association was found between sex role attitudes and whether a person married, age at first marriage, or likelihood of divorce. Although traditionalists had indicated in college that they wanted to have larger families than other students, they did not differ in the number of children, the timing of the birth of a first child, or their plans for having more children in the future. During college, sex role attitudes were linked to women's educational plans, but not to men's. Traditional women were less likely than egalitarians to plan to attend graduate school and to seek a doctoral degree and were more likely to major in a "feminine" field in college. At the time of our follow-up, 93% of participants had finished college and a third of both sexes had a master's degree or higher. For men sex role attitudes were unrelated to educational attainment or employment history. Among women, those with traditional sex role attitudes were less likely than other women to obtain a college or graduate degree. Half of all women had been employed full-time since completing school, and most had been in the labor force to some degree. However, variations in the extent of women's labor force participation were unaffected by sex role attitudes.

When our study began in the 1970s, most couples were matched on their sex role attitudes ($r = .46$), and sex role attitudes were unrelated to measures of relationship satisfaction, closeness, and love or to breakups over a 2-year period. Sex role traditionalism, however, did play a significant role in the ultimate fate of the person's college dating relationship. Of the original 231 dating couples, 73 eventually married each other, and 50 of these couples were still married in 1987. Women in the most traditional third of the sample were more likely than other women to marry their college sweetheart and to stay married to him. Fully 43% of traditionalists married their college boyfriend, and not a single one of these marriages ended in divorce! In contrast, only 26% of women in the most egalitarian third of the sample married their boyfriend, and half of these marriages ended in divorce. Similar but weaker trends were found for men.

We can only speculate about the reasons for this pattern. In college traditional women were oriented toward marriage and typically did not have plans for graduate education or a full-time career. So if a traditional woman found a suitable partner in college, she had no reason to look further. In contrast, although egalitarian women expected to marry, their immediate plans after college often included graduate school or launching a career. Consequently they were less likely to marry their college boyfriend but not less likely to marry someone else during a 15-year period. Although gender ideology did not affect the marital status of our sample as a whole, women's attitudes had significant effects on the long-term outcome of relationships begun in college.

Currently Chuck and I are continuing analyses of our follow-up data. With Khanh-Van Bui we are testing Caryl Rusbult's (1983) investment model of commitment and stability in relationships, both during college and over a 15-year period. With Paula Vincent we are investigating ways women have combined commitments to work and to family. We also are toying with the possibility of conducting another follow-up, perhaps using in-depth telephone interviews as well as a mailed survey.

Reflections

I began this chapter by suggesting that feminist social scientists work at the intersection of two worlds—the world of their discipline and the world of feminist scholarship. Most of the time, I have found the interaction between these two perspectives on research to be mutually enriching. In my experience, social psychologists have been supportive of feminist concerns and analyses. My experiences with feminist scholars outside of psychology have been more mixed.

I was attracted to feminism for fairly simple reasons. Feminist perspectives helped me understand my own life experiences and relationships in new and more insightful ways. Feminist analyses challenged traditional ideas and showed how patriarchal social arrangements constrain the life choices of women and men. Feminist activism sought to improve the lives of women and to work toward a more just society that places a high value on women as well as men. Feminist values have added a sense of passion and purpose to my research. I have found feminist scholarship nourishing when it has inspired me by examples of creative studies, raised new research questions, and offered provocative analyses and interpretations.

After 20 years as a feminist academic, however, I am concerned that students and researchers sometimes perceive feminism not as a source of inspiration, but as a set of rules. Undergraduates ask me earnestly whether feminists can wear makeup or stay home full-time to raise young children. Behind such questions is a view of feminism as a set of prescriptions—do this, don't do that. As a teacher I try hard to combat this view, suggesting that feminists should think critically about the choices they make but that feminism does not provide "correct" answers.

Analogous questions sometimes arise among feminist researchers. A few years ago I taught a graduate seminar on the psychology of gender. Most of the students in the class proudly identified themselves as feminists. These students' research projects addressed such important issues as acquaintance rape, power in male-female relationships, depression among women, and sexism in language. Hoping to broaden students' understanding of feminist scholarship, we read many feminist critiques of traditional psychology, of research methods, and of science. To my horror, the impact of this exposure to women's studies was to cause some students to question their feminism. Like most psychologists, these graduate students were committed to rigorous empirical research, trained in using quantitative methods, and proud of their sophisticated statistical skills. Like the college students worrying that feminism proscribes wearing short skirts or dyeing one's hair, these young researchers worried that they were violating feminist principles by using questionnaires or analyses of covariance in their research. Again I found myself arguing that feminism urges us to be critical of traditional theories and research methods but does not dictate "proper" thinking or methods. I was so perplexed by this experience that I ultimately wrote a paper arguing that all methods, both qualitative and quantitative, are potentially appropriate for feminist research in psychology (Peplau & Conrad, 1989). The unproductive feminist debate over research methods appears to be ending. A consensus seems to be emerging among feminist social scientists that feminists should encourage the widest possible variety of research methods (Jayaratne & Stewart, 1991). Reinharz (1992) concludes that feminism is a perspective, not a method, and she documents that, in practice, feminist research is using increasingly diverse methods. In our own work, we have varied the choice of method, depending on our goals. In the Boston Couples Study, we had the resources to use a variety of methods geared to specific purposes. To survey the experiences of 462 young adults, we used questionnaires. To provide a richer picture of the lives of individual couples, we used in-depth interviews. To test specific hypotheses about fear of success or male threat from female competence, we used laboratory experiments. Similarly in our studies of gay and lesbian relationships, a primary goal was to refute harmful stereotypes that same-sex relationships are inferior to heterosexual ones. To make this point convincingly, we found it helpful to use fairly large samples and standardized measures of relationship functioning, to conduct statistical analyses, and to make comparisons among gay, lesbian, and heterosexual couples.

Today feminist scholars are taking the lead in emphasizing the importance of cultural and ethnic diversity in human life. As a resident of Los Angeles, one of the most multicultural cities on the planet, this is a particularly salient issue for me. In retrospect, one of the striking features of the research described in this chapter is that it is based on white, middle-class samples. My more recent research has begun to broaden. A collaborative project with Vickie Mays and Susan Cochran studies the relationships of African American lesbians. A study of how college students influence dating partners to use a condom includes students from several ethnic groups. I also am trying to incorporate a broad range of diversity issues into all of the courses I teach. Recently Zick and I completed a new project together—an introductory psychology textbook (Rubin, Peplau, & Salovey, 1993). We have made a concerted effort to incorporate gender and cultural diversity into this text. These important changes in my work have been inspired in large part by feminist critiques of current research and teaching.

Yet as important as I believe it is to encourage greater diversity in our research, I worry that feminists now may perceive new and unrealistic standards for feminist research. Reinharz (1992) gives poignant examples of feminist researchers castigating themselves because their work fails to fully encompass one type of diversity or another. In truth, no single study and no individual researcher can address all of humankind or all types of relationships at once. As researchers, our studies are always constrained by the opportunities and resources available to us and by our particular intellectual talents and limitations. Our goal should be to move the field of family studies toward a more inclusive understanding of diverse relationships, not to require individual studies to meet a diversity litmus test.

I recently met a senior male professor from another university and asked him about a graduate school classmate who teaches in his department. "Oh," he replied, "blondie is still into that women's studies stuff." His sexist remark is a reminder of the many feminist challenges that lie ahead. But it is also a reminder that many scholars have made a long-term commitment to feminist research and teaching. I have enjoyed watching and participating in the development of feminist studies of close relationships during the past 20 years. I am also fascinated by the ways in which the feminist movement actually has changed the nature of the relationships we study, enabling us all to lead lives less constrained by arbitrary convention.

References

Abbott, S., & Love, B. (1972). *Sappho was a right-on woman: A liberated view of lesbianism.* New York: Stein & Day.

Bernard, J. (1972). *The future of marriage.* New York: World.

Berscheid, E. (1992). A glance back at a quarter century of social psychology. *Journal of Personality and Social Psychology, 63,* 525-533.

Blasband, D., & Peplau, L. A. (1985). Sexual exclusivity versus openness in gay male couples. *Archives of Sexual Behavior, 14*(5), 395-412.

Brown, L. S. (1989). New voices, new visions: Toward a lesbian/gay paradigm for psychology. *Psychology of Women Quarterly, 13,* 445-458.

Caldwell, M. A., & Peplau, L. A. (1984). The balance of power in lesbian relationships. *Sex Roles, 10,* 587-600.

Cassell, J. (1977). *A group called women: Sisterhood and symbolism in the feminist movement.* New York: David McKay.

Cochran, S. D. (1978, April). *Romantic relationships: For better or for worse.* Paper presented at the Annual Meeting of the Western Psychological Association, San Francisco.

Cochran, S. D., & Peplau, L. A. (1985). Value orientations in heterosexual relationships. *Psychology of Women Quarterly, 9,* 477-488.

Ehrmann, W. (1959). *Premarital dating behavior.* New York: Holt.

Falbo, T., & Peplau, L. A. (1980). Power strategies in intimate relationships. *Journal of Personality and Social Psychology, 38*(4), 618-628.

Ferree, M. M. (1990). Beyond separate spheres: Feminism and family research. *Journal of Marriage and the Family, 52,* 866-884.

Gagnon, J. H., & Simon, W. (1973). *Sexual conduct: The social sources of human sexuality.* Chicago: Aldine.

Garnets, L., Hancock, K. A., Cochran, S. D., Goodchilds, J., & Peplau, L. A. (1991). Issues in psychotherapy with lesbians and gay men: A survey of psychologists. *American Psychologist, 46*(2), 964-972.

Harry, J., & Lovely, R. (1979). Gay marriages and communities of sexual orientation. *Alternative Lifestyles, 2,* 177-200.

Hill, C. T., Peplau, L. A., & Rubin, Z. (1981). Differing perceptions in dating couples: Sex roles vs. alternative explanations. *Psychology of Women Quarterly, 5,* 418-434.

Hill, C. T., Peplau, L. A., & Rubin, Z. (1983). Use of contraceptives by college dating couples. *Population and Environment: Behavioral and Social Issues, 6*(1), 60-69.

Hill, C. T., Rubin, Z., & Peplau, L. A. (1976). Breakups before marriage: The end of 103 affairs. *Journal of Social Issues, 32*(1), 147-168.

Hill, C. T., Rubin, Z., Peplau, L. A., & Willard, S. G. (1979). The volunteer couple: Sex differences, couple commitment and participation in research on interpersonal relationships. *Social Psychology Quarterly, 42,* 415-420.

Hooker, E. A. (1957). The adjustment of the male overt homosexual. *Journal of Projective Techniques, 21,* 17-31.

Horner, M. S. (1970). Femininity and successful achievement: A basic inconsistency. In J. Bardwick, E. M. Douvan, M. S. Horner, & D. Gutman (Eds.), *Feminine personality and conflict* (pp. 45-76). Belmont, CA: Brooks-Cole.

Jayaratne, T. E., & Stewart, A. J. (1991). Quantitative and qualitative methods in the social sciences: Current feminist issues and practical strategies. In M. M. Fonow & J. A. Cook (Eds.), *Feminist strategies for the study of gender* (pp. 85-106). Bloomington: Indiana University Press.

Kelley, H. H., Berscheid, E., Christensen, A., Harvey, J., Huston, T., Levinger, G., McClintock, E., Peplau, L. A., & Peterson, D. (1983). *Close relationships.* San Francisco: Freeman.

Kurdek, L. A. (in press). Lesbian and gay couples. In A. R. D'Augelli & C. J. Patterson (Eds.), *Lesbian and gay identities over the lifespan.* New York: Oxford University Press.

Millett, K. (1970). *Sexual politics.* Garden City, NY: Doubleday.

Must Wellesley go co-ed to survive? (1969, December 16). *Harvard Crimson,* p. 3.

Parsons, T. (1954). The kinship system of the contemporary United States. In *Essays in sociological theory* (rev. ed.). New York: Free Press.

Peplau, L. A. (1972). Patterns of social behavior: The case of sex roles. In *Psychology today: An introduction* (pp. 487-505.) Del Mar, CA: CRM.

Peplau, L. A. (1976a). Fear of success in dating couples. *Sex Roles, 2,* 249-258.

Peplau, L. A. (1976b). Impact of fear of success and sex-role attitudes on women's competitive achievement. *Journal of Personality and Social Psychology, 34,* 561-568.

Peplau, L. A. (1979). Power in dating relationships. In J. Freeman (Ed.), *Women: A feminist perspective* (2nd ed., pp. 106-121). Palo Alto, CA: Mayfield.

Peplau, L. A. (1991). Lesbian and gay relationships. In J. C. Gonsiorek & J. D. Weinrich (Eds.), *Homosexuality: Research findings for public policy* (pp. 177-196). Newbury Park, CA: Sage.

Peplau, L. A., & Cochran, S. D. (1980, September). *Sex differences in values concerning love relationships.* Paper presented at the Annual Meeting of the American Psychological Association, Montreal.

Peplau, L. A., & Cochran, S. D. (1981). Value orientations in the intimate relationships of gay men. *Journal of Homosexuality, 6,* 1-19.

Peplau, L. A., & Cochran, S. D. (1990). A relationship perspective on homosexuality. In D. P. McWhirter, S. A. Sanders, & J. M. Reinisch (Eds.), *Homosexuality/ heterosexuality: Concepts of sexual orientation* (pp. 321-349). New York: Oxford University Press.

Peplau, L. A., Cochran, S., Rook, K., & Padesky, C. (1978). Women in love: Attachment and autonomy in lesbian relationships. *Journal of Social Issues, 34*(3), 7-27.

Peplau, L. A., & Conrad, E. (1989). Beyond nonsexist research: The perils of feminist methods in psychology. *Psychology of Women Quarterly, 13,* 381-402.

Peplau, L. A., & Gordon, S. L. (1983). The intimate relationships of lesbians and gay men. In E. R. Allgeier & N. B. McCormick (Eds.), *The changing boundaries: Gender roles and sexual behavior* (pp. 226-244). Palo Alto, CA: Mayfield.

Peplau, L. A., & Gordon, S. L. (1985). Women and men in love: Gender differences in close heterosexual relationships. In V. E. O'Leary, R. K. Unger, & B. S. Wallston (Eds.), *Women, gender and social psychology* (pp. 275-291). Hillsdale, NJ: Lawrence Erlbaum.

Peplau, L. A., Hill, C. T., & Rubin, Z. (1993). Sex-role attitudes in dating and marriage: A 15-year follow-up of the Boston Couples Study. *Journal of Social Issues, 49*(3), 31-52.

Peplau, L. A., Padesky, C., & Hamilton, M. (1982). Satisfaction in lesbian relationships. *Journal of Homosexuality, 8*(2), 23-35.

Peplau, L. A., & Perlman, D. (Eds.). (1982). *Loneliness: A sourcebook of current theory, research and therapy.* New York: Wiley-Interscience.

Peplau, L. A., Rubin, Z., & Hill, C. T. (1976, November). The sexual balance of power. *Psychology Today,* pp. 142, 145, 147, 151.

Peplau, L. A., Rubin, Z., & Hill, C. T. (1977). Sexual intimacy in dating relationships. *Journal of Social Issues, 33*(2), 86-109.

Pleck, J. H. (1976a). The male sex role: Definitions, problems, and sources of change. *Journal of Social Issues, 32*(3), 155-164.

Pleck, J. H. (1976b). Male threat from female competence. *Journal of Consulting and Clinical Psychology, 44,* 608-613.

Pleck, J. H., & Sawyer, J. (Eds.). (1974). *Men and masculinity.* Englewood Cliffs, NJ: Prentice-Hall.

Reinharz, S. (1992). *Feminist methods in social research.* New York: Oxford University Press.

Risman, B. J., Hill, C. T., Rubin, Z., & Peplau, L. A. (1981). Living together in college: Implications for courtship. *Journal of Marriage and the Family, 43,* 77-83.

Rubin, Z. (1969). *The social psychology of romantic love.* Unpublished doctoral dissertation, University of Michigan, Ann Arbor.

Rubin, Z. (1970). Measurement of romantic love. *Journal of Personality and Social Psychology, 16,* 265-273.

Rubin, Z., Hill, C. T., Peplau, L. A., & Dunkel-Schetter, C. (1980). Self-disclosure in dating couples: Sex roles and the ethic of openness. *Journal of Marriage and the Family, 42*(2), 305-317.

Rubin, Z., & Mitchell, C. (1976). Couples research as couples counseling: Some unintended effects of studying close relationships. *American Psychologist, 31,* 17-25.

Rubin, Z., Peplau, L. A., & Hill, C. T. (1981). Loving and leaving: Sex differences in romantic attachments. *Sex Roles, 7,* 821-835.

Rubin, Z., Peplau, L. A., & Salovey, P. (1993). *Psychology.* Boston: Houghton Mifflin.

Rusbult, C. E. (1983). A longitudinal test of the investment model: The development (and deterioration) of satisfaction and commitment in heterosexual involvements. *Journal of Personality and Social Psychology, 45,* 101-117.

Scarborough, E., & Furumoto, L. (1987). *Untold lives: The first generation of American women psychologists.* New York: Columbia University Press.

Thompson, L. (1992). Feminist methodology for family studies. *Journal of Marriage and the Family, 54*(1), 3-18.

Waller, W. (1938). *The family: A dynamic interpretation.* New York: Dryden.

3

Studying Women's Sexualities

Feminist Transformations

KRISTINE M. BABER

From a social constructivist perspective, stories we tell about ourselves are re-creations and reflect more about how we currently make sense of our lives than about what really happened in the past. Writing about myself as a feminist and as a feminist researcher involves searching back, trying to make my life explicit to myself, looking for motives, tracing patterns, and filling in gaps. The fabric is far from seamless, and a variety of interpretations may be just as valid as the one presented here.

I identify myself as a feminist, but I constantly am revising what that means and reflecting on the implications for my research, my teaching, my political activities, and my personal relationships. I cannot identify a profound experience that led to "becoming feminist" and do not see feminism as an "end state" (Stanley & Wise, 1991). Rather I appropriate Patti Lather's (1991) concept and think of myself as a "constantly moving subjectivity" (p. xix) and my feminism as a personal construct that is revised, elaborated, and experienced as a series of transformations that reflect my changing experiences and consciousness.

My first awareness of the importance of gender and difference occurred at age 5. I won a contest by coloring a picture of a nurse, and my prize was awarded during a visit to a hospital. Asked what I wanted to

AUTHOR'S NOTE: I would like to thank Katherine Allen, Susan Frankel, Leigh Leslie, and Donna Sollie for providing comments and suggestions as I wrote and revised this chapter.

be when I grew up, I responded that I would be a doctor. I was quickly informed that only men could be doctors; women could be nurses. I was confused and angry but had to admit that I had never seen a woman doctor.

A montage of other childhood and adolescent experiences contributed to my understanding of what it meant to be female. I remember my shock and fear at seeing my aunt after my uncle had beaten her, my anxiety at being around another uncle who sexually harassed me, and my frustration at watching my mother negotiate the constraints of her marriage. But I also have positive images of women taking control of their lives: a great-aunt who chose to have no children and happily devoted herself to teaching, my grandmother proudly taking me riding in a car she had bought herself, and my books on the lives of famous women that I read and re-read.

This tension between perceptions of women as oppressed and my knowledge of women as strong, achieving, and powerful persisted. My own life and my observations of other women's lives convinced me that being female in our society limits our experiences and opportunities but that resistance and persistence might offset some of these limitations. My experiences and observations, however, were untheorized and unarticulated until the early 1980s, when I began reading feminist research and literature and structuring a feminist consciousness in a more formal way.

I believe that being born female in our society predisposes one to be a feminist. I do not think my observations of difference between women and men in power, opportunities, and experiences are unique. Situated as I am—a white, middle-class, well-educated woman with an academic position—I have the opportunity to reflect on and theorize about women's achievements and resourcefulness, as well as their oppression and victimization. Because of the relative privilege of my life, I see who I am as a feminist to be what I *do* as a feminist. In other words, I use the resources I have to address structural inequities, to make the world safer for women and other marginalized groups, and to celebrate the strengths and contributions of women. To be consistent with these beliefs, I have served on women's commissions, sexual harassment and rape prevention committees, campus climate committees, sexual harassment hearing boards, a community family planning board, and community task forces. I also am a core faculty member in women's studies at the University of New Hampshire and speak publicly about women's issues. All of these activities have pushed me to reflect on and clarify my position as an activist feminist in all areas of my life.

I try in this chapter to weave together the themes, experiences, and observations I see contributing to who I am as a feminist researcher. I first identify my feminist perspective and then trace the path of my research, leading up to my current project on women's sexualities.

My Postmodern Feminist Perspective

A postmodern feminist perspective guides my recent work and characterizes the way I think about gender relations, social change, and my role as a researcher, teacher, and social activist. It provides me with an epistemology and an ontology, that, in turn, guide my praxis (Stanley, 1990). Postmodernism takes as a basic assumption multiple meanings, multiple realities, and multiple truth claims (Cheal, 1991; Hawkesworth, 1989). It opens spaces for a plurality of points of view and brings into consideration those on the margins of dominant discourse and theory (Cheal, 1991). This perspective allows me to accommodate contradictions and dialectical tension, encourages me to acknowledge and celebrate diversity, and pushes me to move beyond essentialistic and dichotomous thinking. In activities as diverse as teaching my course on race, class, gender, and families and reflecting on myself as a heterosexual feminist, I use a postmodern feminist approach in organizing my ideas and thinking about political activity to bring about change. Therefore, in my class we not only read about and discuss diverse family types but also work on "action projects" in which students use the information to integrate material on marginalized families into a preschool curriculum or write letters to legislators about family-relevant bills. In my personal life, a postmodern perspective accommodates the tension between my feminist position that women have been systematically oppressed and exploited by men and my personal decision to live in a committed relationship with a man.

I find postmodern feminism to offer a unique perspective for exploring the complexity and ambiguity in women's lives and their intimate relationships, but it is also a controversial approach rejected by many feminists who see it as a threat to the solidarity of the women's movement. A deconstruction of "women" as a category raises concerns about the potential risks inherent in illuminating the differences among women (Bordo, 1990; Hawkesworth, 1989; Lugones & Spelman, 1983; Offen, 1990; Pierce, 1991). In my work with Katherine Allen, we struggled with the ethical and epistemological dilemmas involved in moving from feminist standpoint theory to a postmodern feminist perspective. Our article in *Psychology of Women Quarterly* (Allen & Baber, 1992) grew out of our own intense discussions about the thinking guiding our work and the implications of postmodern feminism.

In our book *Women and Families: Feminist Reconstructions* (Baber & Allen, 1992), we used a postmodern feminist perspective to explore women's experiences in families—specifically their intimate adult relationships, their sexualities, reproductive decisions, caregiving issues, and paid and family work. The dialectical aspect of women's lives, particularly the tension between caring for others and caring for ourselves, was a pervasive theme in our book. We looked at the variety of ways women balance these tensions and considered both similarities and differences among women. We wanted to provide an accessible treatment of a postmodern feminist perspective, deconstruct traditional thinking about women and their experiences, include lesbians and their families, and present a feminist vision of changes that might improve women's lives.

Our observations of diversity in women's experiences and perspectives were difficult to accommodate with standpoint theories. Comparing just our own experiences as women and as feminists, we realized that no single standpoint captures all women's experiences (Hawkesworth, 1989). We realized that our knowledge claims were partial, fragmented, and incomplete (Flax, 1990), and we struggled with our inability to represent adequately the experiences of women whose race, class, ethnic group, or other identities differed significantly from our own. We decided to take a point of view situated in our own lives and to encourage others to add their voices to the discussion (Baber & Allen, 1992).

Writing the book, spending 3 years reviewing research on women and families, elaborating my own feminist perspective, and working closely with Katherine in a completely collaborative manner was critical to the direction my future empirical work would take. The book, in many respects, bridged important segments of my research life.

Looking Back

My graduate training in family studies prepared me well to assume an academic position but was very traditional in nature. My family theory course focused on systems theory, social exchange theory, family developmental theory, and conflict theory; feminism was not mentioned as a theoretical perspective or an angle of vision from which to critique more traditional approaches. I took seven courses in statistics and research methodology, but qualitative strategies were never addressed.

Even lacking a formal exposure to feminist theory and methodology, I knew when I began doing research that I wanted to explore issues significant to women. I chose to study for my dissertation the childbearing decisions of women over age 30 and justified this choice by referring to the rapid increase in the late 1970s and early 1980s in numbers of older women having their first child or deciding to remain child free. I perceived these women to have taken control of their sexual and reproductive lives and to have demonstrated great agency in choosing whether and when to have children.

Sexual Agency

I would like to look back and trace a coherent and logical path through my various research projects. My postmodern feminist perspective urges me, however, to accept the fragmentation in my work even as my constructivist orientation encourages me to search for common themes in work I have done.

From my current vantage point, I believe that the notion of sexual agency implicitly ties together much of my earlier work and is becoming explicit in my current research. My thinking about sexual agency is based on Judith Long Laws's (1980) discussion of the empowering capacity to choose and control one's sexual life and related experiences. Sexual agency evolves over time and is rooted in the individual's experiences and evaluations of those experiences. To further elaborate an understanding of women's development of sexual agency, Laws called for work that searches out and explores the continuities between sexuality and other aspects of life. Reproduction and childbearing are intimately tied to women's sexuality, and both have been identified as key factors in women's subjugation.

Elizabeth Moen (1979) argued that control over reproduction is power. For women to have control over their bodies, they not only need to regulate the number of children they have but also should possess the individual right *to* have children and to have economic independence. In addition, the timing of childbearing is critical. Women often need to delay the birth of their first child to complete their education and secure employment.

Taking Control:
Delaying or Forgoing Childbearing

My dissertation research (Baber, 1984; Baber & Dreyer, 1986) focused on childbearing decisions of women and their partners and looked specifically at child-free couples and those who had delayed having a child until after the woman was 30 years of age. Although some research on child-free couples (Bram, 1978; Feldman, 1981; Houseknect, 1979; Veevers, 1976, 1979, 1980) existed at the time, only Daniels and Weingarten (1979, 1982) had published their research on what was referred to as "late first-time parenthood." I was interested particularly in the decision-making process that brought women to make what were at that time still seen as variant, if not deviant, childbearing decisions. How did they think about themselves and their choices? What influenced them to resist normative expectations to have a child during their 20s? What played into their decisions about having or not having a child during the fourth decade of their lives? How influential were these women relative to their partners?

I interviewed 40 women and their partners, half delayed childbearers and half child free. Although I was interested particularly in the women and their perceptions, I believed it important to interview their male partners as well. Childbearing decisions usually are made in context, and I was interested in differences and similarities in the thinking and experiences of these delayed-childbearing men and women. Recently Liz Stanley and Sue Wise (1991) emphasized that feminist research should not concentrate exclusively on women's experiences, but rather should be concerned with all aspects of women's realities. Investigations of women's interactions with men provide critical information for understanding the context within which many women function and can suggest strategies for bringing about change.

Women who participated in the childbearing study were at least 30 years of age, had no history of fertility problems, and neither they nor their partners ever had been a parent. The delayed-childbearing women were pregnant with their first child, and the child-free women had never given birth. In-depth interviews with participants explored their thinking about having children, their decision-making process, and their relationship dynamics. Each person also completed a series of questionnaires to provide information about demographic variables, perceptions of self, and attitudes about gender roles.

Consistent with demographic data, the women in these couples were well educated and career oriented. Many also spoke of relationship variables, sense of self as mother, and influence of friends and family as being important aspects of their thinking about having or not having children. These women had taken active steps to control their reproductive lives, were knowledgeable contraceptors, sometimes resorted to abortions, and most of the delayed childbearers were able to conceive when they were ready to do so.

The women were more influential in the decision-making process than were their male partners, whether the decision was to have or not to have a child. Women's thinking about the decision process was more complex than the men's; they spontaneously discussed more costs and benefits of having children, worried about juggling babies and careers, and reflected on how their decisions were influenced by family members. The delayed-childbearing women had more traditional views of themselves in relationship to mothering and more traditional attitudes about spousal equality than did the child-free women. Both groups of women highly valued their careers, and delayed-childbearing women struggled with plans for managing conflicting demands. The tension between career and mothering was powerfully illustrated in the words of one expectant mother: "I was thinking of getting a computer terminal for the house, renting one for a few months so theoretically I could be breastfeeding the baby with one arm and using the word processor with the other arm if I wanted to" (Baber, 1984, p. 133).

A later study (1989) that I conducted with a group of 50 women who had become mothers after age 30 provided more information about women's control of their reproductive lives and indicated that women actively negotiated fertility decisions with their partners. One 40-year-old woman who was a business manager explained:

> He was ready before I was. I wanted to have a child too, but I was at the point in my mind of saying, "I won't have a child unless I want to have a child." I wanted some of that control. . . . Because I was the one taking the pill and controlling my body, I ultimately made that decision. I had the influence to say, "Yes, now is the time" even though psychologically, he was ready before I was. (Baber, 1989, p. 8)

These women believed that having a sense of control over their fertility and defining parenting as a choice allowed them to come to mothering with a sense of readiness and competence they might not otherwise have had. A 32-year-old consultant explained:

> Because I made a conscious choice and I wanted very much to have a child, I value the time I have with my daughter, enjoy her accomplishments, and willingly devote the time and energy required. By waiting until I was ready, I can view the child care responsibilities as an experience I consciously sought. This gives me more patience, understanding, and happiness as a parent than I would have had if I were younger.

Another woman, aged 39 and a college professor, expressed similar sentiments:

> I am more comfortable about myself and defining myself as a person with individual needs. I think I am a better parent because I define parenting as a choice I made, not as something I did to please my parents or his parents. I think I am a more knowledgeable parent because of my age.

Almost without exception these women and their partners were well educated, career oriented, and verbalized easily their thoughts and experiences related to decisions and negotiations about having or not having children. I was intrigued with the process of this research and the information collected. Many of the participants were people with whom I felt I easily could have developed a friendship because we shared so much in common.

Denying the Personal

I was in my early 30s, married for about 10 years, and voluntarily child free when I started doing research on childbearing decisions. My partner and I felt quite certain that we would not have children, but we reconsidered the possibility from time to time. Most of the couples I interviewed and many of the people with whom I discussed the research project asked whether I was doing this research to help me make a decision about having a child myself. Although some asked jokingly, many asked seriously. I denied, even to myself, that my own situation was any part of my motivation for doing this research. Trained to believe that a researcher should be objective about the topic of her research, I could not admit my own interest without thinking that I would seriously compromise my work.

Looking back, it is clear that my personal interest in these couples, in these women, and in their lives and decisions was a driving force in my work. I learned from them and reaffirmed my own commitment to remaining child free, but in the name of objectivity I missed the opportunity to collaboratively explore shared experiences. I resisted discussing my own feelings, experiences, and choices, and the rich narrative that we might have co-constructed went undeveloped. Now the acceptance of a personal starting point for feminist research has become so widespread that "some people have come to almost expect a link between the personal experience of the researcher and the research project in which she is engaged" (Reinharz, 1992, p. 260). Although such a linkage is not necessary, it need not be denied if it exists.

Delayed Childbearing:
Short-Term Phenomenon or Adaptive Pattern?

During the early and mid 1980s, the national fertility rates for women aged 30 to 39 continued to increase, while rates for other age groups declined or remained constant (U.S. Bureau of the Census, 1986). However, some people questioned whether delayed childbearing was a cohort phenomenon that would pass with the baby boom (Baldwin & Nord, 1984).

In 1986 I collected data from 250 unmarried undergraduate women to explore their thinking about having children, the timing strategies they would employ, and how they planned to integrate paid work and family roles (Baber & Monaghan, 1988). Questionnaires with many open-ended items allowed women to explain their expectations. All of the women planned to work after graduation and identified a total of 71 occupational choices. Only three of the women planned to remain single, and only six planned to have no children. The women planned to have their first child at a mean age of 28—about 5 years later than their mothers' average age at their first birth. Women planning nontraditional careers such as electrical engineering, agribusiness, and military intelligence planned to have fewer children and planned to wait longer to have the first child.

Other than waiting to have their first child until after they had established their careers, these young women lacked clear plans about balancing mothering and demanding careers. More than half expected to take at least a year off from work after the birth of their child, and the vast majority expected to have a partner assume equal responsibility for child care and housework. Many of these young women believed it was their personal responsibility to make their lives work. If they were organized enough, flexible enough, and handled their responsibilities well enough, they believed, they could do it all.

Studying Women's Sexualities

Accurate information about sexuality and reproduction is necessary to a sense of control over one's reproductive life. In teaching human sexuality at the university level, however, I learned how little sexual and reproductive information many of my students (who were primarily women) had. Most had never had a formal sexuality education course in high school or the opportunity to explore relationship development, sexual decision making, or reproductive life plans in other classes.

Discussions with women friends and colleagues about how they had acquired sexual information emphasized how much mystification exists around sexuality in general and female sexuality in particular. Through these discussions, community workshops that I conducted, and my experiences teaching human sexuality, I clarified for myself a deepening interest in exploring women's sexuality and learning how women develop sexual agency.

My current work focuses on women's thinking about and experiences with sexuality. Katherine and I used the concept of *sexualities,* rather than sexuality, in our book (Baber & Allen, 1992) to signify the multiplicity of women's sexual experiences. We devoted an entire chapter to women's sexual experiences to denote the importance of sexual relationships in women's lives and to consider it apart from its reproductive aspects. We considered problems involved in doing research on sexual topics including the limitations of language and ways in which existing social norms control even our conceptualizations of how sexuality is or might be. We also considered whether sexualities were biologically determined or socially constructed and used Judith Long Laws and Pepper Schwartz's (1977) concept of *sexual scripts* to explore the tension between stability and variability in the various aspects of women's sexualities, particularly sexual orientation. Reported differences between women and men and the relationship between sexuality and power also were investigated.

We know little about how women experience and think about their sexual relationships. How important is sexuality to women? How satisfying are their sexual interactions? Catharine MacKinnon (1989) claims that sexuality is the arena within which male dominance is created and maintained, that women have been limited to experiencing sexuality on men's terms. Ruth Colker (1991) agrees that patriarchy has made sexuality a critical component of women's lives and that, in a transformed society, the importance of sexuality in women's lives might disappear. She suggests that the energy women spend on sexual connectedness, love, and compassion may be evidence of their brokenness, rather than signify personal interest and desire.

The Social Construction of Sexualities

Women's sexuality generally is conceived by feminists and others to be socially constructed in response to social, political, and economic influences (Fine, 1988; Golden, 1987; Laws & Schwartz, 1977; McWhirter, Sanders, & Reinisch, 1990; Rust, 1993; Vance, 1984). The concept of *sexual scripts* (Laws, 1980; Laws & Schwartz, 1977) is particularly useful in understanding the process by which women construct an understanding of their sexual identity and the process of sexual relationships. *Sexual scripts* are the implicit rules that individuals develop for themselves regarding the who, when, what, where, and how of their sexual behaviors and activities. Individuals' sexual scripts are developed in the context of societal norms and expectations about appropriate male and female behavior and reflect cultural messages from parents, friends, religious and educational sources, partners, and the media. Sexual scripts include a subtext about the use of power, about communication regarding sexual activity, and about sexual negotiations (Baber & Allen, 1992). We know little about how women develop sexual scripts, how they deconstruct and reconstruct them, and how they use them to guide their sexual activities.

Although primary socialization regarding sexuality appears to be extremely potent in influencing later thinking and behaviors (Laws & Schwartz, 1977), the constructivist notion of sexual scripts is dynamic and accommodates the idea of change over time. Intervention can help young women challenge traditional sexual scripts that may prevent them from acting assertively and developing sexual agency. The prevailing discourses of female sexuality even among feminists, however, are discourses of sexuality as violence and/or victimization (Fine, 1988). Sex is depicted as dangerous and women as vulnerable potential victims of male sexuality. This construction of women only as the objects and victims of male sexuality leaves no room for women to explore and develop their own sexual interests and desires. Michelle Fine (1992) notes that feminist writings persistently have represented women's victimization and consistently have ignored, "indeed misrepresented, *how well young women talk as subjects,* passionate about and relishing their capacities to move between nexus of power and powerlessness" (p. 178).

The challenge in our teaching and research on women's sexuality is to emphasize the pleasure and agency, as well as the danger and victimization, that characterize contemporary women's sexual experiences. In her classic article "Pleasure and Danger: Toward a Politics of Sexuality," Carole Vance (1984) warned:

> To focus only on pleasure and gratification ignores the patriarchical structure in which women act, yet to speak only of sexual violence and oppression ignores women's experiences with sexual agency and choice and unwittingly increases the sexual terror and despair in which women live. (p. 1)

Existing Research on Women's Sexualities

Much of the current research on sexuality investigates behaviors or problems and employs traditional research methodology. Research rarely takes seriously women's sexual interest and desire or reveals the variety and complexity of women's sexual experiences. Philip Blumstein and Pepper Schwartz's (1983) now classic study of American couples provided a window on the sexual relationships of heterosexual, gay, and lesbian couples. They investigated frequency of sexual behaviors and people's expectations about, perceptions of, and satisfaction with their sexual relationships. Findings indicated the pervasive influence of traditional gender scripts and suggested clear differences in the ways males and females constructed their sexuality. Women were "keepers of fidelity" (Blumstein & Schwartz, 1983, p. 302) for whom sex functioned as a strong emotional and physical bond. Men were more likely to seek sexual variety and found the emotional aspect of sexuality less salient.

This study raised new questions about the nature of female sexuality because lesbians reported fewer partners and lower frequency of sexual activity, thereby supporting the position of those who saw women to be passive partners and less interested in sexual activity. Blumstein and Schwartz (1983) suggested lesbians' lower level of activity might be due to traditional female socialization that made them uncomfortable with sexual aggressiveness and therefore less likely to initiate sexual activity with a partner. An alternative explanation is that lesbian and heterosexual women may define sex and sexual activity differently, therefore "counting" differently (Frye, 1990). Regardless of explanation, these findings hint at the apparent heterogeneity among women regarding their sexual behaviors.

A survey of 868 nurses (Davidson & Darling, 1988) explored the relationship between the number of lifetime sex partners and women's enjoyment of their sexual experiences. The researchers eliminated lesbian respondents from their analysis, but results reveal considerable diversity even among women with male partners. Women reported a range of 1 to 75 sexual partners, with older women, divorced or separated women, and never-married women having higher numbers of partners. The vast majority of women, regardless of the number of partners, indicated satisfaction with their sexual experiences.

New data from a cross-sectional national survey of sexual behavior in the United States (Janus & Janus, 1993) revealed differences between career women and homemakers. Information from 1,347 men and 1,418 women identified differences between the two groups of women that were as great as or greater than among women and men. In some cases the employed women expressed attitudes about sexuality that were more liberal than the men's. For example 65% of the career women thought oral sex was very normal, compared with 43% of the homemakers and 59% of the men; 36% of the career women strongly agreed that sex and intimacy are two different things, but only 21% of the men and 25% of the homemakers gave this response.

In the Janus and Janus (1993) study, career women masturbated more frequently than homemakers, were more likely to have an orgasm during lovemaking, were more likely to think that sex is deliciously sensuous, and were less likely to believe that their sex partner's pleasure was more important than their own. These women also were just as likely to self-identify as homosexual (4%) or bisexual (5%) as were men; only 1% of the homemakers self-identified as lesbian or bisexual.

Janus and Janus (1993) did not provide an analysis of behavior or attitudes by sexual orientation, but prior research suggests it is an important analytic category. A study that included 407 lesbians and 370 heterosexual, college-educated women (Coleman, Hoon, & Hoon, 1983) revealed that although both groups of women were satisfied with their sexual experiences, lesbians reported somewhat higher levels of sexual satisfaction. They experienced sexual activity more often, had orgasms more frequently, and had a greater number of partners. These results stand in stark contrast to those of Blumstein and Schwartz (1983) and emphasize the importance of exploring diversity within, as well as between, lesbian and heterosexual women's experiences.

Studies such as these raise provocative questions. To answer them, we need more information about how women construct their sexual satisfaction and how critical choice and control are to defining their experiences as pleasurable and satisfying. We also need a clearer understanding about how women balance pleasure and danger in navigating their sexual feelings and negotiating with intimate partners. My current research focuses on young women's sexual knowledge and how they construct themselves as sexual beings.

Young Women's Thinking About Their Sexualities

This research project is the first that I am beginning with an explicitly feminist theory and methodology. A friend and colleague, Susan Frankel, and I are undertaking a program of research on women's constructions of sexuality and reproductive issues. We both have a passionate interest in these topics and are starting from our own personal and professional experiences. I teach human sexuality, conduct community workshops and institutes on sexuality and HIV/AIDS topics, and serve on the board of directors of our local family planning clinic. Susan is the director of the Center for Health Promotion and Research at the University of New Hampshire, conducts research on abortion rights, and develops conferences on women's health issues.

Our process has been excruciatingly reflexive as we explore and negotiate our theoretical perspective, develop our methodology, challenge our methodology, question why we are doing the research, discuss how we feel as we do the research, and try to identify how what we are doing could be used to help women.

We began our inquiry by sending out letters to a randomly selected group of undergraduate women, inviting them to participate in a discussion group composed of 8 to 10 college-age women. We were interested in learning what sexuality and reproductive health issues are important to women in their late teens and early 20s and how they think about their own experiences. We also wanted to determine what information they have about sexuality and from whom they received it. The discussion format we used with our first two groups was collaborative, provided data appropriate for qualitative analyses, and allowed the women to voice their ideas and direct the flow of conversation.

This is a research approach that Francesca Cancian (1992) calls a "mild" participatory technique because it draws on active involvement and collective knowledge to produce more valid descriptions and explanations of an area of interest than might traditional methods. Judith Daniluk (1993) used a group format with older women to discuss their sexual experiences and found that within a group, through the telling of each member's story, meanings could be negotiated and insights developed in a rich and collaborative manner.

We were concerned initially that women might feel uncomfortable talking in a group about their sexual experiences. This was not a problem for most of the women; the majority spoke almost immediately about their relationships, problems, and experiences. Although we expected the conversations to produce very rich data, we were surprised at the power of the group discussion technique. The women shared experiences, asked one another for more information, developed positions about existing social norms, and sometimes together deconstructed conceptualizations of women's sexuality that they found to be constraining, exploitive, or just invalid.

One of the methodological issues that Susan and I faced involved the tension between our "being there" as women with our own sexual experiences and "being there" as researchers trying to do research with an emancipatory purpose without making the women objects of our inquiry. Because this was not a fully collaborative project, avoiding some degree of objectification was difficult (Lather, 1991); we tried to minimize this as much as possible. We began the discussions by asking, "What sexual and reproductive health issues do you think are important to women of your age today?" We wanted the women to lead the discussions and, therefore, we asked questions only to clarify information, reflect on a general theme, or draw others into the conversation.

Discussions were tape-recorded and analyzed for themes and general categories that characterized the conversations. We initially were struck, particularly in the first group, by how strongly the discourses of danger and victimization (Fine, 1988) reverberated through the women's discussion of their sexual experiences. They talked with great intensity about fear of pregnancy, feeling used by male partners, and sexual harassment. Listening to the tapes, however, we became aware of a subtext we interpreted as sexual agency. Remembering Fine's (1992) admonition not to ignore how well young women talk as subjects, we listened for indications of these women defining themselves as active agents in their sexual experiences and resisting sexual scripts that constructed them as passive victims. They spoke of addressing sexism, "deciding" whether or not to have sexual activity with a certain partner, and "playing around with two people, seeing how people are different" and seeing who can make you feel "that way." The women shared experiences and then gave each other advice about how to deal with sexuality issues and develop a sense of control. Although this information was personal, it also reflected a political stance. One woman talked about the effects of living in a "masculine-defined society" wherein women have been led to believe that the only power women can achieve is through a man. She pointed to *Cosmopolitan* covers as examples of messages women receive that the "only power you can possibly gain is using your looks and your sexuality." She argued that "powerful men are definitely attractive, but powerful women are attractive, too. We're just never told that we can be powerful. Work on being assertive. Work on working for equality. Work on educating people that we don't have to live oppressed" (Baber & Frankel, 1993, p. 12). Another woman added: "And learn that your sexuality is for you—not for someone else, not for some other girl, not for a guy."

This sense of taking control and making decisions included choice of partners. Most of the women were involved in relationships with men, but there was an openness on the part of several to relationships with other women. In encouraging others to pay attention to their own desires, one woman urged:

> I would say do what you want to do, don't let anyone tell you what your role is. You're supposed to have sex with men and enjoy it. I had the enjoyment part down, but I was also having sex with women because it was what I wanted to do. There's a friend of mine and we get together to do the things that most other people wouldn't do with us—just the things that we want to do that we both agree on. (Baber & Frankel, 1993, p. 10)

The topic of sexual orientation raised a variety of issues among the women. Feelings ranged from the desire of the woman quoted above to the concern of another woman who admitted her greatest fear in knowing a lesbian would be whether that woman might be attracted to her. The women voiced a great awareness of homophobia and how difficult it would be for a person to be "out" on campus. They also spoke of actively challenging homophobia, particularly among family members, but stopped short of addressing it in each other in the group.

Several women identified bisexuality as even more taboo than being gay or lesbian. In one group two of the women indicated they had bisexual interests. One woman was currently in a relationship with a man who also identified as bisexual. "It just so happens that we are in our relationship, a loving relationship, and we've chosen each other. But it doesn't mean that we couldn't have chosen someone else." She voiced discomfort with gay and lesbian friends who think she is confused or has copped out: "In a way you can't identify unless you decide one way or the other."

Paula Rust's research (1993) confirms the difficulties faced by women whose own psychosexual experiences contradict social constructions of heterosexuality. She argues that individuals select their sexual identities from the options they perceive to be open to them. Because bisexuality is not generally identified as an authentic form of sexuality, those whose sexual thoughts, feelings, and behaviors involve both same- and opposite-sex partners try to fit themselves into the more accessible options of heterosexuality or homosexuality.

Rust's (1993) research with 346 lesbian-identified and 60 bisexual-identified women challenged linear and unidirectional developmental models; her findings suggest that most individuals do not progress through orderly stages, but rather often switch back and forth among identities. Great variation was found in the coming-out process for women within each group. Two thirds of the lesbian-identified women had wondered whether they were bisexual, although fewer than half had ever identified themselves as such. Most bisexuals had both wondered whether they were lesbians and identified themselves as such at some point. An important piece of information from this study is that the average age at which these women reported their first same-sex attraction was 15 for the lesbian-identified and 18 for the bisexual-identified women. They first questioned their heterosexual orientation at 17 and 20 years of age, respectively. These data suggest that late high school and college years may be critical periods for helping young women explore all aspects of their sexuality, including sexual orientation.

In our discussions with these women, we were surprised that HIV/AIDS was not a more compelling issue for them. Both groups raised it as the first issue in response to our initial question about critical concerns, but there was little spontaneous discussion about it as the conversation moved from topic to topic. Unplanned and unwanted pregnancies were more feared than HIV.

Almost all of the women acknowledged receiving information about HIV through programs on campus. Some still admitted having intercourse without using a condom. One woman had intercourse with two men without using condoms: "I've done it and I know I'm completely stupid." She said she had thought about it and, "I feel really irresponsible. I think it was an insecurity thing and I was embarrassed." Research indicates that attitudes, beliefs, and knowledge about HIV often are not translated into behaviors with male partners (Osmond et al., 1993). Women may not have the power, or may not perceive they have the power, to negotiate condom usage with a partner.

Women in the groups identified other sources of sexuality information, such as the media, friends, partners, and parents. Mothers particularly were mentioned, often ambivalently, as sources of information. Except for two women whose mothers were health care providers, the women questioned the usefulness and validity of their mothers' information and were skeptical about their mothers' ability to accept them as sexual beings. In contrast, the two women whose mothers were health care providers felt very positive about sharing sexual information with their mothers. The one whose mother worked at Planned Parenthood said when she "lost her virginity," her mother was the first person she told.

The topics of virginity and "the first time" demonstrated how these young women deconstructed commonly accepted sexual beliefs and reconstructed conceptions that were more meaningful to them. Although many adhered to the accepted notion that one is a virgin until experiencing penile-vaginal intercourse, a woman with considerable sexual experience commented: "There are many things that I am still a virgin at. There are so many ways to lose your virginity—not just male-female intercourse." Another woman talked about a friend who had an unsatisfying sexual experience and became a "virgin" again 4 months later so that she could lose "it" (again) with someone she loved. She spoke of virginity as a state of mind and noted that the male involved "never knew."

Contradiction and ambivalence characterized the women's stories about experiences, friends, and intimate relationships. One woman spoke of fear of being alone and miserable and feeling incomplete without a male partner. Another said being in a relationship was a big responsibility that really made her feel tied down, but she was afraid to get out of it. The women agreed there was tremendous pressure to have a boyfriend by graduation, but several spoke of developing a sense of autonomy:

> Right now I'm really just coming to terms with forgiving myself for going out with this guy. Use and abuse—this was the relationship. It's really hard for me right now, but I'm the happiest that I've ever been right now. I've got my life planned until 1997. And now I totally love being by myself, getting to know

myself and being in control. I'm just loving being by myself and being in control. (Baber & Frankel, 1993, p. 9)

One of my personal and professional goals is to facilitate the process of young women developing a sense of control over their sexual and reproductive lives. Susan and I intend to develop and implement groups for high school women that will be a cross between the inquiry-oriented discussion groups we did with the college-age women, and more didactic sessions that would provide information about reproductive and sexual topics. The project will be collaborative in that the young women themselves will identify the issues for discussion and determine what information they need. In our dual roles as researchers and educators, we will not only continue to collect data about the ways in which young women construct themselves as sexual beings but also provide information these young women can use in their everyday lives.

We are convinced a group setting provides a comfortable environment within which young women can explore and deconstruct sexual scripts. Themes of sexual agency can be acknowledged and elaborated, while skills can be developed that will provide a foundation for that sexual agency. By helping young women develop expanded vocabularies and constructs about sexual interest, desire, behavior, and identity, we can provide an opportunity for them to consider the variety of possible sexual scripts. We hope this process will contribute to young women feeling more confident in making assertive, responsible, and self-aware decisions about their sexual and reproductive lives.

Ethical Concerns

Ethical issues create tension and demand attention in any research project. Sexuality is a sensitive area in which to do research, particularly with minors, and parental permission is required. Our plans to actively include mothers should facilitate the consent process and enhance the effects of the project.

Mothers are a potentially powerful source of sexual and reproductive health knowledge if daughters have confidence in the validity and usefulness of their information. Nearly all of the adult women in a qualitative study (Brock & Jennings, 1993) on mother-daughter sexuality education wished their mothers had talked to them openly and comfortably. The women wanted positive information and discussions about feelings and choices. Most remembered limited discussions; strong, negative, nonverbal messages; and frequent use of warnings and rules. The limited research conducted with young women suggests that those who had open discussions with their mothers about their sexuality were more likely to emphasize pleasure, curiosity, and desire in their stories about sexual initiation (Thompson, 1990).

Mothers with current information who feel comfortable talking with their daughters are more likely to be positive sources of information. We plan to hold discussion groups for mothers to discuss sexuality and reproductive issues and to learn new skills for talking with their daughters. We will gather data from both the young women and their mothers before and after the project to explore the intergenerational transmission of information about sexuality and reproductive health issues.

The question of how to involve "the participants" in the research process also raises ethical dilemmas (Acker, Barry, & Esseveld, 1983). In this project we want women to determine the topics important to them and the direction in which the discussion moves. However, we believe that some critical issues need to be addressed in the groups. At what point do we exert our "expertness" regarding factual information or move the discussion toward a subject not yet considered? HIV/AIDS is a compelling example. Reports issued in the summer of 1993 by the Centers for Disease Control and Prevention and the United Nations Development Programme identified women in their teens and early 20s as the group now being infected with HIV at the fastest rate (Rensberger, 1993). It seems unethical and irresponsible to be in a setting discussing sexual issues and not spend a significant amount of time on HIV/AIDS, including work on translating knowledge and attitudes into behaviors.

Postscript: Prevailing Tensions

Becoming and being a feminist researcher adds an additional layer of tensions to the ethical and epistemological challenges involved in the research process, perhaps particularly for women in academe. Like many of my colleagues, I have appointments in both a discipline-oriented department (family studies) and women's studies. As my writing, research, and teaching become more ardently feminist, I sometimes worry about being "too feminist" for my department. Yet I also wonder whether I am seen as "not feminist enough" by my women's studies colleagues as I explore postmodern feminism (an orientation some disdain because of perceived threats to feminist solidarity) and teach in a traditional department.

My feminist orientation also challenges me to be constantly self-reflexive in conceptualizing and teaching core courses at both the undergraduate and graduate level (Cancian, 1992). How do I teach graduate theory and methods courses so as not to perpetuate the very systems of thought and methodologies I challenge? I agree with Shulamit Reinharz (1992) that researchers must learn the disciplinary methods, rules of logic, statistical procedures, and other research techniques relevant to their disciplines even if it is only to critique them. So my solution is to do both—teaching and critiquing traditional theories and methodologies and exposing students to alternative approaches. Rather than set up dualistic oppositions, I try to prepare my students to be postmodern scholars who can accommodate the tension between traditional and emerging theoretical perspectives, develop a repertoire of methodologies they can use as appropriate, and apply their knowledge and skills to socially relevant issues.

A core tenet in feminist research is that our work should be political and have as its goal social change (Allen & Baber, 1992; Flax, 1990; Jayaratne & Stewart, 1991; Reinharz, 1992). A commitment to social action pervades my teaching, my community activities, and my research. This activist orientation, however, generates tensions for me. Working on local problems to bring about social change demands significant time and energy. Much of the work is political, invisible, and frequently not "countable" as scholarly activity for tenure and/or promotion. As a tenured faculty member, I feel much freer to become involved with controversial issues such as condom availability at the high school or time-consuming projects such as serving on a task force to develop training for law enforcement personnel in handling sexual assault cases. On the one hand, the time I spend in these activities is time diverted from my "scholarly" research and writing. On the other hand, these are choices I make knowledgeably. I relish being involved in these projects that actually have immediate social effect, and I use these experiences to enhance my teaching and writing whenever possible.

Tensions between scholarly work and activist work, the demands of trying to respond to multiple constituencies, and the challenges of taking a reflexive position in relation to my own work simultaneously encourage and discourage me. But the research I do with women, exploring their thinking and their experiences, is rewarding and purposeful. Working with others who take seriously the lives and experiences of women supports me through the inevitable transformations I experience as a feminist researcher and teacher.

References

Acker, J., Barry, K., & Esseveld, J. (1983). Objectivity and truth: Problems in doing feminist research. *Women's Studies International Forum, 6,* 423-435.

Allen, K. R., & Baber, K. M. (1992). Ethical and epistemological tensions in applying a postmodern perspective to feminist research. *Psychology of Women Quarterly, 16,* 1-15.

Baber, K. M. (1984). Delayed childbearing: Psychosocial aspects of the decision-making process. (Doctoral dissertation, University of Connecticut, 1983). *Dissertation Abstracts International, 44,* 3174A.

Baber, K. M. (1989, November). *Elaborating our understanding of motherhood: The experiences of delayed childbearing women.* Paper presented at the Annual Meeting of the National Council on Family Relations, New Orleans.

Baber, K. M., & Allen, K. R. (1992). *Women & families: Feminist reconstructions.* New York: Guilford.

Baber, K. M., & Dreyer, A. S. (1986). Gender-role orientations in older child-free and expectant couples. *Sex Roles, 14,* 501-512.

Baber, K. M., & Frankel, S. L. (1993). *Revising the scripts: Young women's reflections on their sexualities.* Unpublished manuscript.

Baber, K. M., & Monaghan, P. (1988). College women's career and motherhood expectations: New options, old dilemmas. *Sex Roles, 19,* 189-203.

Baldwin, W. H., & Nord, C. W. (1984). *Delayed childbearing in the U.S.: Facts or fiction.* Population Reference Bureau Bulletin 39.

Blumstein, P., & Schwartz, P. (1983). *American couples: Money, work, sex.* New York: William Morrow.

Bordo, S. (1990). Feminism, postmodernism, and gender-skepticism. In L. J. Nicholson (Ed.), *Feminism/Postmodernism* (pp. 133-156). New York: Routledge.

Bram, S. (1978). Through the looking glass: Voluntary childlessness as a mirror for contemporary changes in the meaning of parenthood. In W. B. Miller & L. F. Newman (Eds.), *The first child and family formation* (pp. 368-391). Chapel Hill, NC: Carolina Population Center.

Brock, L. J., & Jennings, G. H. (1993). Sexuality education: What daughters in their 30s wish their mothers had told them. *Family Relations, 42,* 61-65.

Cancian, F. M. (1992). Feminist science: Methodologies that challenge inequality. *Gender and Society, 6,* 623-642.

Cheal, D. (1991). *Family and the state of theory.* Toronto: University of Toronto Press.

Coleman, E., Hoon, P. W., & Hoon, E. F. (1983). Arousability and sexual satisfaction in lesbian and heterosexual women. *Journal of Sex Research, 19,* 58-73.

Colker, R. (1991). Feminism, sexuality, and authenticity. In M. A. Fineman & N. S. Thomadsen (Eds.), *At the boundaries of law: Feminism and legal theory* (pp. 135-147). New York: Routledge.

Daniels, P., & Weingarten, K. (1979, Spring). A new look at the medical risks in late childbearing. *Women and Health,* pp. 17-21.

Daniels, P., & Weingarten, K. (1982). *Sooner or later: The timing of parenthood in adult lives.* New York: Norton.

Daniluk, J. C. (1993). The meaning and experience of female sexuality: A phenomenological analysis. *Psychology of Women Quarterly, 17,* 53-69.

Davidson, J. K., & Darling, C. A. (1988). The sexually experienced woman: Multiple sex partners and sexual satisfaction. *Journal of Sex Research, 24,* 141-154.

Feldman, H. (1981). A comparison of intentional parents and intentionally childless couples. *Journal of Marriage and the Family, 43,* 593-600.

Fine, M. (1988). Sexuality, schooling, and adolescent females: The missing discourse of desire. *Harvard Educational Review, 58,* 29-53.

Fine, M. (1992). *Disruptive voices: The possibilities of feminist research.* Ann Arbor: University of Michigan Press.

Flax, J. (1990). *Thinking fragments: Psychoanalysis, feminism, and postmodernism in the contemporary West.* Berkeley: University of California Press.

Frye, M. (1990). Lesbian "sex." In J. Allen (Ed.), *Lesbian philosophies and cultures* (pp. 305-315). Albany: State University of New York Press.

Golden, C. (1987). Diversity and variability in women's sexual identities. In The Boston Lesbian Psychologies Collective (Eds.), *Lesbian psychologies* (pp. 19-34). Urbana: University of Illinois Press.

Hawkesworth, M. E. (1989). Knowers, knowing, known: Feminist theory and claims of truth. *Signs, 14,* 533-557.

Houseknect, S. K. (1979). Childlessness and marital adjustment. *Journal of Marriage and the Family, 41,* 259-265.

Janus, S. S., & Janus, C. L. (1993). *The Janus report on sexual behavior.* New York: John Wiley.

Jayaratne, T. E., & Stewart, A. J. (1991). Qualitative and quantitative methods in the social sciences: Current feminist issues and practical strategies. In M. M. Fonow & J. A. Cook (Eds.), *Beyond methodology: Feminist scholarship as lived research* (pp. 85-106). Bloomington: Indiana University Press.

Lather, P. A. (1991). *Getting smart: Feminist research and pedagogy with/in postmodernism.* New York: Routledge.

Laws, J. L. (1980). Female sexuality through the life span. In P. B. Baltes & O. G. Brim (Eds.), *Life-span development and behavior* (pp. 207-252). New York: Academic Press.

Laws, J. L., & Schwartz, P. (1977). *Sexual scripts: The social construction of female sexuality.* Hinsdale, IL: Dryden.

Lugones, M. C., & Spelman, E. V. (1983). Have we got a theory for you! Feminist theory, cultural imperialism and the demand for "the woman's voice." *Women's Studies International Forum, 6,* 573-581.

MacKinnon, C. (1989). *Toward a feminist theory of the state.* Cambridge, MA: Harvard University Press.

McWhirter, D. P., Sanders, S. A., & Reinisch, J. M. (Eds.). (1990). *Homosexuality/heterosexuality.* New York: Oxford University Press.

Moen, E. W. (1979). What does "control over our bodies" really mean? *International Journal of Women's Studies, 2,* 129-143.

Offen, K. (1990). Feminism and sexual difference in historical perspective. In D. L. Rhode (Ed.), *Theoretical perspectives on sexual difference* (pp. 13-20). New Haven, CT: Yale University Press.

Osmond, M. W., Wambach, K. G., Harrison, D. F., Byers, J., Levine, P., Imershein, A., & Quadagno, D. M. (1993). The multiple jeopardy of race, class, and gender for AIDS risk among women. *Gender and Society, 7,* 99-120.

Pierce, C. (1991). Postmodernism and other skepticisms. In C. Card (Ed.), *Feminist ethics* (pp. 60-77). Lawrence: University of Kansas Press.

Reinharz, S. (1992). *Feminist methods in social research.* New York: Oxford University Press.

Rensberger, B. (1993, July 29). HIV increasing fastest among young women, report says. *Boston Globe,* p. 15.

Rust, P. C. (1993). "Coming out" in the age of social constructivism: Sexual identity formation among lesbian and bisexual women. *Gender and Society, 7,* 50-77.

Stanley, L. (Ed.). (1990). *Feminist praxis: Research, theory, and epistemology in feminist sociology.* New York: Routledge.

Stanley, L., & Wise, S. (1991). Feminist research, feminist consciousness, and experiences of sexism. In M. M. Fonow & J. A. Cook (Ed.), *Beyond methodology: Feminist scholarship as lived research* (pp. 265-283). Bloomington: Indiana University Press.

Thompson, S. (1990). Putting a big thing in a little hole: Teenage girls' accounts of sexual initiation. *Journal of Sex Research, 27,* 341-360.

U.S. Bureau of the Census. (1986). Fertility of American women: June 1985. *Current Population Reports,* Series P-20, No. 406.

Vance, C. (1984). Pleasure and danger: Toward a politics of sexuality. In C. Vance (Ed.), *Pleasure and danger: Exploring female sexuality* (pp. 1-27). Boston: Routledge & Kegan Paul.

Veevers, J. E. (1976). Voluntarily childless wives: An exploratory study. *Sociology and Social Research, 57,* 356-366.

Veevers, J. E. (1979). Voluntary childlessness: A review of issues and evidence. *Marriage and Family Review, 2,* 126.

Veevers, J. E. (1980). *Childless by choice.* Toronto: Butterworth.

4

You Can't Be a Woman
in Your Mother's House

Adult Daughters and Their Mothers

ALEXIS J. WALKER

According to a grandmother in Apfel and Seitz's (1991, p. 426) study of
African American adolescent daughters and their mothers, "You can't be
a woman in your mother's house." Although the statement was made by
a very young grandmother—the mother of an adolescent mother—it captures one of the fundamental issues in the relationships between adult
daughters and their mothers: autonomy. Ideally each woman must have a
sense of individuality and uniqueness. This is as true for the older generation—the mother—as it is for the younger—the daughter. Two prominent feminist theorists have written about the issue of autonomy for
women, focusing their attention on mothers of young children. Chodorow
(1978) wrote that women place greater emphasis on relationships relative
to men because daughters are less motivated than sons to separate completely from their mothers. Ruddick (1982, 1989) wrote of the inherent
conflict necessitated by the fact that mothers and their children are sepa-

AUTHOR'S NOTE: My work on this chapter benefitted enormously from the helpful
comments of Leigh Leslie, Donna Sollie, Katherine Allen, and Rosemary Blieszner, and
particularly from several lengthy and penetrating conversations with Stephen Marks. I am
grateful to each of these colleagues, especially for how they have helped me see my own
work in new ways.

rate beings, and that what fosters the growth of one does not always foster the growth of the other.

After a number of years of research on mother-daughter relationships in adulthood, I have become convinced of the importance of feelings of autonomy for both generations. I did not begin my research with autonomy in mind, but the pattern of findings has led me to the inevitable conclusion that mothers and daughters relate best when they have a sense of independence from each other. Mothers are not wholly defined by their attachment to children; they are people too. Daughters, although they may cherish their connection to their mothers, are not exactly like their mothers; they, too, are unique human beings.

In this chapter I describe more than a decade of research on mothers and daughters, pointing to the emergence of autonomy as a central factor in this intergenerational tie. I then discuss the research process, a frequently unexamined aspect of the work we do.

Background

Since 1979, when I completed graduate work in human development and family studies, I have been focusing on the relationships between mothers and their adult daughters. My commitment to feminism, however, predates this research focus. And although my feminist world view has influenced my professional work, the influence has not been as direct as one might expect. Recently I have been attempting to integrate feminist principles systematically into all aspects of my professional life and to be more cognizant of how being a feminist both directly and indirectly influences my work.

When I first chose a population of maternal grandmothers, daughters, and granddaughters for a small research project funded by the College of Arts and Sciences at the University of Oklahoma, I did so, on the surface, for an unimaginative and pragmatic reason: I had learned in graduate school that women were more likely than men to volunteer for research. On an intuitive level, however, I felt strongly that women's intergenerational ties were distinctive from and more powerful than men's, and I wanted very much to focus on them. I was pleased to have an acceptable methodological reason for limiting my sample by gender.

As is true for most members of my cohort, I did not learn about feminist approaches or methods in graduate school. Instead I learned conventional research methodology and theoretical perspectives. Although I knew from my own experience and that of my friends that women's intergenerational relationships were emotionally closer than those of men, I did not articulate this position. I was more interested in demonstrating that frequency of contact was unrelated to how family members felt about each other, contrary to the literature's assumption that emotional closeness predicts such frequency. Because I lived 1,100 miles from my parents and still felt close to them, I knew this assumption was not true. After I received the small grant and collected the data, Linda Thompson worked with me in addressing this question. Our findings revealed what I later learned Bert Adams had shown in 1968: Contact between college student women and their mothers is related to emotional closeness only within moderate geographical distances—that is, when people have some discretion about whether to visit family (Walker & Thompson, 1983). If one lives on the same block as one's mother, contact is probably frequent. If one lives 500 miles away, contact is influenced by income: One must be able to afford long-distance telephone calls and airfare to ensure contact. Within a moderate range, however, there is an element of choice. One could make the effort to drive 1½ hours or so to visit one's mother, but there would be a legitimate excuse not to do so. Emotional closeness plays an important role: The stronger and more positive the emotional tie to one's mother, the more one would choose to go that extra distance to see her.

We identified variations in daughter-mother aid patterns in this sample and related these variations to attachment or emotional dependence. We focused on two sets of intergenerational pairs: (a) student women and their middle-aged mothers and (b) these same middle-aged women and their mothers. We identified four types of reciprocity in both older and younger pairs: (a) mother-dependent: mother received more aid from daughter than she gave; (b) daughter-dependent: daughter received more aid from mother than she gave; (c) high reciprocity: both mother and daughter gave high levels of aid to their intergenerational partner; and (d) low reciprocity: both mother and daughter gave low levels of aid to their intergenerational partner. Each type contained information about both the level and reciprocity of aid. Not surprisingly, mother-dependent patterns were more likely in older pairs, while daughter-dependent patterns were more likely in younger pairs. The high-reciprocity pattern was equally likely in both (Thompson & Walker, 1984).

In older pairs, mothers reported higher levels of attachment than daughters, and both mothers and daughters reported the highest levels of attachment in the high-reciprocity pattern. In younger pairs, however, attachment varied by aid pattern and generation: The dependent partner in nonreciprocal relationships reported less attachment. Here were the first hints of the role of autonomy in mother-daughter ties. We theorized that, on the one hand, nonreciprocity may be more comfortable in older pairs because of a long history of aid exchange that probably balances over time (e.g., Beckman, 1981). A balanced history would not jeopardize feelings of autonomy. On the other hand, it was also possible that older pairs might have long since resolved any struggle over autonomy. In younger pairs, however, partners seemed more sensitive to relationship imbalances. Without a long history of interaction, dependency may threaten feelings of autonomy and may cause mothers and daughters to pull away from their relationships with each other.

What other experiences might weaken mother-daughter ties? Linda wondered what would happen if women experienced major life changes or transitions such as marriage, employment, children reaching adulthood and leaving home, and widowhood. Would these transitions change women's connections to their intergenerational partner, say, push them closer together or pull them apart? So with Carolyn Morgan, from the University of Oklahoma, we investigated the impact of the following variables, singly and in combination, on aid and contact: marital status, employment status, and launching status. We expected, as had been suggested in the literature, that a first marriage, employment, and children leaving home might pull women away from larger family connections. When I think about our assumptions now, I am alarmed at the way we succumbed to conservative thinking: If you take women away from families and children away from women, you diminish their involvement in and commitment to family life. We could not have been more wrong.

Because our expectations were guided by our assumptions, we were startled by the results: Except for married student women who were less close to their mothers than single students, role status or even combinations of role statuses were remarkably unrelated to interdependence between mothers and daughters. For the most part, we concluded, transitions do not seem to draw women away from ties with their mothers or daughters. Well. How could we explain these findings?

Fundamentally this was a "no results" paper; that is, the independent variables had no influence on the dependent variable(s). And we all know how difficult it is to publish a paper with no significant findings. Yet lack of statistical significance did not mean the findings were without value.

Our assumptions had led us astray. Without having developed much of an argument, we submitted the paper to the *Journal of Marriage and the Family*. Predictably, it was rejected.

For lack of direction, that manuscript sat on my desk for nearly 2 years while I read and thought more about the relationships between mothers and daughters. Empirical literature was scant, although there was the work of feminist psychologist Nancy Chodorow (1978). (I was not yet familiar with Sara Ruddick's theory of maternal thinking.) Chodorow focused attention on the mother-daughter relationship as the origin of women's strong connections to others. She described the particular difficulty women face in becoming autonomous beings. Girls identify with their mothers, she wrote, while boys identify with their fathers. But both girls and boys have strong attachments to their mothers because of the intense focus of mothers on infants and small children. With time, however, boys pull away from their mothers and orient more toward fathers. This pulling away primes boys to be autonomous. Because girls identify with their mothers, however, they have little motivation to pull away. They retain strong ties, Chodorow argued, and thus are less prepared to navigate the world independently.

Our data focused on adult women, presumably those who already had established some level of autonomy. They, too, argued for the stability, the invulnerability, of the mother-daughter bond. Perhaps Chodorow (1978) was correct: The early structure of the mother-daughter relationship may establish a pattern that is relatively permanent. We concluded that the suppositions in the literature regarding women's movement away from family connections with life transitions were erroneous. We rewrote the manuscript, stressing the constancy of mother-daughter ties and the structural constraints toward mother-daughter relationship stability, and published it in a feminist journal (Walker, Thompson, & Morgan, 1987).

Overall, we found a lack of connection between residential proximity and emotional closeness, variation across mother-daughter pairs in patterns of reciprocity, generational differences in response to dependency, and relationships that were stable in quality over time. Although scant additional empirical literature was available, we had no doubt that at least some of the presumptions in the intergenerational literature about the mother-daughter tie were without foundation. I was convinced that we needed to know more about the relationships between mothers and daughters. I wanted to pursue my interest but thought the connections between two generations might be better illuminated if I focused on a select group of pairs of mothers and daughters, those in a similar context. I remembered a lesson from research methods: To identify influences on the dependent variable, research participants should face similar stimuli; that is, the mothers should be in a position similar to each other, and the daughters should be in a position similar to each other.

A Focus on Family Caregiving

The context I chose was parental caregiving: the giving of care by adult children to their frail, aging parents. I selected this context for several reasons. I had observed my mother and my uncles' wives, but especially my aunt, take care of my father's mother throughout a 17-year decline into dementia. I also knew that my mother provided considerable assistance to her parents even though they would not then have met a formal definition of dependency; they were fully able to meet their daily needs without her help. Many of my mother's friends were taking care of their aging parent(s), as were a number of my own friends' mothers. So I thought I knew a bit about parental caregiving from my own observations.

I was aware that gerontologists were increasingly interested in family caregiving, although not from a family studies perspective. Their attention was focused on the growing number of elders with a need for assistance and the decreasing likelihood of their receiving help from family members, given the smaller number of children per family and the increasing employment of middle-aged women (potentially caregiving daughters) in successive cohorts. Notice the assumption that employed women may not meet their familial obligations, an assumption that has been invalidated several times by empirical data (e.g., Brody & Schoonover, 1986; Finley, 1989; Matthews, Werkner, & Delaney, 1989; Stoller, 1983, 1990). They also were concerned about the stress resulting from caregiving and the ways in which this stress might be minimized. Although I, too, saw the increasing numbers of aging parents with needs for assistance and the smaller numbers of potential caregivers as an escalating social problem, I also was curious about the connections between caregivers and care receivers. As it turned out, the parental caregiving context provided a perfect opportunity to pursue the issue of autonomy. Here the frail, elderly mother depends on the aid provided by her adult daughter. In this culture, dependence is at odds with autonomy. So how are aging mothers affected by dependence? And what of the mother-daughter relationship? How is it influenced, changed, affected when the mother is dependent on the daughter? This question has occupied my research attention since 1986.

Problems With the
Family Caregiving Literature

Although there is much empirical literature on family caregiving, for the most part it reflects neither a family nor a close relationship approach; that is, the relational context of caregiving is ignored. Indeed, few caregiving studies specifically focus on one particular relationship type (e.g., spouse, adult child), although several are centered on husbands and/or wives as caregivers. Studies of adult children as caregivers frequently combine sons and daughters together, simultaneously overlooking the fact that the vast majority of adult-child caregivers to aging parents are daughters and ignoring variation within and between genders.

The dependent variable of focus is primarily the stress of caregiving to caregivers operationalized by caregiver burden scales or depression measures (e.g., Kinney & Stephens, 1989; Zarit, 1989) despite the fact that caregiver burden scores consistently are found to be relatively low (e.g., Stoller & Pugliesi, 1989). Little attention is paid to the positive aspects of caregiving and care receiving (Matthews, 1985; Motenko, 1989; Stueve, 1982). In addition, research on family caregiving attends to caregiving tasks but minimizes its less tangible, affective aspects such as the meaning of caregiving to the caregiver (see Allen & Walker, 1992b).

Finally, aging family members are seen as passive, dependent care recipients, rather than as active relationship partners (e.g., Stueve, 1982). Having read this literature, I, too, expected relationship quality to decline with caregiving—that is, that there would be only negative outcomes for both mothers and daughters. I ignored the findings from my own research in which older mother-daughter pairs had relationships that seemed to be insensitive to dependency and in which mother-daughter ties appeared to be stable over time. I believed what I read in the literature and used social exchange theory to articulate my position.

Social Exchange Theory

Social exchange theory is ideally suited to a capitalist system such as that in the United States, but it irritates feminists, myself included, because it focuses on individual maximization of outcomes and overlooks altruistic behavior. It deflects attention from the origins of power differences and depicts people as freely able to make choices in relational interactions (Glenn, 1987). If people only do things to benefit themselves, how can we explain the everyday behavior of mothers and of women as partners? The inconsistency between social exchange theory and feminism has been a constant struggle for me. Social exchange theory is outcome centered, rather than women centered. It cannot account for and even ignores the relentless, unrecognized sacrifices women make for the people they love. So I was grateful when Katherine Allen introduced me to the work of Ruddick (1982, 1989).

In the meantime, to satisfy reviewers, editors, funding agencies, and my need to integrate my findings in some way with those of others, I relied on social exchange theory (Thibaut & Kelley, 1959). But I drew mostly from its application to the study of close relationships (e.g., Kelley, 1979). First, and not of minor significance, it is the theory I know and understand best because it was the organizing theme of my graduate training centered on close relationships. Second, it requires the researcher to attend to the relationship itself, as influenced and understood by its participants; that is, it acknowledges that the relationship exists beyond each partner. Third, any thorough study of relationships from this framework requires attention to the perspective of both partners. Each partner is likely to experience the relationship in a unique way. Therefore, one cannot understand it fully without data from both relationship participants. Fourth, it facilitates exploration of relationship participants' unique definitions of what is rewarding or costly, as only partners can tell us what is valuable or distressing to them. Fifth, it is compatible with the notions of *independence, dependence,* and *interdependence,* three concepts essential to the understanding of mother-daughter relationships in later life because of their relation to the concept of *autonomy.* For me these characteristics have justified the use of social exchange theory to explain my findings, but I hope to expand what I am learning about mother-daughter relationships into an explicitly feminist model of women's intergenerational ties.

Frail Elderly Mothers and Their Caregiving Daughters

For the past 6 years, I have worked to develop a research practice more directly tied to my feminist ideology. I have centered my efforts on a topic of interest to women: the unpaid labor of family caregiving. It is an area of study with the potential to improve the quality of women's daily lives. I have placed women at the center of inquiry and focused attention on what women do. My experiences with the participants in my research have shaped my view of mother-daughter relationships and strengthened my confidence in autonomy as a defining characteristic. What have I learned about family caregiving and about mother-daughter relationships in later life?

With the help of colleagues, I have confirmed the similarities between caregiving/care receiving pairs and pairs of aging mothers and adult daughters in which mothers are self-sufficient. The literature on parental caregiving reflects an underlying assumption that sudden events trigger caregiving; that is, caregiving occurs after a history of intergenerational independence. Our study includes a comparison group of elderly, self-sufficient mothers and their middle-aged daughters. We have reports of daily activities with and for their intergenerational partners from these women, as well as from those in the "dependent" pairs. The data have shown that despite the mother's poor health and physical dependence, frail elderly women and their daughters have much in common with self-sufficient women and their daughters (Walker & Pratt, 1991). Although caregiving daughters give assistance to their mothers frequently and spend considerable time providing help, the daughters of self-sufficient mothers also help their mothers on a routine basis in the same categories of activities in which caregiving daughters engage, such as household tasks, food preparation, and personal care. These findings suggest that caregiving occurs against the backdrop of a history of intergenerational assistance.

When we think about the lives of our own mothers, most of us have ample evidence to support this conclusion. When I was a child, my mother often purchased items at the grocery store for my grandmother, took her a sample of the dessert left over from last night's dinner, phoned, or just dropped by to visit. She still does these things, but she does them more often and spends more time doing them because now my grandmother must have her help. If we look at our own lives or those of the women we know, the findings from my research with mothers and daughters are sustained. But researchers have not been driven by what we know to be true about women's lives, so these obvious findings have a place in the literature on family and close relationships.

A second major finding has been the pivotal role of relationship quality in intergenerational caregiving. The experience of giving or receiving care is dependent, in part, on how one feels about the giver or receiver

(Walker, Martin, & Jones, 1992): Daughters who feel closer to their mothers do not feel as pressed for time, as frustrated, or as anxious as daughters who feel less close. Relationship quality is less important for care receivers than physical health in determining care-receiving outcomes, but it still matters: Mothers who feel closer to their daughters are less angry in receiving care. For those who study close relationships, these findings may seem obvious. But the literature on family caregiving has not taken a dyadic approach. It primarily has sampled caregivers and focused on their individual concerns. It has given little attention to relationship quality and relationship processes. The focus has been on the burdens of caregiving without consideration for the relationship context, the way people in the caregiving situation feel about each other.

A serendipitous finding has been the significance of the care receiver as a contributor to the relationship with the caregiver: Elderly care receivers play an active role in their relationships with caregivers, particularly in the provision of socioemotional support. They see themselves as active relationship partners, and their daughters see them that way as well (Walker, Pratt, & Oppy, 1992). I believe that ageist biases have contributed to the idea that aging persons are passive and dependent. It is striking to see how widespread these biases are within the gerontological literature. I learned that when we really listen to our research participants, we find many of our assumptions to be in error.

Finally, consistent with feminist principles, we have verified the diversity in relationships between caregiving daughters and their mothers (Walker & Allen, 1991). These intergenerational relationships differ in the extent to which the women receive rewards from interacting with each other, experience costs in their interaction, handle conflicts that arise in their relationship, and express feelings of concern for each other. Contrary to the opinion of many regarding mother-daughter relationships, we have not found them to be mostly stormy and conflicted, though some are. Many of the women, mothers and daughters both, describe their intergenerational partner as their best friend.

Both mothers and daughters in these "intrinsic" pairs (Walker & Allen, 1991) find the relationship rewarding. They experience few costs relative to rewards. They have few, if any, conflicts, they are able to keep their disagreements from spilling over into all areas of their interactions, and they both express concern for the welfare of their intergenerational partner. Intrinsic relationships are reflected accurately in this comment from a care-receiving mother: "Every day I wait for my daughter to come. She don't have to come every day, but she just does it on her own. It might not be for a long time if she's got other things to do, but she always comes. We're just like sisters." In these pairs, daughters and mothers both respect each other's autonomy. Each person is seen as an adult, and daughters work hard to sustain their mothers' sense of independence.

A second set of relationships is somewhat more ambivalent. In these pairs, both partners experience positive aspects of the relationship, but at least one, usually the daughter, reports significant negative outcomes too. The high level of costs tempers the rewarding aspects of the relationship for daughters. Conflict is more common in these ambivalent pairs, and concern for the other's outcomes does not appear to be mutual: Daughters express concern for their mothers more than the reverse. Ambivalent relationships are reflective of this daughter's feelings: "Mother is very appreciative, but she reminds me occasionally that she has money in this house, too. I wouldn't be in as good a situation as I'm in without her. I feel a big responsibility toward her, but I wouldn't let it interfere with my happiness." In ambivalent pairs, there is a sense of frustration in daughters that their mothers expect them to be helpful and are not as appreciative as they could be. Daughters in ambivalent pairs hint at a lack of respect from their mothers for their own autonomy. They believe that their mothers treat them like children.

Finally, some pairs may be described accurately as conflicted. These relationships appear to be unrewarding for both mother and daughter. Costs are heavy, rewards few, and both seem focused on their own outcomes, rather than on those of the intergenerational partner. Partners in conflicted intergenerational pairs seem to insist on their own autonomy without regard to the tangible connection they have with each other. A mother describes a conflicted relationship: "If I say yes, she might say no. . . . We don't always agree: I'm an older type; she is modern. She's an extrovert; I'm an introvert. . . . She thinks I'm dependent on her. I say, 'Not when I'm well.' "

An Evolving Feminist Perspective
on Mother-Daughter Relationships

The findings described above were derived primarily from studies using a social exchange perspective. Recently, however, I have been working toward a feminist perspective on mother-daughter relationships in adulthood. My collaboration with Katherine Allen is in pursuit of that goal. Consistent with feminist principles, for example, we have attended to the meaning that caregiving has for the caregiver. We believe it is the researcher's perspective that has led to an overemphasis on caregiving burdens. From the viewpoint of an observer, it appears that caregiving would be fraught with anguish, misery, and suffering. And, for some, it is. But if we listen to caregiver daughters, those who tend to the needs of a woman they love, the mother who cared for them when they were dependent children and to whom they are still very much attached, we find more complex motives and outcomes.

In one study we set out specifically to attend to positive outcomes and/or meanings of the caregiving experience for caregivers. We applied our perspective to interview data from 29 pairs of mothers and their caregiving daughters (Allen & Walker, 1992b). We found evidence for three types of positive outcomes: companionship, concern and caring, and appreciation and gratitude.

Some of these intergenerational partners saw each other as friends. For example, a daughter told us: "We go once a month to the theater; we have lunch two to three times a week; we go out to dinner at least once a month; we take long drives." Another mother-daughter pair played Scrabble every day. In separate interviews members of such pairs showed affection for each other and respect for each other's autonomy. We also found considerable evidence of concern and caring. A daughter whose mother could not walk unaided and who slept most of the time told us: "I keep her socks pulled up; mother really likes that." A mother with debilitating osteoporosis said of her only child: "I hate to have her do so much—If I'd had two kids, maybe they could have divided the work she does for me." Finally we found appreciation and gratitude. One mother told us: "The things my daughter does overwhelm me sometimes." Another said: "I wanted to do this study because my daughter deserves to get credit for what she's done for me." A daughter reported: "[My family and I] never do anything for her but what she's very grateful." This study confirmed the active role care-receiving mothers play in intergenerational dyads and produced substantial evidence of positive caregiving outcomes for both caregivers and care receivers. Thus we confirmed that a feminist orientation facilitates the discovery of some of the missing facets of the caregiving literature.

Katherine introduced me to Ruddick's (1982, 1989) theory of maternal thinking, a worldview that derives from the practice of mothering or caring for a fragile being. In Ruddick's model the labor of mothering is in response to the three demands of raising children: to preserve their lives, to nurture them and foster their growth as unique human beings, and to train them to be acceptable members of society (Ruddick, 1982, 1989). Together the emotional and physical labor of caring creates in mothers attentive love, the joint practice of preservation, nurturance, and training.

We applied Ruddick's theory to data from in-depth interviews (Allen & Walker, 1992a). We looked for similarities in and differences between the thinking and practice of caregiving to children and the distinct but related caring provided by adult daughters to their frail, elderly mothers. As Ruddick suggested, we focused our study on the actual work that caregivers do and the way they see that work, because it is the work that leads to maternal thinking. In Ruddick's (1982, 1989) model a mother's attachment to her child causes her to focus on the child's health and safety. We saw evidence of this preservation in caregiving daughters; that is, in caregiving, daughters focused on their mothers' health and safety. One widowed daughter told us: "When mother broke her wrist, before she moved in with me, I wrote her every day so the person who took her mail to her could check on her."

Ruddick (1982, 1989) suggested that perceiving the children as separate from the self motivates mothers to foster their growth and autonomy. Caregiving daughters saw their mothers as separate, autonomous beings and worked to maintain that autonomy. A daughter whose mother was confined to bed told us: "We have a speakerphone that we use when I make a call for her, so that she can hear, too." A daughter whose mother had to move to a foster home following a stroke reported: "I take her to the apartment complex where she used to live so she can visit with her friends."

Finally Ruddick (1982, 1989) proposed that mothers must train their children to become acceptable members of society. But Ruddick (1989, p. 47) also suggested that "the teaching of healthy children differs from the teaching of the ill or the elderly." In the United States, autonomy in adulthood is socially valued. We found numerous attempts by daughters to maintain their mothers' autonomy in spite of their increasing frailty. Perhaps these attempts can be viewed as efforts in pursuit of acceptability. We suspect that more effort would be devoted to helping mothers be acceptable to society when mothers are cognitively impaired. The mothers in our study were cognitively intact, their disabilities physical in nature. For them it was probably less necessary for their daughters to foster acceptability. The behavioral problems associated with cognitive decline, however, would provide multiple opportunities to train an acceptable being.

One woman in our study, a married daughter, revealed: "We built our home so mother could live in the basement. It has the plumbing and everything." The connection among the three tasks of preservation, growth, and acceptability is evident in her plan for her mother's future. When the mother is no longer able to live on her own, she will move in with her daughter. The daughter can keep a close eye on her, watching for signs of failing health. Yet the mother will live in separate quarters, thus helping to maintain her own and her daughter's autonomy. This pattern of coresidence should be acceptable to society, as the mother would not be wholly dependent.

Overall, then, we found evidence that adult daughters preserve their mothers' lives, foster their growth, and help them remain independent. Thus we were able to extend Ruddick's theory to encompass a different kind of caring labor. As in caring for children, the motives for parental caregiving arise from the needs of the elderly parent and occur within a relational context.

This review of my research confirms that autonomy has emerged as a significant component of mother-daughter relationships. It is important for both generations, mothers and daughters. In the future I intend to explore the issue of autonomy from a longitudinal view. The research described herein focused on mothers and daughters at one point in time. What happens when there is a steady or sudden decline in the mother's health? Can a daughter continue to foster her mother's autonomy in such circumstances? Notice that increasing needs on the part of the mother place greater restrictions on the daughter when she is the primary source of care. Is it possible for the daughter to maintain her autonomy in such instances? And what of a mother who experiences cognitive decline? Is the daughter's sense of her mother as an autonomous being sustained? Or does she now think of her mother as dependent, much like a child? These questions and more, no doubt, will occupy my attention for years to come. Whatever the focus, I intend to pursue my efforts toward implementing a feminist research practice.

Feminism and the Research Process

The research in which I have been involved has received funding from the National Institute on Aging. I mention this external funding because it is an important constraint on research design. Although external funding agencies do provide support for innovative approaches, including feminist ones, by far most funded research employs the dominant methodologies prominent within social science today. Members of the review panels for private and public funding agencies are among the most celebrated researchers in their particular fields of study (e.g., developmental and social psychology, sociology, gerontology). They have lengthy and impressive records of external research support and are the authors of a nearly uncountable number of articles published in the most highly valued journals. When they review research proposals or manuscripts, they look for research that follows the dominant paradigm(s) in sampling, design, measurement, and analysis. Essentially this approach maintains the status quo; that is, support and reinforcement are given for quantitative designs that employ measures with demonstrated validity and reliability and well-accepted analytical techniques. Only occasionally are contributions that address new research questions or unique populations supported. This statement about the status quo will not surprise feminist researchers who have struggled for financial support and labored to publish in the journals that will earn them tenure and promotion.

I believe what is needed to understand mother-daughter relationships in the context of family caregiving is a number of descriptive studies that combine detailed observations with in-depth, qualitative interviews. These studies should be exhaustive in their focus. This sort of work, beginning at the point of women's caring labor, is central to feminist thinking (e.g., Thompson, 1992). If the caregiving literature was grounded in such studies, we might not be predisposed to see all care recipients as passive and dependent. We might be sensitized to the interdependence of individuals in a relationship. And certainly we would have room in our conceptualizations for positive and negative outcomes, for both the struggles and pleasures of family life. Yet researchers who pursue this sort of research with necessarily small samples have difficulty both securing external support and publishing in mainstream journals. Such studies do not maintain the status quo.

Years ago, despite a commitment to feminism and political activism, I made the choice to follow the acceptable or mainstream path. I did so because of a desire for job security and because I wanted to be successful. I chose an academic career and continue to choose to work within the constraints of the academic system. I had another important reason as well. As I mentioned earlier, in graduate school I was trained in traditional ways of thinking about research. I did not learn qualitative approaches to research questions, nor did I learn feminist theories. This training has shaped my research questions and approaches. Sometimes I feel as if I am two separate persons: I feel constrained to pursue conventional academic goals through my research, and feminist goals through advocacy for women on campus, in my profession, and in my community. Although the distinction is somewhat arbitrary, these feelings of separateness are more common than I would like.

Of course, as feminists have argued persuasively, ideology influences one's work and one's daily life. Feminism has influenced my choice of research topic, the design of my research, the research process, and the conclusions I reach. Although my political position has influenced the way I conduct my research, the influence is less than I desire; specifically, although I have made somewhat superficial changes in research design, I have made more dramatic changes in the research process.

Research Design

I firmly believe I have received external support for my research, in part, because of my use of conventional methodology. Yet I have learned from feminist scholars such as Kathleen Gerson (1985), Carol Gilligan (1982), Arlie Hochschild (1989), and Lillian Rubin (1979), among others, how important it is to pay attention to one's research participants and to listen to their comments, reactions, and ideas around and outside of structured research questions. Consequently, when I developed my research protocol, I included a number of truly open-ended questions, not just follow-up questions, to compel people to elaborate on their responses. Although I was not trained in grounded theory research, studies such as *Worlds of Pain* (Rubin, 1976) and *In a Different Voice* (Gilligan, 1982) led me to keep extensive notes and to impress on staff members the need to write down exactly what the women said throughout data collection. These field notes have become invaluable to me. They are providing a richer understanding of the processes of caregiving and care receiving and the properties of the mother-daughter relationship. For me this use of field notes and a handful of open-ended items within a structured questionnaire has been a small step on my long path toward feminist research practice, a practice I am learning from my colleagues and my students.

The Research Process

For 5 years I worked with a research staff including a co-principal investigator, a clerical assistant, and four graduate research assistants, although specific personnel varied over time. Having read Acker, Barry, and Esseveld (1983), I knew about the power inherent in the principal investigator's position. Having worked as a research assistant, I knew about the powerlessness of the graduate student. I was determined to break down the hierarchy of the research process by involving members of the staff as much as possible in research decisions. This involvement proved to be an elusive goal.

One objective was to have all staff members involved with research participants. For example, throughout data collection I was determined to conduct as many interviews as the graduate assistants did. For the first 9 months of the project, I did so. This was an undeniably enriching experience. I came to know well a number of the women in the study and still have contact with several of them. In fact I recently received an invitation to a daughter's 50th wedding anniversary. I care about these women, some more than others, of course, and have been captivated by their history and experiences. Conducting interviews was invaluable to me as a researcher. I quickly saw how my own biases had led me to exclude from scrutiny important aspects of these women's lives.

As I indicated earlier, one of my interests was in recognizing and carefully detailing the actual caregiving labor of the daughters. Rather than ask for reports on typical days or questioning respondents about the average amount of time per week or month spent in specific categories of activities such as indoor maintenance, I adapted a procedure from Atkinson and Huston (1984) in which each daughter reconstructed her previous day in terms of activities with and/or for her mother. With this method it was evident to me immediately that we were gathering only some of the information about relationship activities. When I called daughters to ask about their day, they reported on their own activities, but they also told me what their mothers had done for them! I was astonished. From my reading I was certain that aging family members were passive in their receipt of care. I could not have been more wrong. The mothers in my study prepared meals for their daughters, helped them with the care of their children, mended their clothes, accompanied them to church, worked on hobbies with them, served as a sounding board for ideas and problems, and provided invaluable emotional support. This was not true of all mothers, of course, but even those who were dying or otherwise confined to bed could be and often were significant sources of comfort and love for their daughters.

It now seems so obvious to me and to others to whom I mention it that care-receiving mothers are active relationship participants. But this was not evident from the family-caregiving literature, and I certainly would not have thought to include information on mothers' activities without having participated in interviews with respondents (see Lyman, 1989, and Stueve, 1982, for criticisms). I have been reminded that reciprocity is a key aspect of later-life, mother-daughter relationships, so mothers' contributions must be studied as well as daughters'. Subsequently I secured supplemental funding from the National Institute on Aging to add to our procedures reports of daily activities from care-receiving mothers.

This "discovery" would not have occurred had I not conducted interviews myself. When I discussed at staff meetings the help provided by mothers to daughters, the other interviewers agreed that they had heard similar reports from daughters but that they had not thought them worth mentioning. The insight I gained from conducting interviews myself is exemplary of the benefits of the feminist process. My interest in sharing with students the labor of data collection and in hearing for myself what the mothers and daughters in the study had to say led to an important modification of the research design, as well as to a better understanding of the subject at hand. It was not without trial and hardship in the rest of my life, however. Besides conducting interviews, I had a full-time job and my work responsibilities were increasing. It became more and more difficult to take the time to conduct interviews and to do the follow-up telephone calls required for reports on daily activities. And it was increasingly difficult to leave my office in midday to gather data. Here I found daily occupational responsibilities to be in direct conflict with feminist practice.

This conflict was true in a number of other ways. For example, I had hoped to be part of a research team, rather than to have a research staff. Early on, all those involved with the project, including the clerical assistant, agreed to read articles related to the research for discussion at staff meeting. Although the level of interest was high at first, in practice our discussions were less and less beneficial. Given the demands of course work, it became more difficult for graduate students to read these "extra" articles in addition to their assignments as research assistants. I found it hard to find time to assemble reading lists. Nor could I rely on other staff members to recommend articles, as they either knew little about the research area or were unwilling to make suggestions. Concurrently staff meetings became increasingly devoted to discussions of issues regarding data collection and data coding. The idea of scheduling additional meeting time to facilitate a conceptual discussion, even without the foundation of a common reading list, was resisted. It was apparent that I was far more interested in daughters and mothers as caregivers and care receivers than were other members of the staff.

My aspiration to involve all staff members with respondents also was less than successful. With the permission of respondents, I arranged for the clerical assistant to accompany staff members once or twice on interviews so that she could get a better feel for what we were doing. Although the first clerical assistant was pleased to do so, the second was not interested in this sort of contact. Nor was the coinvestigator interested in conducting interviews.

Initially I had hoped that all staff members could share authorship on any papers we presented and/or published. This sharing would involve participation by seven authors plus work without pay by potential additional authors who were interested in and working on aspects of the project, such as literature reviews or data analysis. Those who put more effort into data analysis, conceptualization, and writing and who spent time reading and thinking about the subject at hand were reluctant to see their names diminished among a sea of coauthors. So the rule was changed to require "effort beyond ordinary job responsibilities" for coauthorship. Again most of those students working on the project for pay were not sufficiently interested to spend extra time in the pursuit of a particular research question.

To be sure, some of these difficulties may have resulted from the size of the graduate program at Oregon State University. If I had been at a larger institution with more graduate students, perhaps it would be easier to put together a team of people with common interests. But most feminists who focus on family or close-relationship issues are in comparable programs, and many do not even have the opportunity to work with doctoral students. It is also true that few of us, myself included, have the luxury of coinvestigators, graduate students, and other staff members who share our feminist ideology.

It would be easier to realize a feminist research practice if we were not also implementing feminist principles in other aspects of our professional lives. It takes extra time and energy to integrate material and methods from a feminist perspective into our teaching, for example. I spent an entire summer reading everything I could find on feminist pedagogy to prepare for a course on gender and family relationships. Having always used a traditional lecture format, the transition to feminist pedagogy has not been an easy one, and I still struggle to find a way to make all students in the course feel valuable. I find it difficult, for example, to foster the contributions of students opposed to a woman's choice or of those convinced that it is neither harmful nor problematic for women to bear most of the burdens of family labor, without alienating feminist students or feeling as if I am sacrificing my own integrity and self-respect.

It also takes incredible initiative and stamina to confront the common academic ways of doing things that result, only sometimes unwittingly, in sexual discrimination at the departmental, college, and university level. Someone must be available to students, staff, junior and senior faculty, and even administrators whose daily tasks become more onerous when the system does not support women. Someone must respond to the latest financial or other crisis faced by the Women's Studies Program, to support the women students on campus who are fighting the Miss All-University Pageant, to strengthen the resolve of the token woman in a particular department, and to require the administration to address the issues and concerns of women in the university community. This is true in terms of national service to the profession as well: Senior feminist faculty must be available to champion the cause of women in the discipline and to sustain the struggle for additional incremental and larger advances.

My focus on the inability to implement an exclusively feminist practice does not mean there have been no successes. Indeed, as I described above, I did have the opportunity to get to know and learn personally from some of my respondents. Another important success has been my collaborative efforts with feminist colleagues. Through my political activism, both inside and outside of academic and professional issues, I have had the extraordinary good fortune to develop friendships with feminist peers, an exhilarating experience. To me there is no substitute for a shared political ideology in discussing research and professional issues. Together we have helped each other obtain tenure and promotion, secure raises, procure desirable academic and professional positions, and contend with the daily obstacles encountered in the struggle to live a feminist life.

A prominent benefit of these friendships has been the opportunity to join efforts on specific research projects. It has been immensely gratifying to work with these colleagues. Here is a context in which each participant brings to the project her own unique knowledge and abilities; together we create our own feminist process. These joint feminist efforts simultaneously serve as models for graduate students and new professionals and are essential for my professional survival. In the process of working with and learning from my colleagues, I have found (a) the freedom to reject the notion that there is one feminist way of doing things and

(b) the support I need to make steady and consistent changes over time toward achieving my goals of feminist practice.

Conclusion

Being a feminist in an academic setting is, in some ways, a reproduction of the experience for women of family life: The university is a locus of both struggle and support. There are the constant struggles of working within a patriarchal system, some of which I described above, and the tremendous opportunities to choose one's own collaborators and to follow one's own interests and point of view. In everyday life I try to focus on the opportunities and the support. I am passionate about my feminism, my research, my teaching, all aspects of my academic life. Being a feminist sustains and enriches me as a person and continues to make me a better researcher.

Most importantly, it has provided colleagues ways to bolster and enrich me. My feminist sisters and brothers have been and continue to be both forgiving and supportive of my professional work. They are a ready sanctuary from the patriarchal system in which we are embedded, and they have helped shape me as teacher, researcher, colleague, and friend. Being a feminist has empowered me to allow my colleagues to have a major impact on my professional life. Together we are learning about the complexity of women's life experiences. In the future, as some among us rise to positions atop our respective fields, feminist voices will help shape the status quo through service as university administrators, as reviewers on funding committees, and as editors of leading journals. Then we will be poised to explore and understand fully the reality of women's daily lives.

References

Acker, J., Barry, K., & Esseveld, J. (1983). Objectivity and truth: Problems in doing feminist research. *Women's Studies International Forum, 6,* 423-435.

Adams, B. (1968). *Kinship in an urban setting.* Chicago: Markham.

Allen, K. R., & Walker, A. J. (1992a). Attentive love: A feminist perspective on the caregiving of adult daughters. *Family Relations, 41,* 284-289.

Allen, K. R., & Walker, A. J. (1992b). A feminist analysis of interviews with elderly mothers and their daughters. In J. F. Gilgun, K. Daly, & G. Handel (Eds.), *Qualitative methods in family research* (pp. 198-214). Newbury Park, CA: Sage.

Apfel, N. H., & Seitz, V. (1991). Four models of adolescent mother-grandmother relationships in Black inner-city families. *Family Relations, 40,* 421-429.

Atkinson, J., & Huston, T. L. (1984). Sex role orientation and division of labor in early marriage. *Journal of Personality and Social Psychology, 46,* 330-345.

Beckman, L. J. (1981). Effects of social interaction and children's relative inputs on older women's psychological well-being. *Journal of Personality and Social Psychology, 41,* 1075-1086.

Brody, E. M., & Schoonover, C. B. (1986). Patterns of parent-care when adult daughters work and when they do not. *The Gerontologist, 26,* 372-381.

Chodorow, N. (1978). *The reproduction of mothering.* Berkeley: University of California Press.

Finley, N. J. (1989). Theories of family labor as applied to gender differences in caregiving for elderly parents. *Journal of Marriage and the Family, 51,* 79-86.

Gerson, K. (1985). *Hard choices: How women decide about work, career, and motherhood.* Berkeley: University of California Press.

Gilligan, C. (1982). *In a different voice: Psychological theory and women's development.* Cambridge, MA: Harvard University Press.

Glenn, E. N. (1987). Gender and the family. In B. B. Hess & M. M. Ferree (Eds.), *Analyzing gender: A handbook of social science research* (pp. 348-380). Newbury Park, CA: Sage.

Hochschild, A., with Machung, A. (1989). *The second shift.* New York: Avon.

Kelley, H. H. (1979). *Personal relationships: Their structure and processes.* Hillsdale, NJ: Lawrence Erlbaum.

Kinney, J. M., & Stephens, M. A. P. (1989). Hassles and uplifts of giving care to a family member with dementia. *Psychology and Aging, 4,* 402-408.

Lyman, K. A. (1989). Bringing the social back in: A critique of the biomedicalization of dementia. *The Gerontologist, 29,* 597-605.

Matthews, S. H. (1985). The burdens of parent care: A critical evaluation of recent findings. *Journal of Aging Studies, 2,* 157-165.

Matthews, S. H., Werkner, J. E., & Delaney, P. J. (1989). Relative contributions of help by employed and nonemployed sisters to their elderly parents. *Journal of Gerontology: Social Sciences, 44,* S36-S44.

Motenko, A. K. (1989). The frustrations, gratifications, and well-being of dementia caregivers. *The Gerontologist, 29,* 166-172.

Rubin, L. (1979). *Women of a certain age: The midlife search for self.* New York: Harper & Row.

Rubin, L. B. (1976). *Worlds of pain: Life in the working-class family.* New York: Basic Books.

Ruddick, S. (1982). Maternal thinking. In B. Thorne & M. Yalom (Eds.), *Rethinking the family: Some feminist questions* (pp. 76-94). New York: Longman.

Ruddick, S. (1989). *Maternal thinking: Toward a politics of peace.* Boston: Beacon.

Stoller, E. P. (1983). Parental caregiving by adult children. *Journal of Marriage and the Family, 45,* 851-858.

Stoller, E. P. (1990). Males as helpers: The role of sons, relatives, and friends. *The Gerontologist, 30,* 228-235.

Stoller, E. P., & Pugliesi, K. L. (1989). Other roles of caregivers: Competing responsibilities or supportive resources. *Journal of Gerontology: Social Sciences, 44,* S231-S238.

Stueve, A. (1982). The elderly as network members. *Marriage and Family Review, 5,* 59-87.

Thibaut, J. W., & Kelley, H. H. (1959). *The social psychology of groups.* New York: John Wiley.

Thompson, L. (1992). Feminist methodology for family studies. *Journal of Marriage and the Family, 54,* 3-18.

Thompson, L., & Walker, A. J. (1984). Mothers and daughters: Aid patterns and attachment. *Journal of Marriage and the Family, 46,* 313-322.

Walker, A. J., & Allen, K. R. (1991). Relationships between caregiving daughters and their elderly mothers. *The Gerontologist, 31,* 389-396.

Walker, A. J., Martin, S. S. K., & Jones, L. L. (1992). The benefits and costs of caregiving and care receiving for daughters and mothers. *Journal of Gerontology: Social Sciences, 47,* S130-S139.

Walker, A. J., & Pratt, C. C. (1991). Daughters' help to mothers: Intergenerational aid versus caregiving. *Journal of Marriage and the Family, 53,* 3-12.

Walker, A. J., Pratt, C. C., & Oppy, N. C. (1992). Perceived reciprocity in family caregiving. *Family Relations, 41,* 82-85.

Walker, A. J., & Thompson, L. (1983). Intimacy and intergenerational aid and contact among mothers and daughters. *Journal of Marriage and the Family, 45,* 841-849.

Walker, A. J., Thompson, L., & Morgan, C. S. (1987). Two generations of mothers and daughters: Role status and interdependence. *Psychology of Women Quarterly, 11,* 195-208.

Zarit, S. H. (1989). Do we need another "stress and caregiving" study? *The Gerontologist, 29,* 147-148.

5

Feminist Reflections
on Lifelong Single Women

KATHERINE R. ALLEN

Beginnings

I began to study older single women as a young graduate student at
Syracuse University in a course entitled History of Western Family Systems and taught by my mentor, Robert Pickett. I was in my second semester of graduate school, and after taking courses in family theory and
research methods, I was already uneasy with the ways intimate life was
characterized in contemporary family studies. Authors portrayed adult
men and women as following neat developmental transitions through normative roles and events, giving little attention to non-normative aspects
of adult life.

Developmental theory enshrined these roles for women in the marital
and parental careers of wife and mother (Hill & Rodgers, 1964). Although
structural-functionalism had fallen into disfavor (Holman & Burr, 1980),
the reductionistic notion of instrumental and expressive roles resisted era-
sure, because it was easy to learn and easy to teach, like returning to
the simple reference of independent and dependent variables when a
problem I was studying holistically became too dense. I eventually
learned that it was more conceptually than empirically useful to think in

AUTHOR'S NOTE: I wish to thank my colleagues Kristine Baber, Vern Bengtson, Karen
Blaisure, Rosemary Blieszner, David Demo, Leigh Leslie, Stephen Marks, Donna Sollie,
Tamara Stone, Linda Thompson, and especially Alexis Walker for their generous assistance
in shaping my ideas for this chapter.

terms of normative roles and stages (Nock, 1979), but even then family theories appeared to use mechanistic ways of conceptualizing individual and social life, unable to handle the fluidity and variability of how I sensed the world to be.

As we were studying the history of Western family systems, I also was raiding my mentor's bookshelves for other texts to supplement my course work. I found that Libby and Whitehurst's (1977) edited book on alternative lifestyles was an important resource for my peers and teachers. In studying this volume, I noticed a contradiction about knowledge of the family that still seems resistant to change. On the one hand, much space was devoted to remote abstract theorizing about the family that comprised the dominant mainstream knowledge base of family studies. On the other hand, the immense diversity that captured my attention seemed compressed into a controversial volume on "alternatives" (Libby & Whitehurst, 1977) or into a single chapter in a decade review on "nontraditional family forms" (Macklin, 1980). This bifurcation of the normative and the non-normative foreshadowed eventual attempts in the field to deal with family diversity and complexity (Elder, 1981), particularly in terms of women's lives (Thorne, 1982).

Dr. Pickett introduced me to a new way of examining individuals and families. With my friend Christine Riley, I read earlier developmental accounts within an emerging framework called the *life course perspective*. Among other startling assertions, this perspective emphasized the variability of an individual's life trajectories and the notion of conflicting interests within the same family (Elder, 1977). The idea of the family as a unity of harmonious perspectives, roles, and careers was challenged by this interdisciplinary way of viewing individual, family, and societal change over time. Demographic studies using a cohort perspective revealed that it was no longer useful to conceptualize adulthood as one undifferentiated pathway. To examine family diversity and change, for example, Uhlenberg (1974) compared five successive groups of women (1890-1894, 1900-1904, 1910-1914, 1920-1924, 1930-1934) in five demographic categories: women who experienced early death; spinsters; childless women; women in unstable marriages with children; and married or widowed women with children. Uhlenberg theorized that the latter was the most preferred category, while the spinster category was the least preferred. This approach enabled me to think in terms of variability across well-defined subgroups of a slice of the population.

With these new ideas in mind, I chose to investigate my own family history as my project for Dr. Pickett's class. The emerging ideas in the scholarly literature on contemporary alternative lifestyles and historical family diversity that challenged the unitary model of family development coincided with observations I had made about my own family. Many women in my family did not marry, but they did not fit the pejorative stereotype of old maid or the image evoked by Uhlenberg's (1974) empirical label of "spinster." In fact, the older unmarried women in my family had more personal freedom than the married mothers and grandmothers: They worked outside the home, traveled, had their own money, drove their own cars, and went to the movies. They had full lives that were not described in any of the standard texts I was reading, nor did Libby's (1977) account of "creative singlehood as a sexual life-style" describe their experience. And though marriage and motherhood were held as the expected paths to adult status in my family, the choices of the single women were not denigrated overtly. Indeed these women were fully integrated into their families of origin and the larger kin group. Why were older unmarried women so invisible in mainstream accounts of family life when they were so vital in my own family? More importantly, why did we not have an adequate language with which to describe their life course experiences? Uhlenberg's (1974) unexamined use of the term *spinster* became a rallying point for my work on women who did not marry or become mothers. This marginalized group of women had been noticed, but they still were categorized in stereotypic ways. And even I continued to define them as "never-married, childless women," not yet having a picture big enough to break free from the mainstream conceptualization that defined women by what they were not—in this case, not wives and not mothers.

During this semester-long project, I spent a week with one of my older unmarried aunts. She helped me trace six generations of my family back to 1802. While examining my family history, I observed that only one child per family of origin reproduced prodigiously and that most of the women were eccentric, tiny, and unmarried.

Years later, after I wrote my dissertation and was turning it into my first book (Allen, 1989b), I learned from an article by Dixon (1978) that my Irish ancestors followed the "Western European marriage pattern," in which only one or two children in a large family married and had children. Dixon's portrayal of economic and demographic pressures that led to late marriage and a high proportion of people who never married explained the macrostructure in which this pattern emerged. Using this explanation, I could account for the many women and men who did not marry or have children in those six generations of my family. But I still had not yet answered all of my questions about their lives, nor did I have a language or theory to explain their visibility in my own family of origin and their exclusion from the family studies literature.

Although I found some answers in the data I collected for my dissertation, insights also emerged as I lived my own life. For example, in 1985, when I was preparing to teach my first qualitative research methods course as a new assistant professor at Texas Woman's University, I resonated with the narrator in Mary Gordon's (1985) novel *Men and Angels:*

> There was that hunger that she felt, that women felt, to know details: where women stood in relation to their families, as daughters, sisters, mothers. It wasn't just; it wasn't creditable. Yet one wanted to know, when the women had accomplished something. Whom did they love in relation to their bodies? Whom were they connected to by blood? . . . . But it wasn't the fact of the connection that was interesting; it was how they got around it. The truth of the matter was that for a woman to have accomplished something, she had to get out of the way of her own body. This was the trick people wanted to know about . . . people who were interested in the achievements of women wanted the grossest facts: Whom did they sleep with? Did they have any babies? Were their fathers kind to them, cruel to them? Did they obey or go against their mothers? Infantile questions, yet one felt one had to know. It gave courage, somehow. (p. 50)

Like Gordon's narrator, one motivation for my quest to understand the life course of single women was practical. To paraphrase Gordon's passage about how women got out of the way of their own bodies, I was asking, How did women get out of the way of social prescriptions to marry and have children? My partial answer to this question would come from another stream of my life: my practical experience with the feminist movement. Until an experience in 1987, when I began again to read feminist scholarship, my feminist reading was confined to the occasional classic radical work such as *Sisterhood Is Powerful* (Morgan, 1970), the poetry of Adrienne Rich, and the novels of Margaret Atwood, Mary Gordon, Toni Morrison, Marge Piercy, and others. I subscribed to the feminist journal *Signs* in the early 1980s, but as the press of writing a dissertation and starting my professional career closed in on me, I relinquished that intellectual tie, having little support for my desire to read feminist scholarship. In those later years of graduate school, I was a liberal feminist activist, not a radical feminist scholar. Along with my graduate school friend Jane Gilgun, I worked in the local chapter of the National Organization for Women and was involved for several years in trying to pass the Equal Rights Amendment, but still I was on the edge of the intellectual revolution of women's studies.

These two streams—academic and political feminism—had not yet merged in my own life. My scholarly commitment to women's studies was to come several years later, in 1987, when I submitted a manuscript to the journal *Family Relations* for which Alexis Walker was collecting articles on feminist approaches to family studies. Alexis became a guide and colleague in reading feminist theory and empirical studies. I was pregnant with my son Matthew, and I recall waking up at 4:30 in the morning and sitting at my computer to begin writing a paper on feminist teaching (Allen, 1988). As I sent the manuscript to Alexis, I believed, unreflexively, that my private experience of incorporating feminist principles into my teaching, without one reference to the impassioned feminist literature that already existed, would be accessible to others. The reviews I received of that paper from other feminists led me to examine a multiplicity of pedagogical and theoretical works. The process of critique and the suggestion of whole new literatures to read changed my intellectual life. It was a turning point, and I have devoured feminist writing ever since. In going from the practical to the theoretical, my personal life also changed. I have learned that these dialectics of change are a critical component of feminist praxis.

Thus what began as a student project on family history has become a personal, theoretical, empirical, and political journey. My trek back to 1802 eventually led me to the women I studied for my dissertation, women whose narratives continue to teach me about the integration of theory, research, and practice. They have led me to a new story that I am now able to tell, a story in which feminist consciousness is central.

Initial Analyses

My dissertation (Allen, 1984) involved life history interviews with 30 women, 15 of whom did not marry or bear children, and 15 of whom married, had at least one child who survived to adulthood, became grandmothers, and eventually became widows. A main objective was to examine two trajectories in women's family life course, not as normative and deviant, but as variations. A life course perspective guided the study, grounded in a critique of the application of traditional family developmental theory to aggregate data on female life cycle experience. Previous studies conceptualized marriage and motherhood as normative and other pathways, such as permanent singlehood, as deviant (Glick, 1977; Uhlenberg, 1974). The life course perspective provided a more comprehensive understanding of variations among women by allowing me to examine their experiences within the context of working-class family life.

To locate these 30 women, I contacted 193 women by telephone from a list of referrals provided by former colleagues in the elderly social service network to which I once belonged as a social worker. I interviewed 104 older women in person and determined that 74 were not "eligible" for the complete study. To be eligible, the women needed to be from the 1910 birth cohort (within the range of 1907 to 1914), of working-class status (because nearly all studies of lifelong single women had been with educated, middle- to upper-class privileged women only), and white (in retrospect, this choice was unfortunate; it had been required by a few committee members who believed that a homogeneous sample was essential to obtaining valid qualitative data).

The 30 women in the complete project were interviewed for about 5 hours over the course of three sessions. In the first interview, they were asked about their daily activities and current experiences as older women and then to complete a life events guide to sensitize them to the more in-depth life history questions that comprised the next steps of the interview process. In the second interview, they were asked to describe and reflect on the major events of their lives, with a particular focus on their family experiences. The single women and the widows were asked to comment on how typical they thought their lives had been in comparison with other women whom they thought were similar to and different from themselves in terms of marital and parental careers. These questions dealt with how women in different female life course careers considered their lives to be normative or atypical. They also were asked about their perspectives on the past, present, and future, a strategy designed to establish rapport, gain insight into their subjective meanings about their lives, and offer closure at the end of the interview. In the third session, detailed life history questions were asked about their families, friendships, health histories, and residential, occupational, and educational careers.

The data analysis process yielded 10 major coding categories, each elaborated with several subcategories. Although findings from the study were published in articles (Allen, 1989a; Allen & Pickett, 1987) and elaborated in my book (Allen, 1989b), I will provide a few examples of the initial analysis and interpretation by using quotations from Allen (1989b).

I followed a developmental scheme to present the data, beginning with the harsh realities of childhood in which early loss of parents, child labor, and discrimination due to immigrant heritage characterized many of their lives. Several women lived in orphanages or were cared for on a temporary basis by kin other than their parents, foreshadowing the subsequent engagement of most of the women with family caregiving throughout their lives. This familistic ideology as a way to deal with the ever-present threat of dependency was characteristic of working-class women at the turn of the century (Hareven, 1977; Katz, °3).

As young adults the 30 women follow. .t two pathways (marriage vs. singlehood) to adult status, but three: 10 women married early, 5 women delayed marriage until about age 30, and 15 women did not marry at all. The 10 who married early did so by age 24, some to escape mistreatment and hard work in their families of origin:

> I didn't have any love as a child, but I got love from my husband. I can't understand a woman not wanting to have children because I couldn't wait to have my own. I took care of other people's children from the time I was 7 years old, and I wanted my own. (Allen, 1989b, p. 71)

Others married early because their friends were getting married:

> I always wanted to be married. . . . I think girls of my era did feel that we should be married. My closest girlfriend and I . . . graduated together. She started to date about the same time I started to date. She married, and I was her bridesmaid. They were married in June, and we were married in November, and she was my bridesmaid. (p. 74)

The five women who delayed marriage throughout their 20s did so because they were either needed at home or enjoying being single. Their narratives appeared more similar to those of the women who did not marry at all, contradicting the assumption that women follow a uniform pathway to marriage:

> Well, I thought there for a while I was going to be an old maid because I was 29. . . . I was close to my mother. I took care of her, and when she died of cancer, I was home. (p. 75)

The 15 women who did not marry gave one of four accounts for their singlehood. Only 2 women said they had their "hearts broken" by men who had promised to marry them. The others claimed they had responsibilities in their families of origin to care for or support dependent parents or siblings:

> I had to take my mother into consideration. . . . I wanted to get to work, because I knew we needed the money. So there was just no question. . . . It was my responsibility because my older brother was married, and my other brother was in school, so I was elected. (p. 78)

Three of these never-married women claimed they remained single because they "wanted to accomplish something in life." They did not want to be hindered by the excessive work that marriage and motherhood would bring:

> I had places to go and things to see. And I wasn't going to be stopped, nobody was going to. It took me a long time to get going, but I made it. (p. 82)

Those who said they never wished to marry provided insight into other pathways to fulfillment in adulthood:

> For many people, events like graduating . . . are very exciting, but the ends of things are not exciting to me. Its the getting there that's what interests me. I remember some particular days in my life, but a lot of them had to do with nature. The very good days. (p. 82)

In middle adulthood the women's lives were centered around family caregiving activities. Married women cared primarily for their husbands, children, and grandchildren. Twelve lifelong single women had primary responsibility for aging parents, but only 4 widows provided such care. Nearly all of the women in the sample maintained important relationships with children, either their own or as second mothers to other women's children, as in the example of this lifelong single woman:

> My sister had 4 kids and 13 grandchildren. Since she died, I'm the matriarch of the family. They all come to me, and I'm pretty lucky to have them. (p. 103)

Finally all of the women were single in old age. Most felt free from former caregiving responsibilities. Their lives converged around adjusting to being alone. As one never-married woman said:

> I am not a widow, but I'm the same as a widow. I'm a woman living alone, going home to an empty house. . . . If I go out to places with the senior citizens,

either my friend or his wife will follow me home. . . . This is one of the ways they help me. (p. 112)

Others simply enjoyed taking care of themselves, as one widow noted:

> I never had any desire to remarry. People used to ask me why I never remarry and I said, "if I could find someone to take as good of care of me as I take care of myself, maybe I would consider it." (p. 110)

Some of my choices about theory, method, sample, and analysis seem almost quaint to me now that I have read more extensively in the vast literature on feminist methodology, taught courses on qualitative and feminist research methods, conducted new research projects, and advised more than a dozen qualitative dissertations. But I had proposed my dissertation in 1983, when conducting qualitative research in family studies was unusual and unpopular. At worst it was considered "unscientific," so I was asked to conform to certain research conventions derived from experimental methods. What appealed to me about qualitative methods a decade ago continues to appeal to me today: the opportunity to be an active participant in the research process without assuming the illusion of objectivity that undergirds the positivist tradition. Making a qualitative study look more like a quantitative one is less likely to be asked of a student today. But I did make concessions to get my proposal accepted. At the time it seemed as if I was asked to do more than others who proposed a survey design. In retrospect I realize that the concerns and questions of my teachers and peers forced me to think through and justify every aspect of the project.

Continuities

The work that went into strengthening and clarifying my method and conceptualization at the proposal stage allowed me to collect and analyze valid data that continue to hold up under my current feminist scrutiny. Over time, however, a deeper involvement with feminist theory, teaching, and research, as well as changes in my personal life, have led me to rethink some ways in which I first wrote about these data. In particular, three themes from my original dissertation analysis continue to talk back to me, informing me that I have a more adequate and accurate story to tell. These themes have served as guideposts for my intellectual and personal journey—nudging my unconscious, inspiring my attempts for more inclusive theories about women and their families, and appearing in new projects I have undertaken.

The Pervasiveness of Abuse in Women's Lives

The first theme in my work is that many of the women I interviewed were abused as children and young adults. In my original writings, however, I was unable to describe fully their abuse histories except in socially acceptable ways. I have come to realize that part of my inability to go beyond euphemistic descriptions of *family* violence, abuse, and neglect related to not having a *feminist* language for these experiences. I learned from Kelly (1988) how long it takes women to describe their experiences of being violated and to name their abuse. This was a turning point in my ability to name and then to begin to understand the pervasiveness of abuse in women's lives. Perhaps even more revealing of my socially acceptable account of these abuse histories was that I had not yet come to terms with my own abuse history.

Recollections of one never-married woman (I will call her Nell) from my original study edge me toward greater clarity about the pervasiveness of abuse in women's lives. She lived with and cared for an abusive father until his death at 94. She was raised by her father and stepmother who, she said:

> always kept me under heel. They told me I was clumsy and stupid. I had a hard time getting through school . . . but when I got out and started [working], I found out I wasn't as stupid as I was painted. . . . I felt like I was jumping a hurdle by getting away from my family. (pp. 80-81)

During our interviews she presented herself to me with dignity, grace, and self-respect. Although I failed to explore her painful experiences in detail, I believe I now would take a more probing approach to questions and hunches that emerged when I first interviewed her. As an inexperienced researcher, I was afraid to venture beyond my initial hesitancy and to inquire with greater care and depth about the family life she described. Well-trained not to read into the situation or to extrapolate beyond the data, I realize now that I also may have shrunk from opportunities during the interview to ask her, for example, about her relief when her father died.

Perhaps Nell told me all she was going to, and I was responsible by not inquiring further. I listened well to her narrative and reported it faithfully, but I have learned since that listening well is only part of the process. As I look back over the interviews with Nell and reread the transcripts, she said clearly that her father was abusive to her. Although I did report that she had suffered from these traumatic experiences, at this point in time I would be a more active participant in an interview with her. I would explore with more confidence the contradiction of her escape from her home as a young woman and then her return in midlife to care for her father. Now I would have the courage to ask her about her feelings after his death, rather than to leave the question, planted like a seed in me at that time, unwatered, and thus undeveloped. I now wonder how my silence about certain issues may have silenced her.

Now I would believe her with more faithfulness than I could muster as a beginner in life and in research. I still recall the fragility of her face, like a fine pastry that flakes in your hand or porcelain that cracks when exposed to extreme changes in temperature; not the puffy look of someone who has spent years drinking and smoking, but the look of a woman who has suffered betrayal from her most intimate associates and yet still believes it is her place to continue to care for them. As my feminist consciousness emerges, I feel more urgency and capacity to understand and describe her story than during my initial at-face-value attempt.

I feel self-conscious about these wonderings. Am I revealing too much about the dilemmas I face as a person and a researcher? When I teach classes on qualitative methods, I emphasize the importance of not sliding all the way to the end of the piano keys too quickly—that is, not pushing respondents to tell more or probe in ways that are not exquisitely close to their own words. Caution and respect for another's reticence about self-disclosure are paramount to the trust we develop in conducting research (Allen & Baber, 1992a). But there is always more to the story than one can hear, no matter how many hours are spent with a respondent, as Stacey (1988, 1990) poignantly reveals in her accounts of conducting a feminist ethnography.

Feminism offers a theoretical perspective that allows us to politicize the narratives we hear and tell, so that the structures of domination that govern our lives (racism, sexism, heterosexism, ageism, and classism) can be understood and transformed (hooks, 1989). The process of becoming conscious about structures of domination is an important part of the feminist promise of social change and liberation from oppression. Feminists focus on the tension between the personal ways in which our lives are constrained by such structures and the political activities in which we engage to change those structures.

Thus I have come to realize that there were some things I was not ready to hear when I first listened to Nell. Naming one's abuse history is risky; for some it may never be possible. Personal narratives of survivors reveal how difficult it is for others to hear and believe their stories and how difficult it is for even one woman to believe herself (Bass & Davis, 1988; Kelly, 1988). Patti Davis, former President Reagan's daughter, was interviewed in a *People* magazine article ("A daughter's lament," 1992) regarding her autobiographical book *The Way I See It* (Davis, 1992). A subsequent letter to the editor in the June 8 issue stated, "Wouldn't it be great if Patti Davis got another string for her violin." Glib denial and incredulity are socially acceptable responses to abuse narratives, even among clinicians and other professionals (see Barrett & Trepper, 1992; Schwartz, 1992).

As my feminist consciousness deepened, I could no longer hold the narratives of others at arm's length, as if oppression happened only to others less fortunate than I. Learning to recognize, name, and confront ways in which I had been abused followed my feminist activism on behalf of others. Personal narratives told "from the heart" (Collins, 1990) became a way to stop the subterfuge and hypocrisy in telling only socially acceptable accounts of my experience (Witherell & Noddings, 1991). Learning to reconnect these personal narratives to public, political struggles is a feminist activity in which I am now engaged (hooks, 1989). In my teaching, as in my life, I am on a quest to merge emotional honesty and intellectual insight in the pursuit of social and political change.

What Normative Female Life Course?

The second theme in my work is that older single women's lives provide evidence for the need to rethink the theoretical life course that women in textbooks are supposed to experience. Following Erikson (1950), theories of individual and family development proposed that an individual first develops a secure identity and then, if healthy, goes on to commit oneself to another (who, it goes without saying, is a partner of the other gender within the context of heterosexual legal marriage). After securing a husband, a woman proceeds to motherhood, where she extends her capacity for love and intimacy to nurture her offspring in a generative way. Scholars such as Rubin (1979) and Gilligan (1982) challenged the progression of identity, intimacy, and generativity, suggesting instead that for women, intimacy probably precedes identity. Carrying that observation further, feminist theorists suggest that development may be far more idiosyncratic than previous revisions allowed (see Jordan, Kaplan, Miller, Stiver, & Surrey, 1991). The women I interviewed exemplify the alternative view that there is no socially patterned time or event at which a woman feels she has "grown up." The notion of developmental stages is an incomplete conceptualization for the diversity of women's lives, as Kristine Baber and I propose in our reconstruction of family life from women-centric perspectives (Baber & Allen, 1992). The life stories of these women can be better understood by using a feminist analysis that places them at the center, not one in which a general norm guides the construction of their lives.

A touchstone for this observation that continues to inform my work is another lifelong single woman from my original study (I will call her Meg). She said, completely nonplussed, that she was a child until her parents died when she was 63. She lived alone in the home she had shared with her parents; she was active in the senior center where she spent most days making doll clothes and toys. She was friendly with a man for the first time and had just learned to drive. When I asked whether she ever considered getting married and having children, she replied:

> The thought never crossed my mind. Not a bit. I didn't have anything against men, but maybe I stayed kinda childish for quite a few years. I just wasn't interested in them. (p. 120)

Meg certainly did not fit into the models of adulthood I had learned about in graduate school. I was 30 and she was 73 at the time of our interview, and I saw her as completely different from me—an enigma. I was fond of her and curious about her lack of regret that she had lived under the thumb of her parents until she was what I then considered to be old age. At that time I was unable to grasp that she preferred the way she lived: She was not just a sweet anomaly, but a woman in control of her own life. I did not have a clue about our common ground, nor could I have predicted how profound her experience of not feeling grown up until she was 63 would become for me.

Ten years later I see that marriage and motherhood, two socially acceptable events in the transition to adulthood, did not confer adult status on me either. Rather, like Meg, a more definitive event in my own life course was breaking with my parents' reality about the unambiguous harmony of our family. Ironically, at age 30, I felt more advanced in my adulthood than this elderly woman who was making crafts and toys and going on dates for the first time in her life. At the time of our interview, I was unable to see that she already had disavowed herself of many cultural and familial myths that I still possessed. Chief among these was that a woman needed a husband in order to lead a fulfilling life. Now, at 40, I feel as if I am a novice. Meg taught me about the long, uncharted road toward independence in adulthood and the myriad ways in which women come to understand their own lives and fulfill their intimacy needs.

Why Are Lesbians Invisible in Family Studies?

The third theme in my work follows from this general questioning of the normative female life course. I have come to realize that I avoided questions about women's sexualities in my original interviews, reporting data about sexual education and experiences only if volunteered by the women themselves. The women talked about their lack of sexual knowledge, but mostly in terms of socially acceptable topics such as menstruation and pregnancy (Allen, 1989b, pp. 54-57). Looking back, I realize that I silenced my respondents by not taking a more proactive approach and asking about their sexual histories as an important aspect of life experience. Again a deepening feminist consciousness corresponds with my increasing reflexivity about how even a sympathetic listener can stop women inadvertently from telling their stories.

Avoiding questions about sexuality, particularly lesbian experience, is not new. In another study on lifelong single women, Rubinstein, Alexander, Goodman, and Luborsky (1991) described 8 of the 31 never-married, childless older women in their sample as participants in "same-generation, same-gender companionate relations" (p. S275). The authors noted that these relationships "were more than casual friendships. Generally they included some of the following features: enduringness, subjective closeness, periods of co-residence, extensive traveling together such as on vacations and holidays, and in some cases involvements with the other's extended family" (p. S275). Although this description seems like the kinds of lesbian partnerships described by Blumstein and Schwartz (1983) in their examination of four kinds of intimate relationships (including lesbian couples) and Weston's (1991) work on the families of lesbians and gay men, none of the "same-generation, same-gender companionate relations" described by Rubinstein et al. (1991) were referred to as lesbian.

Shying away from naming or defining women's experiences as lesbian has long been a dilemma for feminist researchers as well. In an explicitly feminist analysis, Taylor and Rupp (1991) discuss why they omitted questions about lesbians from their oral history interviews with elderly participants in their study of the women's movement during the antifeminist climate of the 1940s and 1950s. They noted that some of the women they interviewed, who "had long-term companions and might have been lesbians . . . made derogatory remarks about lesbians in the contemporary women's movement" (p. 126). Following Simon's (1987) experience of interviewing older never-married women and being unable to gain information about their sexual experiences, Taylor and Rupp (1991) chose to avoid questions about lesbian experience out of respect and care for the participants. Citing a generational difference between explicit lesbian-feminists of today and older activists of several decades ago, they followed the feminist principle of learning about their respondents' world from the respondents' perspectives, rather than imposing their own.

I, too, thought about the issue of lesbian experience in the lives of never-married women and decided to steer clear of it. But even then I knew my choice was political; I was protecting myself more than my respondents. I avoided the lesbian issue from the very beginning. I had read Adams's (1972, 1976) work on singlehood and had been frightened away from the topic of sexuality by the following passage:

> Single women, for example, are still the victims of quite outrageous stereotyping in regard to their ascribed characteristics, and their unmarried status is popularly attributed to personal failings, such as lack of sexual attractiveness (whatever that elusive quality may be), unresolved early psychosexual conflicts, narcistic [sic] unwillingness to be closely committed to another individual, latent lesbianism. (Adams, 1972, p. 92)

Regardless of what Adams meant by the phrase "latent lesbianism," to me it was a neon sign saying, "Stay away from the lesbian question." Rather than deal with it directly or break new ground on the topic, I chose to dissociate myself from the issue of sexuality altogether. I was often asked: What was a young, middle-class, heterosexually married doctoral student doing studying never-married, working-class, childless elderly women? My best guess was that it was a road not taken for me—until, that is, the day I realized the road had been there all along. As Stacey (1990) points out, alternative narratives coexist with the ones we choose to privilege.

My research on older single women awakened me to other possibilities, rattling the knobs to doors formerly invisible to me. So fearful was I of reading myself into my research that it seems the text began to read me. I had not so much slammed the doors shut to other experiences; rather, I could see the doors but the knobs were invisible, so I did not think about opening them. I began to change as my feminist awareness deepened. I became more reflexive about how respondents might view me. My former one-way gaze at the women through my lens only, without engaging the possibility of understanding them from their own perspective, inhibited me from exploring all possible aspects of their experience. Now a feminist perspective and the process of maturing enable me to see in new and other ways, extending my vision from a mirror to more of a panorama.

None of the women I interviewed spoke explicitly about her sexuality as an adult. No woman described her sexual history with her husband or suggested she had an intimate sexual relationship with another woman or man. As I rethink the interviews, however, I realize I was blinded by the belief that marital status and sexual experience are entwined. I assumed that the married women had been sexual with their husbands and that the never-married women had been asexual. The prevailing theory of my discipline—that dating, courtship, and marriage follow in a neat progression—did not encourage me to follow up on clues to other processes and feelings I sensed in the interviews. What about Mary, for example, a woman who joined the WAVES during World War II? What else was more compelling to her than marriage?

> Marriage wasn't that important to me, but I used to have girlfriends who would say to me, "You are the first one of our group to have dated, so how come you're not married?" They used to think it was terrible because I'm not married, and I wouldn't ever change places with them. So, I have been very happy with my life. I think it has been fantastic, and I would never want to go back and lead my life again, because if I did, it probably wouldn't have been as good. (p. 118)

Although I cannot speculate about the reasons behind Mary's single status or address the possibility of lesbian experience in particular, Mary's comments suggest the viability of a life without marriage. Furthermore the women in my study lived in mostly same-gender communities in which men were rather absent. Even the widows spent very little time talking about the men in their families—past or present. These observations about the invisibility of lesbians in the family studies literature and the relative absence of men in the daily experience of these older women hint at missed opportunities for further inquiry into their emotional and sexual affiliations.

As I mature, the data I collected for my dissertation continue to inform my thinking about older single women. Although I support the integrity of my original data analysis, I have developed the courage to question the neat transitions from theory to data and back to theory again. Most importantly, I question the omissions that seemed necessary to my survival as a young scholar and a woman not yet aware of certain choices she would make one day. The unfinished business of these three issues has been prominent in my thinking about older single women, leading me to examine what was unarticulated in the way I first wrote about them.

Transformations

The most powerful part of feminist process for me is the responsibility to care about others and the urgency to act toward change. As a social movement, feminism embraces the postmodern tension between the responsibility to otherness and the responsibility to act (White, 1991). The joining of personal and political transformations in my life has been enhanced by a deepening commitment to feminist theory, research, and praxis. I began to change my safe approach by taking seriously the meaning of being a feminist as a way of living and as a way of relating to others politically (Stanley, 1990).

Although unarticulated at first, my work began as a dialogue between theory and life. Along the way I have gained certain privileges that have allowed me to be more deliberate about this dialogue. Obtaining structural advantages, such as tenure, recognition of my teaching, and a network of fine colleagues and students, has freed me to do the kind of reading, teaching, research, and writing that stirs my imagination and allows me to question theoretical standpoints I once held dear. My double vision as a feminist—I am both an insider to the academy as a professor and an outsider as a woman and a lesbian—has fostered my struggle between certain freedoms and constraints in that tension-filled space in which I envision a more authentic way of living, thinking, and being. Feminist sociologists have described this struggle between life and theory as an ever-widening influence from local knowledge to generalized theory—from the particular to the general (see Collins, 1990; Smith, 1987).

Over time I have gained the confidence to trust that my particular experience is more than just that, more than "one woman's experience." I am not saying that a unitary female experience exists; rather, I am suggesting that my private struggles with abuse, life course transitions, and sexual orientation are not so unique after all. Indeed these issues have been present in my life, though I was aware only vaguely that such could be the case as I began my work on lifelong single women. How did they awaken? My explanation lies in the pathway from particular to general and back again through the process of conducting this research and narrowing the distance between myself and those whose lives I have studied.

I began with the theories of my intellectual community and found connections to my own life. When I embarked on this scholarly path, I would have described myself as a scholar, researcher, and theorist—a student of the family. Only incidentally would I acknowledge my status, at that time, as a married, child-free woman. But distinguishing between one's personal and professional identity seems dishonest to me now, as if anyone really could believe that the private life of the inquirer does not matter in the conduct of her research. Acknowledging that I am a woman, a lesbian, a survivor, a qualitative researcher, a theorist, a feminist, a mother, a teacher, and much more seems to be a basic step toward lessening the hypocrisy and subterfuge that attends much of our work as scholars.

Having acknowledged these shifting identities and allegiances, the next part of the process is politicization (hooks, 1989). It involves realizing how the researcher is changed by the process of research. It is not enough to point out simply how our "subjects" are changed by the research process or to report only how we minimized bias. New questions must be asked: How is the researcher changed? What are the benefits of self-awareness and reflexivity as research strategies (Fonow & Cook, 1991)? How can personal narratives transform our social worlds (Krieger, 1991)?

Reflexivity

A growing feminist awareness has allowed me to know in new ways where I read the data too narrowly. I do not know which came first—whether my unarticulated, unrealized knowledge of myself as a potential unmarried woman led me to investigate never-married women, or whether this project itself led me to these insights about abuse, life course, and sexuality.

As a novice researcher, I followed standard conventions of qualitative research; I avoided speculating about issues beyond my data. But now I know that even before I analyzed the data, I avoided collecting data on topics that either did not occur to me or made me uncomfortable. The product, then, is hygienic: Particular data are avoided altogether, and the collected data are cleansed of inconsistencies (Stanley, 1990). Feminist research, however, is excruciatingly self-conscious (Stacey, 1988).

Thus my initial rendering of the data, though I followed standard procedures to ensure their validity, is limited by an adherence to hygienic-qualitative research methods, traditional academic discourse, and my own hesitancy about examining abuse, growing up, and lesbianism in my private life. I continue to embrace the integrity of my original analysis because I view research as a process. I would not be able to critique my own work if I had not actively, even anxiously, pursued the unanswered questions from my original analysis. Other publications on life-long single women corroborate the evidence from my study, for example, the kinds of fictive kin relationships and attachments I found, the presence of family ties, and the life satisfaction among these women (e.g., Rubinstein et al., 1991; Simon, 1987). Thus I do not question the validity of the findings.

I question the enterprise of traditional research that gives no more than lip service to the person of the researcher or the context in which research is validated and accepted. My understanding of feminist theory and my own way of being in the world have allowed me to open that tension-filled space between the integrity of my original project and the socially acceptable—even advocated—distortions that accompany hygienic social science. I have proceeded with my research program by asking more inclusive questions about what I formerly was unable to see. I have allowed my scholarly path to be driven by my own unanswered questions about my life and the lives of others I have observed. Feminist praxis is teaching me how to listen to what I have not explained adequately, how to turn over the stones I could not see before, how to select the ones I am ready to turn over now, how to prepare myself for other explanations of what I see, and how to care so deeply about the lives of those I study that I want to get the story as close to their rendering of their lives as possible.

As I chart the scary waters of a new identity, the women from my dissertation come to mind. When, at age 35, I was looking for role models of how to live a new life, I thought about the women from my study who did not live with men, and I realized that male approval was not central to their well-being as women. No wonder single women are on the fringes of family theories. Now I am free to wonder whether among them were women who loved other women passionately. At the time, I didn't have the words, the questions, the courage, or the support to ask about something so untheorized in mainstream family studies. But the turning points in my own life have allowed me to hear their voices all over again, opening me to the possibilities of new questions and interpretations of women's lives.

New Collaborations

At the present time, my colleagues and I are researching explicitly feminist questions. Alexis Walker and I have applied this same process of uncovering previously unnamed benefits in women's relationship histories to our feminist analysis of mother-daughter caregiving pairs, relying on our friendship and professional collaboration to guide our inquiry (Allen & Walker, 1992). Addressing questions raised by sociologists Bernard (1972) and Stacey (1986), Karen Blaisure and I are considering ways that men and women in feminist marriages work together to "upgrade" marriage for women (Blaisure & Allen, 1994). We are examining also the continued vitality of heterosexuality for women who are feminists, despite the dilemmas created by gender inequity in marriage. Kristine Baber and I have forged a commitment to make feminist ideas accessible and alive for new scholars by proposing practical strategies for family life education (Allen & Baber, 1992b). We have struggled with the promise and the risk of applying postmodernism to feminist research (Allen & Baber, 1992a). In our recent book, we have deconstructed monolithic ideas of women's relationships, sexualities, reproductive decisions, caregiving, and work from a postmodern feminist perspective and offered a new synthesis of the plurality of women's experiences in their families and society (Baber & Allen, 1992).

I began my work on lifelong single women with the question, How are women who do not marry or have children like and unlike women who do? In the process of studying this question, feminism has provided a way of living, a way of conducting empirical and personal inquiry, and a way of theorizing about the world. I have joined other feminists as co-investigators in research, I have transformed my former marriage into a constructive friendship, and I have found a new way to live my own life— with another woman as my partner.

The process of conducting feminist research has allowed me to become more of myself, ironically, a creation that seems to change daily. I have become more relaxed than I ever thought possible, perhaps because I have the freedom to ask the questions that appear on the fault line between theory and my life. I have not done this alone, but through the voices of 104 women, 30 of whom shared several hours from their 70-some years. Even as time has faded the memory of their faces, the experiences I have recorded on paper speak to me about conducting my life and my research with greater clarity and care.

References

Adams, M. (1972). The single woman in today's society: A reappraisal. In H. Wortis & C. Rabinowitz (Eds.), *The women's movement: Social and psychological perspectives* (pp. 89-101). New York: Wiley.

Adams, M. (1976). *Single blessedness: Observations on the single status in married society.* New York: Basic Books.

A daughter's lament. (1992, May 18). *People,* pp. 113-114, 116.

Allen, K. R. (1984). *A life course study of never-married and ever-married elderly women from the 1910 birth cohort.* Unpublished doctoral dissertation, Syracuse University, Syracuse, NY.

Allen, K. R. (1988). Integrating a feminist perspective into family studies courses. *Family Relations, 37,* 29-35.

Allen, K. R. (1989a). Continuities and discontinuities in elderly women's lives: An analysis of four family careers. In D. Unruh (Ed.), *Current perspectives on aging and the life cycle: Vol. 3. Personal history through the life course* (pp. 225-241). Greenwich, CT: JAI.

Allen, K. R. (1989b). *Single women/Family ties: Life histories of older women.* Newbury Park, CA: Sage.

Allen, K. R., & Baber, K. M. (1992a). Ethical and epistemological tensions in applying a postmodern perspective to feminist research. *Psychology of Women Quarterly, 16,* 1-15.

Allen, K. R., & Baber, K. M. (1992b). Starting a revolution in family life education: A feminist vision. *Family Relations, 41,* 378-384.

Allen, K. R., & Pickett, R. S. (1987). Forgotten streams in the family life course: Utilization of qualitative retrospective interviews in the analysis of lifelong single women's family careers. *Journal of Marriage and the Family, 49,* 517-526.

Allen, K. R., & Walker, A. J. (1992). A feminist analysis of interviews with elderly mothers and their daughters. In J. F. Gilgun, K. Daly, & G. Handel (Eds.), *Qualitative methods in family research* (pp. 198-214). Newbury Park, CA: Sage.

Baber, K. M., & Allen, K. R. (1992). *Women and families: Feminist reconstructions.* New York: Guilford.

Barrett, M. J., & Trepper, T. S. (1992). Unmasking the incestuous family. *Family Therapy Networker, 16*(3), 39-46.

Bass, E., & Davis, L. (1988). *The courage to heal: A guide for women survivors of child sexual abuse.* New York: Harper & Row.

Bernard, J. (1972). *The future of marriage.* New York: Bantam.

Blaisure, K. R., & Allen, K. R. (1994). *Feminists and the ideology and practice of marital equality.* Unpublished manuscript.

Blumstein, P., & Schwartz, P. (1983). *American couples: Money, work, sex.* New York: William Morrow.

Collins, P. H. (1990). *Black feminist thought: Knowledge, consciousness, and the politics of empowerment.* Boston: Unwin Hyman.

Davis, P. (1992). *The way I see it.* New York: G. P. Putnam.

Dixon, R. B. (1978). Late marriage and non-marriage as demographic responses: Are they similar? *Population Studies, 32,* 449-466.

Elder, G. H., Jr. (1977). Family history and the life course. *Journal of Family History, 2,* 279-304.

Elder, G. H., Jr. (1981). History and the family: The discovery of complexity. *Journal of Marriage and the Family, 43,* 489-519.

Erikson, E. H. (1950). *Childhood and society.* New York: Norton.

Fonow, M. M., & Cook, J. A. (1991). Back to the future: A look at the second wave of feminist epistemology and methodology. In M. M. Fonow & J. A. Cook (Eds.), *Beyond methodology: Feminist scholarship as lived research* (pp. 1-15). Bloomington: Indiana University Press.

Gilligan, C. (1982). *In a different voice.* Cambridge, MA: Harvard University Press.

Glick, P. C. (1977). Updating the life cycle of the family. *Journal of Marriage and the Family, 39,* 5-13.

Gordon, M. (1985). *Men and angels.* New York: Random House.

Hareven, T. K. (1977). Family time and historical time. *Daedalus, 106,* 57-70.

Hill, R., & Rodgers, R. H. (1964). The developmental approach. In H. T. Christensen (Ed.), *Handbook of marriage and the family* (pp. 171-211). Chicago: Rand McNally.

Holman, T. B., & Burr, W. R. (1980). Beyond the beyond: The growth of family theories in the 1970s. *Journal of Marriage and the Family, 42,* 729-741.

hooks, b. (1989). Feminist politicization: A comment. In *Talking back: Thinking feminist, thinking black* (pp. 105-111). Boston: South End.

Jordan, J. V., Kaplan, A. G., Miller, J. B., Stiver, I. P., & Surrey, J. L. (Eds.). (1991). *Women's growth in connection: Writings from the Stone Center.* New York: Guilford.

Katz, M. B. (1983). *Poverty and policy in American history.* New York: Academic Press.

Kelly, L. (1988). How women define their experiences of violence. In K. Yllö & M. Bograd (Eds.), *Feminist perspectives on wife abuse* (pp. 114-132). Newbury Park, CA: Sage.

Krieger, S. (1991). *Social science and the self: Personal essays on an art form.* New Brunswick, NJ: Rutgers University Press.

Libby, R. W. (1977). Creative singlehood as a sexual life-style: Beyond marriage as a rite of passage. In R. W. Libby & R. N. Whitehurst (Eds.), *Marriage and alternatives: Exploring intimate relationships* (pp. 37-61). Glenview, IL: Scott, Foresman.

Libby, R. W., & Whitehurst, R. N. (Eds.). (1977). *Marriage and alternatives: Exploring intimate relationships.* Glenview, IL: Scott, Foresman.

Macklin, E. D. (1980). Nontraditional family forms: A decade of research. *Journal of Marriage and the Family, 42,* 905-922.

Morgan, R. (Ed.). (1970). *Sisterhood is powerful.* New York: Random House.

Nock, S. L. (1979). The family life cycle: Empirical or conceptual tool? *Journal of Marriage and the Family, 41,* 15-26.

Rubin, L. B. (1979). *Women of a certain age: The midlife search for self.* New York: Harper & Row.

Rubinstein, R. L., Alexander, B. B., Goodman, M., & Luborsky, M. (1991). Key relationships of never-married, childless older women: A cultural analysis. *Journal of Gerontology: Social Sciences, 46,* S270-277.

Schwartz, R. (1992). Rescuing the exiles. *Family Therapy Networker, 16*(3), 33-37, 75.

Simon, B. L. (1987). *Never-married women.* Philadelphia: Temple University Press.

Smith, D. E. (1987). *The everyday world as problematic: A feminist sociology.* Boston: Northeastern Press.

Stacey, J. (1986). Are feminists afraid to leave home? The challenge of conservative pro-family feminism. In J. Mitchell & A. Oakley (Eds.), *What is feminism?* (pp. 208-237). New York: Pantheon.

Stacey, J. (1988). Can there be a feminist ethnography? *Women's Studies International Forum, 11,* 21-27.

Stacey, J. (1990). *Brave new families: Stories of domestic upheaval in late twentieth century America.* New York: Basic Books.

Stanley, L. (Ed.). (1990). *Feminist praxis: Research, theory and epistemology in feminist sociology.* London: Routledge.

Taylor, V., & Rupp, L. J. (1991). Researching the women's movement: We make our own history, but not just as we please. In M. M. Fonow & J. A. Cook (Eds.), *Beyond methodology: Feminist scholarship as lived research* (pp. 119-132). Bloomington: Indiana University Press.

Thorne, B., with Yalom, M. (Eds.). (1982). *Rethinking the family: Some feminist questions.* New York: Longman.

Uhlenberg, P. (1974). Cohort variations in family life cycle experiences of U.S. females. *Journal of Marriage and the Family, 36,* 284-292.

Weston, K. (1991). *Families we choose: Lesbians, gays, kinship.* New York: Columbia University Press.

White, S. (1991). *Political theory and postmodernism.* Cambridge, UK: Cambridge University Press.

Witherell, C., & Noddings, N. (1991). Prologue: An invitation to our readers. In C. Witherell & N. Noddings (Eds.), *Stories lives tell: Narrative and dialogue in education* (pp. 1-12). New York: Teachers College Press.

6

Feminist Perspectives on Friendship

Intricate Tapestries

ROSEMARY BLIESZNER

My seminar students have expressed surprise that "so much" conceptual and empirical material can be applied to the analysis of friendship. In doing so, they implicitly acknowledge that people take friendship more or less for granted. No doubt, if we were asked, most of us readily could cite numerous benefits of friendship, with social and emotional support heading the list. But everyday life offers few chances to analyze friendship; we are more likely to interact socially with little thought about friendship than to engage in abstract inquiry about it. In the scholarly world, too, we find that although some researchers have focused on friendship, in general investigators have devoted more attention to the study of marriage and other family relationships.

Recently friendship has captured new and renewed attention from social psychologists, sociologists, communications experts, and others in fields whose researchers previously ignored friend ties. Perhaps this trend reflects, at least in part, the interest of women and feminists in important aspects of everyday life. My task in this chapter, then, is to review recent

AUTHOR'S NOTE: My long-term collaboration with Rebecca G. Adams contributes much to this analysis. I am grateful for helpful comments on the chapter from Katherine R. Allen, Leigh A. Leslie, Stephen R. Marks, and Donna L. Sollie. I appreciate the support of the AARP Andrus Foundation for some of my research (Adams & Blieszner, 1993a; Lovingood, Blieszner, & Hill, 1987; Mancini & Blieszner, 1992; Mancini, Travis, & Bianchinotti, 1985).

research in the emerging field of friendship scholarship from a feminist viewpoint.

The phrase "emerging feminist perspectives" signifies both my personal development as a feminist and the extent to which friendship research is feminist. Looking first at the personal sense of the phrase, my feminist leanings have roots in a variety of background incidents and are evolving still. Although I grew up in a fairly traditional household, certain elements of my early experiences—helping my father with household repairs and taking public transportation alone to art lessons as a youngster, for instance—fostered a sense of competence and independence that not every young girl back then had a chance to gain. Somehow I acquired convictions about the importance of justice, fairness, and reduction of hierarchies. For example, in high school I stood firmly in the camp of classmates who insisted on selecting participants for a school pageant by random drawing, rather than by voting on the basis of traditional standards of popularity and beauty, and on listing each senior's activities in an appendix at the back of the book, rather than having some graduates' photographs decorated with many lines of accomplishments while others were bereft of any.

College activities typical of students in the late 1960s and early 1970s, such as collecting food and clothing for needy persons, organizing political consciousness-raising weekends, and joining marches in opposition to the Vietnam War, furthered my understanding of social justice issues. Those experiences, and the reading I was doing as a charter subscriber to *Ms.* magazine, raised my awareness of feminist principles. Although that consciousness has long been a part of my personal life, until recently it was integrated into my research and teaching only indirectly. Now, as a result of association with influential colleagues and ongoing study about feminism, I incorporate feminist principles into my professional activities more intentionally and more specifically.

Turning to the second meaning of the phrase "emerging feminist perspectives," my assessment of the social science close relationship literature shows that feminist scholarship in the domain of friendship is less well developed than in other relationship areas such as romantic ties. This is probably the case because friendship is viewed as a relationship among equals, rather than one centered on power differentials. Such an assumption is not necessarily accurate, of course—consider friendship between employer and employee or between teacher and student—but researchers have not tested the assumption with evidence about power and status differences among friends. Yet uncovering previously hidden dimensions of a subject is precisely the interest of feminist scholars. The goal of feminist research on friendship is to broaden our understanding of the diverse types of friend relations and friendship interaction patterns in contemporary society. This goal is significant not only because of the inherent value of human relations but also because of the importance of friendship and other close relationships for provision of social support and maintenance of psychological well-being (Thoits, 1985).

To trace the emergence of feminist perspectives in friendship scholarship, I have chosen the metaphor of tapestries, woven wall hangings or floor coverings depicting magnificent scenes rich in color and detail, to symbolize approaches to understanding the beauty and complexity of friend relationships. I begin with inspection of a gallery of friendship research tapestries: a review and feminist critique of research. Next I move to detailed examination of one particular tapestry, my own. I examine my own conceptual training, examples of my scholarly pursuits in friendship and other close relationships, and my growing understanding of feminism. I conclude with suggestions for more complex tapestry designs: conceptual enhancements and future research needs from a feminist stance.

A Gallery of Friendship Research Tapestries

Tapestries often record intricate pictures of important historical events. Thus, in developing a feminist analysis of friendship research tapestries, I start with a search for the historical roots of current interpretations and then move on to accounts of contemporary studies.

Friendship Research Tapestries in Historical Perspective

The earliest conceptualizations of friendship appeared in the writings of ancient philosophers such as Plato, Aristotle, and Cicero (Pakaluck, 1991). For the most part, they assumed that only men could attain ideal types of friendship because only men possessed the intellectual capacities necessary for it (Murstein & Spitz, 1973-74). These philosophers ignored women's friendships in their discourses. In effect, they denied the importance of women's activities and cast women into "history's shadows" (Ferree, 1990, p. 880), rendering invisible to us the kinds of social interactions that women of antiquity had with men and with other women.

Nevertheless Lopata (1990) points out that in certain periods the social structure afforded women and men similar opportunities to participate in friendship—in hunting-gathering and agricultural societies, for instance, and in the Middle Ages, when social and commercial activity were indistinguishable. Friendships existed across gender, age, and class groups, and personal success was tied to social competence. Lopata asserted, however, that as the nuclear family placed more emphasis on privacy, work was separated from the home setting, and extensive sociability was seen as incompatible with family life. Friendships then were restricted to those of similar gender, age, and class. A parallel transformation occurred in America, where early colonial culture afforded many chances for cross-sex as well as same-sex friendships, but Puritanism brought restricted social opportunities, especially for women. Later the progress of industrialization contributed to separate spheres of work and family experience in which both women and men had intimate same-sex friendships but neither was likely to have nonromantic opposite-sex friendships (Faderman, 1981; Hansen, 1992; Oliker, 1989; Smith-Rosenberg, 1975). For the most part, this pattern endures today, although same-sex nonsexual friendships are less romanticized than in the past.

Contemporary Friendship Research Tapestries

The study of adult friendship has flourished recently (see bibliographies in Blieszner & Adams, 1992; O'Connor, 1992; Rawlins, 1992). The multifaceted tapestries comprising contemporary friendship literature include descriptions of networks, functions, interaction processes, and phases. Although comparisons of women's and men's friendships have been made (see Blieszner & Adams, 1992, for extensive details), most have not been guided by feminist thought.

Characteristics of friend networks. Adults have an average of from 2 or 3 to about 12 friends. Variations in opportunities to make and keep friends over the life course, between the genders, and among class and racial ethnic groups affect the *size* of friend networks. *Homogeneity* influences friendship choices: For the most part, people are friends with those who are similar to themselves. *Density,* or the proportion of a person's friends who know each other, is correlated with *solidarity,* or the level of emotional closeness among friends; that is, the higher the network density, the closer those people are likely to feel to each other.

Friendship interaction processes and functions. Friendships are enacted by means of the thoughts, feelings, and actions of each partner. For example, perceptions that friends share one's values and interests and possess desirable personality traits are important *cognitive* aspects of friendship. Liking and trusting the friend and feeling satisfied with the friendship are significant *affective* processes. Self-disclosure and joint activities are paramount *behavioral* processes.

Friendship serves many functions in people's lives, including provision of social support and advice, companionship, and socialization. Sources and amounts of support vary with demographic attributes such as gender and marital status. For example, both men and women feel closer to the females who give them support than to the males who do so, and widowed women tend to receive more support from their friends than do married women.

Phases of friendship. Friendships are dynamic, moving from acquaintanceship to emotional closeness, from harmony to discord, or from low involvement to high supportiveness through myriad processes. Some acquaintances go on to establish deeper friendships and others do not; qualities initially perceived as attractive may be unappealing on closer examination, or opportunities to further the rapport may not occur. The maintenance phase can embody increasing, decreasing, or stable solidarity, depending on levels of satisfaction, conflict, or self-disclosure in the relationship. Some friendships endure for decades, with partners expecting only their continuation; others fade away gradually through benign neglect or end abruptly because of violations of friendship norms. It is rare, however, that individuals actively terminate friendships.

Despite the wealth of available research, many gaps remain in the friendship literature. Many studies incorporated experimental designs involving strangers interacting for short periods of time—a strategy that feminists call "disembodied." Although valuable for investigating initial attraction, such research has little to say about the transition from first perceptions to enduring friendship. Also it is difficult, if not impossible, to generalize findings because of the tendency to use members of only one sex, age, racial, or ethnic group instead of diverse samples in a given study. We know much about college student friendships but relatively less about those of nonstudent young adults, older adults, persons of color, and members of poor, working, or elite classes. Thus friendship tapestries contain blank spaces that remain to be filled in by creative weavers of friendship scholarship. In the next section I further discuss conceptual and methodological issues from a feminist perspective.

Analysis of the Friendship Tapestries:
A Feminist Critique of Theory and Methods

Female versus male friendship styles. A prevailing theme in recent friendship scholarship has been comparison of friendships as enacted by women and by men, and debate about which group is better at "doing" friendship. On the one hand, some commentators have assumed that men are more capable of engaging in intimate friendship than women are because of their sociobiologically based bonding instincts related to hunting and protection functions and that women's competition for available males interferes with their intimate friendships. On the other hand, others have assumed that men are incapable of close friendship because of their inability to engage in intimate conversation and displays of affection, at which women are more adept. In fact, some would argue that the women's movement enhanced women's possibilities for intimate friendships by providing supportive environments in which women could confide in one another and help each other with their problems (see discussions of these issues in Acker, Barry, & Esseveld, 1990; Booth & Hess, 1974; Candy-Gibbs, 1982; Wellman, 1992; Wright, 1982, 1989).

A theoretical problem in trying to understand whether women's and men's friendship styles differ is the issue of identifying the key components of effective or satisfying friendship—whether a "feminine" or a "masculine" definition of intimacy will prevail, for instance (e.g., Swain, 1989; Wellman, 1992). Depending on whether intimacy is characterized in terms of preference for self-disclosure and emotional support or preference for joint activities and small services, women and men will be deemed differentially successful in accomplishing close friendship. Summarizing many studies, we might conclude that both women and men value intimacy in friendship but achieve it in different ways (Caldwell & Peplau, 1982; Rubin, 1985; Swain, 1989).

It is difficult to understand precisely what such a conclusion means because the research is confounded not only by differential definitions of intimacy but also by method bias between female and male researchers. Evidence of this bias comes from a revealing analysis by Adams (1988) of 41 surveys on older adult friendship. Conceptualizing agentic and communal (Carlson, 1971) aspects of research methods as a continuum on which survey designs could be located, Adams noted a shift from the 1960s to the 1980s toward more communal and feminist tactics. These tactics included (a) defining friendship and examining the content or process of interaction in terms of qualitative characteristics (closeness, confiding, support) instead of in only quantitative terms (number of friends, frequency of contact); (b) asking questions about specific friends instead of about global friendship in general, as if all friends are the same; and (c) using the dyad as the unit of analysis instead of only the individual respondents, thus addressing the integrity of specific relationships.

Not only did communal methods increase in frequency over time but also a larger percentage of studies using such methods was conducted by female rather than male researchers. This gender bias among investigators has important implications for the conclusions we can draw from existing research. Friendships of women and men may be characterized inaccurately, with gender differences exaggerated (*alpha bias*) in some respects and hidden (*beta bias*) in others (cf. Ferree, 1990; Hare-Mustin & Marecek, 1988), depending on the gender of the researcher. As Adams (1988) further pointed out, the above conclusion based on "summing over many studies" is flawed because few studies included both female and male participants. Given that investigators operationalized friendship constructs differently, we really cannot compare results for women and men across studies.

Sources of differentiation in friendship styles. A second, perhaps even more important issue than conceptualization and measurement of the dependent variable is researchers' failure to adequately conceptualize their independent variables (cf. Sherif, 1987). Most friendship research has focused on distinctions between females and males. Although I can point out a few analyses of the implications of race (Franklin, 1992; Peretti, 1976, 1977), class (Franklin, 1992; Hansen, 1992; Rubin, 1976), and sexual orientation (Faderman, 1981; Nardi, 1992; Rose & Roades, 1987), friendship researchers have tended to ignore these characteristics of study participants.

Investigators who did attempt to address gender issues in friendship often reported sex differences (but tended to regard similarities as failure to support hypotheses, cf. Ferree, 1990, and Hare-Mustin & Marecek, 1988) without analyzing the impact of *gender* on friendship. In other words, they failed to differentiate varying theoretical meanings of gender in their unidimensional assessment of the variable *sex* and reported friendship differences between women and men without much explanation, as if the sources of such differences were completely apparent. As a case in point, results showing that white, urban, middle-aged males have more friends than their female counterparts (e.g., Fischer & Oliker, 1983) could be interpreted either in terms of differential opportunities to meet potential friends or in terms of differential gregariousness across the sexes. Similarly, explanations of the findings that middle-aged women's friendships are more intimate than middle-aged men's (e.g., Fox, Gibbs, & Auerbach, 1985) could invoke female psychological capacity or address women's relative freedom to pursue very close relationships without negative social consequences. As shown by these examples, sex is used often as a proxy measure for two different aspects of gender (Adams & Blieszner, 1994; Blieszner & Adams, 1992).

Thus, intentionally or otherwise, some friendship scholars in the field of personal relationships have focused on the influence of *dispositional* aspects of gender (e.g., personality: Mazur, 1989; McAdams, Healy, & Krause, 1984), whereas others have emphasized correlates of *social structural* dimensions (e.g., size or composition of friend networks: Fischer & Oliker, 1983; Nahemow & Lawton, 1975). Sometimes friendship researchers offered theoretical reasons for one focus or the other (e.g., gender socialization: Aukett, Ritchie, & Mill, 1988; Williams, 1985), but often they did not supply any theoretical argument to support their analyses (e.g., Buhrke & Fuqua, 1987). They rarely distinguished, either conceptually or empirically, between the interacting effects of social structure and psychological disposition on women's and men's friendships (Blieszner & Adams, 1992). To disentangle the various predictors of gender similarities and differences, we advocate the approach of Fox, Gibbs, and Auerbach (1985) and Rubin (1985), who included assessment of both dispositional (e.g., emotional reactions, sense of competition, motives associated with friendship) and structural (e.g., number, sex, sources of friends, length of friendships) consequences of gender (Adams & Blieszner, 1993a).

Research designs and methods. New, more feminist approaches to research on friendship have appeared recently (Adams, 1988). Although participant observation studies that included discussion of friendship appeared in the 1950s, 1960s, and 1970s (e.g., Gans, 1962; Hochschild, 1973; Liebow, 1967; Stack, 1974; Whyte, 1956), much research that touched on friendship was based either on laboratory experiments or on surveys. Traditional experimental and survey designs and even observational and structured-question self-report data collection methods exclude women's experiences and the purposes of feminist research (Harding, 1987) and thus are limited in what they can reveal about friendship. Although not necessarily feminist in their orientation, scholars studying friendship nevertheless have acknowledged the need to employ, either alone or in conjunction with quantitative techniques, qualitative methods that permit detailed, open-ended questioning about friend interactions and the meanings that partners ascribe to them (e.g., see Adams, 1987; Allan, 1979; Gouldner & Strong, 1987; Matthews, 1986; Oliker, 1989; Rubin, 1985).

My own work provides an example of an evolving approach that incorporates some of these desirable characteristics in friendship research. My discussion of it includes three parts: a brief summary of the conceptual underpinnings of my research, a sequential review of my studies of friendship and other close relationships, and an overview and feminist analysis of one of my current projects.

Closeup of a Friendship Tapestry

Conceptual Elements

The scene of a tapestry is stitched onto a firm foundational fabric. The *background* of my scholarly tapestry is my undergraduate major in home economics education, which I studied at a small liberal arts college. This context implies that the curriculum was not limited to stereotyped conceptions of home economics (cooking and sewing "for the girls"), but rather focused on multidisciplinary ways of examining and responding to individual and family needs, with attention to the importance of everyday behavior and surroundings for sustaining and enhancing human life—the essence of contemporary views of what feminism is all about (P. Thompson, 1988; cf. Walker & Thompson, 1984).

The *threads* of a tapestry provide the colors and shapes that unite to depict the focal design. One thread in my career progress was the decision to pursue advanced graduate studies. This thread developed as a result of experiences I had while teaching with a master's degree at a small college at which innovative educational programs abounded. One such program involved inviting older adults to take regular courses; another was offering special minicourses to elder citizens. I participated in both options and was delighted to discover the wisdom and perceptive insights that the older students contributed to class discussions. As a result I decided to pursue doctoral work in adult development and aging. Little did I know at the time that gerontology, like home economics, is an inherently multidisciplinary field with an applied orientation toward generating knowledge to enhance the later years of life—an orientation that parallels feminists' concern about research that benefits women's lives (L. Thompson, 1992).

A second thread joined the tapestry when, as a doctoral candidate, I studied principles of life span developmental psychology and became interested in applying them to the study of close relationships. I was intrigued and challenged by the idea of translating this conceptual framework from the individual to the relationship level of analysis. I can see now, although I was not aware of it then, how important life span development and life course concepts are in feminist thought, particularly notions of within- as well as between-group heterogeneity and the impact of sociocultural and historical influences on people's lives (cf. Walker & Thompson, 1984).

My decision to focus on close relationship aspects of gerontology was based on theoretical interest and on the desire to understand more about the family and friend affiliations that are so special in my own life. Thus a third thread shaping my tapestry comes from the intersecting fields of family studies and personal relationship studies. From my present vantage point, I now see feminist roots in these disciplines, as well. Examining family and other relationships in which people spend much of their time corresponds to feminists' call to study everyday, relevant, meaningful experiences (Walker, Martin, & Thompson, 1988).

A fourth thread in my tapestry represents feminist studies. Having come of age during the modern civil rights and women's movements, I have long been aware of the oppression of racism and sexism. My studies of aging processes and aged people have revealed the oppression of ageism to me. More recently I have begun to learn about the oppression of classism and heterosexism. Attempts at feminist analysis of friendship (this chapter) and of widowhood (Blieszner, 1993b) have helped deepen my thinking about many forms of domination. True to the life span perspective that focuses on processes of development and change, I see my tapestry design becoming more complex, with the colors deepening over time. Consonant with feminist praxis, I acknowledge successful and meaningful collaborative partnerships with generous-spirited colleagues.

Design Motifs

In this section I highlight six themes from my research career while demonstrating the evolution of my feminist approaches. My colleagues and I have (a) examined the connections between close relationships and psychological well-being, (b) explored the connections between close relationships and personal development, (c) advocated for broader conceptualizations of age and gender, (d) looked at changes within close relationships, (e) provided feminist interpretations of widowhood and filial responsibility, and (f) encouraged the application of relationship research findings to intervention programs and public policies.

Relationships and well-being. The first motif in my friendship tapestry was my doctoral dissertation research (Blieszner, 1982, 1993a). My initial focus was on variables that contribute to psychological well-being in old age. As I reviewed the literature, I discovered that researchers acknowledged the importance of close relationships for life satisfaction but tended to assess rather superficial aspects of them. For example, measures of the *amount* of social interaction ended up explaining little of the variance in life satisfaction, leading investigators to conclude that measures of the *quality* of interaction were required. Thus I decided to assess subjective dimensions of relationship quality (e.g., relationship satisfaction, intimacy, trust, expectations for giving and receiving six different types of support, the actual frequency of giving and receiving each type of support), along with the more typical behavioral measures of frequency and type of contact. It also seemed important to acknowledge that not all relationships exist at the same levels of emotional closeness and social support; in my design each respondent reported on six relationships at three levels of intimacy (very close, less close, acquainted but not close).

The findings, based on 192 white, elderly women, confirmed a set of hypotheses predicting that the most frequent interactions and the most intense feelings would be associated with the closest persons. Moreover, as predicted, relationships with very close persons accounted for a significant amount (24%) of the variance in life satisfaction, whereas the two less close relationships accounted for lesser, nonsignificant amounts of the variation. The implication is that researchers must differentiate among types of relationships, rather than assume that all have similar characteristics or contribute equally to well-being.

In retrospect I can say that my study broadened notions of important elements of close relationships by addressing their multifaceted aspects, a method advocated in feminist approaches, but at the time I did not construe the study as feminist in orientation. The fact that most of the sample members were women (I did not include the data from 40 men in these analyses) reflects the demographics of the elder segment of the population, not feminist intent. I knew about various forms of oppression, but I did not know about feminist scholarship then. I had participated in social psychology seminars led by Carolyn Sherif, and I understood her discussions of gender bias in selecting research topics, conceptualizing variables, interpreting results, and the like (see Sherif, 1987). But that understanding was disconnected from my research plans (and Sherif's ideas were in formative stages then: She published the above-cited article 6 years after I left graduate school). I was not reading literature on feminist epistemology at the time, nor did I have feminist researcher role models or discussions with anyone about how to incorporate consciousness about oppression into my own research. I believed I was doing good for society by studying a neglected group—older adults—and a neglected topic—close relationships. The explicitly feminist analysis in this chapter is actually quite new in my intellectual life.

Relationships and personal development. A second motif in my research history was grounded in the life span development framework that emphasizes intersecting and reciprocal influences between the larger social context and an individual's personal development. One analysis of the influence of friendship (and marriage) on personal development appeared in a conceptual piece (Blieszner, 1988). I discussed the ways that friendships during the busy middle-age years might help focus attention away from the routine aspects of daily life and toward the spontaneity of recreation, or might ameliorate the perception of the middle years as a time of crisis. In old age, friendships can maintain role continuity despite role losses associated with retirement and widowhood, enhance self-esteem and morale through companionship, and afford opportunities of retaining self-respect and avoiding feelings of dependence because it is easier to reciprocate assistance received from age peers than help from younger persons.

A second view of the influence of relationships on personal development comes from a qualitative, longitudinal study of adults providing care to elderly relatives (Blieszner & Shifflett, 1989, 1990). We examined the impact of a non-normative life event—Alzheimer's disease—on relationship stability and change between spouses and parent-child dyads. We found that although caregivers reported declining feelings of intimacy for their spouse or parent over the course of the study, they nevertheless retained a strong commitment to preserving the relationship and continuing to provide care for the patient. These results suggested that the caregivers developed personal strength and courage as they met the challenge of coping with Alzheimer's disease.

A third example is a large random-sample survey study of the effects of social support on psychological well-being in old age (Mancini & Blieszner,

1992; Mancini, Travis, & Bianchinotti, 1985). The findings revealed that morale, affection, and friend network interaction—variables that help maintain healthy functioning in the later years—were all significantly associated with availability of social support.

The common thread running through these three pieces is the notion that friendship and other close relationships contribute to personal development and well-being. Although none of these studies were designed explicitly as feminist inquiries, it seems to me that they reflect feminist and gerontological concerns about research that is useful and that examines meaningful domains of participants' lives. Moreover, use of qualitative methods in the investigation of the effects of Alzheimer's disease on close affiliations enabled us to explore fully the meaning of relationship changes as the disease progressed, an approach not previously reported in the caregiving literature. More importantly, the results of that study challenge models of relationship dissolution that harbor the narrow assumptions that all close relationships are romantic and that relationship termination always occurs completely, under the control of at least one of the partners (e.g., Duck, 1982).

Multidimensional conceptions of age and gender. A third motif in my friendship tapestry emerged from a very productive collegial relationship with Rebecca G. Adams. A sociologist, she strengthened my understanding of the importance of analyzing age and gender as representing socially structured sets of opportunities and constraints. In turn, I relied on my developmental and social psychological background to reinforce for her the importance of acknowledging internal developmental and dispositional aspects of age and gender. From these expanded conceptualizations of age and gender—more feminist than can be found in extant literature—together we crafted an edited book (Adams & Blieszner, 1989), a monograph (Blieszner & Adams, 1992), articles (Adams & Blieszner, 1993b, 1994), and a funded research project (Adams & Blieszner, 1993a) that elucidated these principles in the context of adult friendship. For example, our organizing conceptual framework integrates both structural and developmental aspects of age and gender. We employed this framework in designing the questionnaire for our study of older adult friendship. We not only asked basic demographic questions (e.g., age, sex) about the respondents and their friends but also administered scales tapping psychological dimensions of the respondents' age (developmental maturity) and gender (gender identity). Further, we secured respondents' opinions about the effects of age and gender on their friendships and their perceptions of the effects of their own personality on their friendships.

Collaborating has enabled us to clarify our own thinking, understand each other's fundamental theoretical position, and thus strengthen our theorizing about influences on friendship.

Relationship development. Research and writing on the formation, maintenance, and dissolution or loss of close relationships represents a fourth motif in my friendship tapestry (Adams & Blieszner, 1993a; Blieszner, 1994; Blieszner & Mancini, 1992; Shea, Thompson, & Blieszner, 1988). Here the focus has been on demonstrating the dynamic nature of close relationships, applying principles of individual-level life span development and life course change to the dyadic level of analysis. For example, relationships remain stable or change as a consequence of direct actions that participants take: making special efforts to call and visit with a favorite friend, deciding to end a friendship with someone who violated norms about borrowing money. Indirect events, too, can have an effect: Contact is lost with coworkers after a change in employment, a person becomes too frail to attend class reunions. In addition, results show the almost infinite variety of relationships that can be defined as friendship, such that the research celebrates a form of diversity that mainstream feminists have yet to consider.

Widowhood and filial responsibility. Other investigations, though not about friendship, lent themselves explicitly to feminist analysis and thus have sharpened my consciousness about application of feminist principles in my current and future friendship research. One study concerned widows' and widowers' abilities to perform everyday household tasks and to maintain an independent lifestyle in the absence of their spouses (Lovingood, Blieszner, & Hill, 1987). The results revealed that bereaved women are better able to maintain their own home and independent lifestyle than are bereaved men, largely because the men have not acquired basic skills necessary for preparing meals, cleaning, maintaining clothing, and so on. The gender-based division of household tasks renders elderly widowed men, who depend on outside helpers for fundamental sustenance, quite vulnerable to loss of their independent living status, depending on the strength or fragility of their support network. Furthermore, in applying a socialist-feminist perspective to self-sufficiency and economic aspects of widowhood (Blieszner, 1993b), I argued that a capitalistic, patriarchal society oppresses both widowed women and widowed men, with differential effects based on class and racial ethnic group membership. In general, widows possess the social and homemaking skills that sustain the independent lifestyle preferred by most elderly people, but they and minority group widowers are unlikely to have sufficient economic resources; white widowers tend to have adequate finances, but they and other widowers are unable to provide acceptably for their own fundamental survival needs.

Another feature of this motif is a feminist analysis of the effects of gender on filial responsibility as expressed from adult children to their parents (Blieszner & Hamon, 1992). Research shows that as with other aspects of family reproductive work, women—usually daughters and daughters-in-law—provide more assistance in general to elderly parents than sons do and also help more than sons do with direct hands-on, intensive, instrumental, and emotional support tasks. In contrast, the help given by sons typically involves financial management, advice, heavy chores, and shopping. We observed that most parental caregiving research has not been conducted from a feminist standpoint. Thus we advocated feminist analyses to (a) examine gender as a construct evoked through everyday filial interactions (not a predetermined attribute of daughters and sons), (b) connect personal experiences of parental caregiving to the larger social context in which it takes place, (c) seek previously hidden reasons for adopting the caregiving role, (d) propose models of shared filial responsibility among adult children, rather than spend further research resources on determining whether daughters versus sons should aid parents or are more motivated to do so, (e) enable research participants to contribute to identification of important caregiving research questions and interpretation of the results, and (f) provide data that can be used to enhance the ability of both daughters and sons to choose their filial duties and to carry them out without being oppressed by them.

Application of friendship research. The sixth and final motif in my friendship tapestry is a conceptual analysis of the uses to which friendship research might be put (Adams & Blieszner, 1993b). Social interventions occur constantly in the form of programs, services, environmental design, policies, and other formats. Given the importance of social relations for personal well-being, it is our contention that attempts to change or manipulate people's lives ought to be informed by social relationship research. Thus investigators of friendship and other relationships have the responsibility to specify the practical implications of their findings, and practitioners who design social interaction interventions have the obligation to apply research findings as they discharge their responsibilities. This line of reasoning is consonant with the feminist dictum "the personal is political" and with the associated plea for research that is both useful and not harmful to people's lives. The everyday implications of friendship research have rarely, if ever, been specified, however.

An example of how friendship research might be applied comes from our study of older adult friendship (described below). We included measures of psychological well-being in the interviews, and we analyzed the implications of various structural, process, and phase aspects of friendship for mental health in old age. In addition, we developed a brochure for gerontologists who work with older adult clients to provide suggestions about using the study results in their programs and activities.

Toward More Intricate Friendship Research Tapestries

Using one of my current research projects as an example, I illustrate an application of feminist concerns to the study of friendship. Then I discuss suggestions for feminist conceptualizations of future research on friendship.

A Tapestry in Progress

Rebecca Adams and I are engaged in research on older adult friendship (Adams & Blieszner, 1993a). The purposes of the study are to examine the effects of gender and age (assessed in terms of both social structural and psychological characteristics) on friendship interaction patterns and to evaluate the connection between friendship patterns and psychological well-being.

We interviewed 53 women and men in three elderly age groups, asking both structured and open-ended questions designed to address the purposes stated above. We used multiple data collection techniques to enhance the reliability of our results and to gain greater insight about friendship patterns than has been achieved previously in survey research. Using Thompson's (1992) agenda for feminist research in family studies as a guide, I analyze now the extent to which our study addresses three major themes of feminist scholarship: feminist agenda, epistemology, and ethics.

Feminist agenda. First, Thompson emphasized the importance of conducting research *for* women, not just *about* them. Our study incorporated several elements of research aimed at enhancing women's lives. For example, our look at the mental health implications of friendship has the potential of yielding useful information for those who plan and provide services to older adults, most of whom are women. By asking about the contexts in which respondents meet and interact with friends, we grounded their personal friendship experiences in the larger social context. We embraced diversity in terms of age, gender, race, and class by conducting the study in a metropolitan area and by using random-digit dialing to identify the sample. We can challenge prevailing concepts of gender in several ways: (a) We inquired explicitly about power and status relations between friends, (b) the data (and software that permits linking of textual with numerical information) enabled us to explore both differences and similarities between women and men, as well as diversity within each gender group, (c) we measured both structural and dispositional aspects of gender, and (d) the interview format enabled respondents to offer their own meanings about particular friendships in their lives.

Besides these, Thompson mentioned two other aspects of research for women: identifying how women struggle against and adapt to oppression, and promoting a vision of nonoppressive relations. Because friendships in our society are voluntary relationships and are governed by weaker norms than other relationships, they may be less susceptible to an oppressive character than work or family relationships. Nevertheless any relationship probably can be oppressive; our study did not deal explicitly with how women are oppressed by or contend with oppression in friendship. But we did ask about problems in friendships and reasons for terminating friendships; we can seek examples of oppressive aspects of friendship in replies to those questions.

Epistemology. With respect to truth, reality, and objectivity, our study dealt with several of the aspects Thompson deemed important for feminist inquiry. One area of epistemology concerns the connection between the researcher and the researched. Rebecca and I conducted pilot interviews and study interviews, but we also had the help of other interviewers. The interviewers went to the respondents' homes or other locations of their choice in an effort to maximize respondents' comfort and convenience in the research process. We did not conceal the topic or purposes of the study from the participants.

Another aspect of epistemology is acknowledging women's experiences as valid sources of knowledge. Our design included women and men. Each interview was tape-recorded and transcribed verbatim so that each participant's own words could be heard.

The last facet of epistemology is value-sustaining and politicized inquiry. On the one hand, our research topic gives credence to an informal relationship that has long been ignored by mainstream disciplines such as sociology and psychology. On the other hand, we have not really analyzed how our beliefs and politics have shaped this study. We often discussed our personal friendship experiences as we developed the study but have not explicitly outlined how our position as elite members of society affects our selection of variables or interpretation of the data. This latter task is a next step in the stitching of our own friendship tapestry.

Ethics. Finally, Thompson's third domain of feminist methods was ethical considerations, wherein she challenged us to think about exploitation versus empowerment of research participants and oppressive objectification. I think our methods conveyed respect for the participants and treated them ethically. The participants provided their own definition of friendship and gave us their own version of friendship experiences. We recognized that they are authorities on their own lives by asking them to tell us their interpretations of the effects of gender and age on friendship opportunities and constraints. We paid respondents a small fee in recognition of the value of their sharing time and friendship experiences with us. We sent the results, written in an accessible style, to those who requested them.

New Motifs for Feminist
Friendship Research Tapestries

The warp and woof of friendship tapestries have been stretched—many studies of adult friendship exist. But as I have shown throughout the discussion, much embellishment of the tapestries with feminist threads and design motifs remains to be done. In this concluding section I splice together some of my own idea threads with those of others to suggest fresh research directions for friendship.

In my view the threads for such endeavors are found in the life span/life course, family/personal relationship, and feminist theoretical perspectives. These threads must be integrated so that one needle can pull them through the background fabric and apply the stitches of particular inquiries. This integration means that researchers interested in the functions of friendship, for example, must employ explicitly concepts and methods that have not necessarily adorned previous research. That is, they should (a) examine the structural and cultural context in which friends participate (e.g., Wellman, 1992); (b) ground their research questions in social science theory that is scrutinized carefully from a feminist framework; (c) include samples of respondents that represent diversity of ages, genders, classes, and racial ethnic groups and interpret the results in terms of the socially structured implications of those characteristics; (d) carefully operationalize both independent and dependent variables to allow for all kinds of functions—not just preconceived ones—to surface; (e) use data collection and analysis techniques that highlight unexpected findings instead of obscuring them and enable respondents to accurately portray their own experiences; and (f) provide ideas about the practical implications of their results.

Besides innovative approaches to familiar themes such as friendship functions, we need research on new topics that could contribute to generation of more intricate feminist friendship motifs. Rather than assume equal status and power among friends, we must examine the effects of hierarchy on their relationships. Rather than ignore negative aspects of friendship, we must acknowledge that they can be problematic, as well as helpful (e.g., Rook, 1989), and explore the causes and consequences of conflict and dissatisfaction. Rather than pretend that friendship is only a benign influence in individuals' lives, we must investigate its effects at the societal level, such as the ways it upholds the traditional institution of marriage (e.g., Oliker, 1989), reproduces class structure, and furthers economic and political interests (O'Connor, 1992). Rather than trivialize women's friendships, we must seek insights about the extent to which they might transform social structure (O'Connor, 1992). Research attention to issues such as these would display more fully the rich colors, textures, and patterns of friend relationship tapestries.

References

Acker, J., Barry, K., & Esseveld, J. (1990). Feminism, female friends, and the reconstruction of intimacy. In H. Z. Lopata & D. R. Maines (Eds.), *Friendship in context* (pp. 75-108). Greenwich, CT: JAI.

Adams, R. G. (1987). Patterns of network change: A longitudinal study of friendships of elderly women. *The Gerontologist, 27,* 222-227.

Adams, R. G. (1988, November). A gender-informed approach to friendship in late life. In T. M. Calasanti (Chair), *Incorporating gender into theory and research on aging.* Symposium presented at the 41st Annual Scientific Meeting of the Gerontological Society of America, San Francisco.

Adams, R. G., & Blieszner, R. (Eds.). (1989). *Older adult friendship: Structure and process.* Newbury Park, CA: Sage.

Adams, R. G., & Blieszner, R. (1993a). *Older adult friendship patterns and mental health.* Final report to the AARP Andrus Foundation, Washington, DC.

Adams, R. G., & Blieszner, R. (1993b). Resources for friendship intervention. *Journal of Sociology and Social Welfare, 20,* 159-175.

Adams, R. G., & Blieszner, R. (1994). An integrative conceptual framework for friendship research. *Journal of Social and Personal Relationships, 11,* 163-184.

Allan, G. A. (1979). *A sociology of friendship and kinship.* London: Allen & Unwin.

Aukett, R., Ritchie, J., & Mill, K. (1988). Gender differences in friendship patterns. *Sex Roles, 19,* 57-66.

Blieszner, R. (1982). Social relationships and life satisfaction in late adulthood. *Dissertation Abstracts International, 43,* 2366B. (University Microfilms No. 82-28863)

Blieszner, R. (1988). Individual development and intimate relationships in middle and late adulthood. In R. M. Milardo (Ed.), *Families and social networks* (pp. 88-101). Newbury Park, CA: Sage.

Blieszner, R. (1993a). Resource exchange in the social networks of elderly women. In U. G. Foa, J. M. Converse, Jr., K. Y. Törnblom, & E. B. Foa (Eds.), *Resource theory: Explorations and applications* (pp. 67-79). New York: Academic Press.

Blieszner, R. (1993b). A socialist-feminist perspective on widowhood. *Journal of Aging Studies, 7,* 171-182.

Blieszner, R. (1994). Close relationships over time. In A. L. Weber & J. H. Harvey (Eds.), *Perspectives on close relationships* (pp. 1-17). Boston: Allyn & Bacon.

Blieszner, R., & Adams, R. G. (1992). *Adult friendship.* Newbury Park, CA: Sage.

Blieszner, R., & Hamon, R. R. (1992). Filial responsibility: Attitudes, obligations, and roles. In J. W. Dwyer & R. T. Coward (Eds.), *Gender, families, and elder care* (pp. 105-119). Newbury Park, CA: Sage.

Blieszner, R., & Mancini, J. A. (1992). A life span developmental perspective on relationship loss. In T. Orbuch (Ed.), *Close relationship loss* (pp. 142-154). New York: Springer Verlag.

Blieszner, R., & Shifflett, P. A. (1989). Affection, communication, and commitment in adult-child caregiving for parents with Alzheimer's disease. In J. A. Mancini (Ed.), *Aging parents and adult children* (pp. 231-243). Lexington, MA: Lexington.

Blieszner, R., & Shifflett, P. A. (1990). The effects of Alzheimer's disease on close relationships between patients and caregivers. *Family Relations, 39,* 57-62.

Booth, A., & Hess, E. (1974). Cross-sex friendship. *Journal of Marriage and the Family, 36,* 38-47.

Buhrke, R. A., & Fuqua, D. R. (1987). Sex differences in same- and cross-sex supportive relationships. *Sex Roles, 17,* 339-352.

Caldwell, M. A., & Peplau, L. A. (1982). Sex differences in same-sex friendship. *Sex Roles, 8,* 721-732.

Candy-Gibbs, S. E. (1982, November). *The alleged inferiority of men's close interpersonal relationships: An examination of sex differences in the elderly widowed.* Paper presented at the 35th Annual Scientific Meeting of the Gerontological Society of America, Boston.

Carlson, R. (1971). Sex differences in ego functioning: Exploratory studies of agency and communion. *Journal of Consulting and Clinical Psychology, 37,* 267-277.

Duck, S. (1982). A topography of relationship disengagement and dissolution. In S. W. Duck (Ed.), *Personal relationships, 4* (pp. 1-29). London: Academic Press.

Faderman, L. (1981). *Surpassing the love of men.* New York: William Morrow.

Ferree, M. M. (1990). Beyond separate spheres: Feminism and family research. *Journal of Marriage and the Family, 52,* 866-884.

Fischer, C. S., & Oliker, S. J. (1983). A research note on friendship, gender, and the life cycle. *Social Forces, 62,* 124-133.

Fox, M., Gibbs, M., & Auerbach, D. (1985). Age and gender dimensions of friendship. *Psychology of Women Quarterly, 9,* 489-501.

Franklin, C. W., II. (1992). "Hey, Home—Yo, Bro": Friendship among black men. In P. M. Nardi (Ed.), *Men's friendships* (pp. 201-214). Newbury Park, CA: Sage.

Gans, H. J. (1962). *The urban villagers.* New York: Free Press.

Gouldner, H., & Strong, M. S. (1987). *Speaking of friendship.* New York: Greenwood.

Hansen, K. V. (1992). "Our eyes behold each other": Masculinity and intimate friendship in antebellum New England. In P. M. Nardi (Ed.), *Men's friendships* (pp. 35-58). Newbury Park, CA: Sage.

Harding, S. (1987). Introduction: Is there a feminist method? and Conclusion: Epistemological questions. In S. Harding (Ed.), *Feminism and methodology* (pp. 1-14 and 181-190). Bloomington: Indiana University Press.

Hare-Mustin, R. T., & Marecek, J. (1988). The meaning of difference: Gender theory, postmodernism, and psychology. *American Psychologist, 43,* 455-464.

Hochschild, A. R. (1973). *The unexpected community.* Berkeley: University of California Press.

Liebow, E. (1967). *Tally's corner.* Boston: Little, Brown.

Lopata, H. Z. (1990). Friendship: Historical and theoretical introduction. In H. Z. Lopata & D. R. Maines (Eds.), *Friendship in context* (pp. 1-22). Greenwich, CT: JAI.

Lovingood, R. P., Blieszner, R., & Hill, P. P. (1987). *Continuity of household task performance during widowhood.* Final report to the AARP Andrus Foundation, Washington, DC.

Mancini, J. A., & Blieszner, R. (1992). Social provisions in adulthood: Concept and measurement in close relationships. *Journal of Gerontology, 47,* P14-P20.

Mancini, J. A., Travis, S. S., & Bianchinotti, R. C. (1985). *Family interaction and psychological well-being: An analysis of older parent-adult child relationships.* Final report to the AARP Andrus Foundation, Washington, DC.

Matthews, S. H. (1986). *Friendships through the life course.* Beverly Hills, CA: Sage.

Mazur, E. (1989). Predicting gender differences in same-sex friendships from affiliation motive and value. *Psychology of Women Quarterly, 13,* 277-291.

McAdams, D. P., Healy, S., & Krause, S. (1984). Social motives and patterns of friendship. *Journal of Personality and Social Psychology, 47,* 828-838.

Murstein, B. I., & Spitz, L. T. (1973-74). Aristotle and friendship: A factor-analytic study. *Interpersonal Development, 4,* 21-34.

Nahemow, L., & Lawton, M. P. (1975). Similarity and propinquity in friendship formation. *Journal of Personality and Social Psychology, 32,* 205-213.

Nardi, P. M. (1992). Sex, friendship, and gender roles among gay men. In P. M. Nardi (Ed.), *Men's friendships* (pp. 173-185). Newbury Park, CA: Sage.

O'Connor, P. (1992). *Friendships between women.* New York: Guilford.

Oliker, S. J. (1989). *Best friends and marriage.* Berkeley: University of California Press.

Pakaluck, M. (1991). *Other selves: Philosophers on friendship.* Indianapolis, IN: Hackett.

Peretti, P. O. (1976). Closest friendships of black college students: Social intimacy. *Adolescence, 11,* 395-403.

Peretti, P. O. (1977). Closest friendships of black college students: Structural characteristics. *Human Relations, 30,* 43-51.

Rawlins, W. K. (1992). *Friendship matters.* Hawthorne, NY: Aldine.

Rook, K. S. (1989). Strains in older adults' friendships. In R. G. Adams & R. Blieszner (Eds.), *Older adult friendship* (pp. 166-194). Newbury Park, CA: Sage.

Rose, S., & Roades, L. (1987). Feminism and women's friendships. *Psychology of Women Quarterly, 11,* 243-254.

Rubin, L. B. (1976). *Worlds of pain.* New York: Basic Books.

Rubin, L. B. (1985). *Just friends.* New York: Harper & Row.

Shea, L., Thompson, L., & Blieszner, R. (1988). Resources in older adults' old and new friendships. *Journal of Social and Personal Relationships, 5,* 83-96.

Sherif, C. W. (1987). Bias in psychology. In S. Harding (Ed.), *Feminism and methodology* (pp. 37-56). Bloomington: Indiana University Press.

Smith-Rosenberg, C. (1975). The female world of love and ritual: Relations between women in nineteenth-century America. *Signs, 1,* 1-29.

Stack, C. (1974). *All our kin.* New York: Harper Colophon.

Swain, S. (1989). Covert intimacy: Closeness in men's friendships. In B. J. Risman & P. Schwartz (Eds.), *Gender in intimate relationships: A microstructural approach* (pp. 71-86). Belmont, CA: Wadsworth.

Thoits, P. A. (1985). Social support and psychological well-being: Theoretical possibilities. In I. G. Sarason & B. R. Sarason (Eds.), *Social support: Theory, research and applications* (pp. 51-72). The Hague, The Netherlands: Martinus Nijhoff.

Thompson, L. (1992). Feminist methods for family studies. *Journal of Marriage and the Family, 54,* 3-18.

Thompson, P. J. (1988). *Home economics and feminism: The Hestian synthesis.* Charlottetown, PEI, Canada: Home Economics Publishing Collective.

Walker, A. J., Martin, S. S. K., & Thompson, L. (1988). Feminist programs for families. *Family Relations, 37,* 17-22.

Walker, A. J., & Thompson, L. (1984). Feminism and family studies. *Journal of Family Issues, 5,* 545-570.

Wellman, B. (1992). Men in networks. In P. M. Nardi (Ed.), *Men's friendships* (pp. 74-114). Newbury Park, CA: Sage.

Whyte, W. H. (1956). *The organization man.* New York: Simon & Schuster.

Williams, D. G. (1985). Gender, masculinity-femininity, and emotional intimacy in same-sex friendship. *Sex Roles, 12,* 587-600.

Wright, P. H. (1982). Men's friendships, women's friendships, and the alleged inferiority of the latter. *Sex Roles, 8,* 1-20.

Wright, P. H. (1989). Gender differences in adults' same- and cross-gender friendships. In R. G. Adams & R. Blieszner (Eds.), *Older adult friendship* (pp. 197-221). Newbury Park, CA: Sage.

PART II

The Role of Work in Close Relationships

7

Studying Workplace Intimacy

Havens at Work

STEPHEN R. MARKS

Four themes frame the telling of this research story. The dominant theme is the progression of my research on coworker relationships through several data sources. A second theme highlights some points of connection with feminist thinking. Of my various data sources, some lend themselves to feminist analysis better than others. My intent here is to suggest that feminist thinking need not stop in these latter instances; we still can look at *how* our data constrain us, and note the questions that might yield a deeper feminist analysis. A third theme concerns some ethical matters emerging in the process of this research. The larger issue here concerns morals, or values, and how they shape our research. What does feminism contribute to our moral sensibilities? What is our position when we find that the people we are studying are contravening these values? The fourth theme is more personal: How has my own life experience shaped my research questions, my feminist inclinations and my moral sensibilities? I begin on this personal level and return to it at the end of the chapter.

AUTHOR'S NOTE: Everyone should have the kind of advice and support that was my good fortune to get. I am especially thankful for the penetrating readings and detailed suggestions from Alexis Walker, Katherine Allen, Anisa Zvonkovic, Leigh Leslie, Donna Sollie, Ralph LaRossa, Joan Marks, and Kyriacos Markides.

What Is a Coworker?
Early Impressions

As a child I had no active concept of what a coworker was. My upper middle-class upbringing in Miami Beach provided me with little first-hand experience of "ordinary" people doing their work in the company of one another. I do remember two women who came regularly to my home, from what was called the "colored" part of Miami: one to clean our house and cook our meals, and the other to do our laundry. They often would talk together while they worked. Their conversations seemed close and private; they protected themselves from my prying ears, perhaps because I was the boss's son, perhaps because they simply wanted a space for themselves alone.

My father was a "self-made" Jewish doctor who, despite his protestations that we would wind up in the "poorhouse" if we were not very careful, made it plain that we were not ordinary. The proper answer to "What are you going to *be* when you grow up?" could only have been some kind of professional, so the work life of these two "maids," as they were called in my household, was nothing to take note of or to become curious about. The message I got was that people like them work for people like us, and as long as they do their jobs, their lives are not to be seen as part of a pattern in which I am also involved.

When I would visit my father at his workplace—his office—I encountered the same kind of drama that played out at home. The nurses who worked for him were his "girls," and neither their work nor their relationships were ever considered as significant in their own right, apart from their support of his own doctorly calling (medicine was God's only chosen profession). He would not hire young, married, childless women: "They'll just get pregnant and quit on me," he would say with a note of derision. He always spoke and acted as if the women he employed were not quite appreciative enough of the wonderful opportunity he was providing them. They were anything but his "coworkers" to him, and my own concept of work was identified squarely with his. He did not *have* any coworkers, much like the lord of the manor has no co-lords. Work to me was thus a solitary enterprise, accompanied at most by a chorus of cheering and grateful subordinates.

My mother had to find her place within this traditional patriarchal arrangement. While I was growing up, she was charged with the bookkeeping at his office, managing our household, and providing general emotional support services to my father and my sister and me. The household management included supervising the women who looked after us and who did most of the other household work except the shopping, which she did. She also edited and typed my father's medical manuscripts and did the unrelenting errands he sent her to do. And she was held responsible for anything that went wrong with my sister and me or with the household. What was my mother's position? There was certainly no perception of her as his bona fide coworker or his partner. For that matter, her work was not reckoned as real work—not by him, not by us children, not by the surrounding upper middle-class culture, and dimly, if at all, by herself. She did her best to make his needs and triumphs her own. What she was, I see now by hindsight, was his "wife."

I think the seed of some of my feminist sensibilities took root in this male-defined household in reaction to my father's arbitrary claims over women, though it was only much later that I could get beyond framing the issue in terms of my own claims over women, beginning with my claims over my mother's attention—a contest with my father that I invariably lost. That story is well beyond the scope of this chapter, but it is worth noting that when I interviewed married people for my book *Three Corners* (1986), I was primed to look at how these couples were dealing with the same patriarchal legacy that provided the undergirding of my own upbringing. I especially wanted to explore male control of the public realm of work—how that control was linked to the power to construct the private domain of marriage and family. Thinking about that issue in terms of the microdynamics of married life, I was led to a feminist version of the resource theory of power, which suggests that the partner with the most resources from outside the relationship has the most power inside the relationship. Because, in a consumer society, "income" becomes the prime resource, and because jobs are the basis of independent incomes, male rule in marriages is tied up with restricting females' full access to the job market. In short, the strings of patriarchy are pulled through the male purse. Here was a way I could understand the emotional and power dynamics both within my own family and within the couples who were telling me their stories.

Exploring the Public/Private Split

My next project was conceptual and theoretical, and it continues today after some 7 years. In search of a keener understanding of the work-family connection, I turned my attention to current notions of the public/private split. Theorists, social critics, and family social scientists, including family historians, all seemed to see the home and family world as the one place where intimacy might still happen, a "haven in a heartless world," in the phrase popularized by Lasch (1977; see my critique in Marks, 1994.) Even when analysts conceded that many families are hard put to meet all of their emotional burden (e.g., Hareven, 1982; Laslett, 1978), they still seemed to be assuming that families are the only intimate game in town.

Something bothered me about this conceptualization of the public/ private divide, and I drew on feminist work to get an adequate handle on it. For example, the literature on domestic violence made it plain that for many people the family is characterized more by terror than by "heart." (My own family was not terrifying, but it was often tense. As a boy I thrilled to the anticipation of my father coming home with his daily tales of lives saved and his aura of importance, but I soon learned that once he did get home, more reliable havens were to be found elsewhere.) Feminist thinkers also alerted me to the gendered *phenomenology* of the home world as a haven. Women have been charged with compulsory emotional service to their family members; that is, a wife and mother's job has been to *make* the family a haven for her husband and children, although the job descriptions of "husband" and "children" never included making the family a haven for her. That was certainly the case in my own family, in which no one ever wondered whether he or she was doing enough to meet my *mother's* needs, and I recall times when she would complain, exasperatedly, that all she seemed to be was a doormat. Again, then, the feminist critique resonated well with my own experience.

As I struggled to make sense of the public/private split, my focus soon shifted to the "heartless world" side of the haven-in-a-heartless-world formulation. Feminist thinkers had unmasked the arbitrariness of positing the home as an emotional haven, but sociologists rarely challenged the notion that the world outside the family is inherently heartless (for exceptions, see Gans, 1988; Peterson, 1985; Siltanen & Stanworth, 1984; see also the literature on friendship, such as Rawlins, 1992). I reasoned that one location where many adults encounter the "outside," public world on an almost daily basis is the workplace. Here I had a concrete way of exploring the "heartless world" presumption. Are workplaces always cold, impersonal, heartless places? Or are some workplaces replete with caring, nurturing, and intimacy? I began to ask my students: "How many of you, in your most recent job, had at least one coworker with whom you regularly shared things about yourself that you would not share with very many people?" Almost everyone had at least one such person. "And how many of you ever kept a job you would otherwise have quit, if not for your relationship with one of your coworkers?" Far fewer affirmations here, but surprisingly many—perhaps around 20%. I decided I was on to something.

Of course, I knew that many workplaces are awful places, but so are many homes and other settings. Still, the question of frequency did seem important. I knew from my own experience that intimate companionship with certain of my coworkers has been a staple of my work life, and now I had found out that the same was true for many of my college students. But just how general is this phenomenon of workplace intimacy? In my own case, is it simply a privilege and perquisite of my professional job and hence of social class? For my students, is it simply youthful openness, or perhaps innocence, or orientation toward the privileges of the educated that allows them to jump over the constraints to engaging their coworkers?

One day while shopping for some shirts at a discount chain, I stopped momentarily to watch two storeworkers—women in their middle years, working, no doubt, for near-minimum wages. Their job was to refold all of the clothing that customers had left in disarray, and they had managed to locate their activity well within earshot of one another. They folded vigorously, but while they did so, they also talked personally to each other about their lives; this had the feel of a well-practiced routine. Here was an instance of workplace intimacy among working-class people. I began to suspect that perhaps most workplaces are replete with such intimacy, and if this is so, it makes little sense to carve up the world into a heartless public domain on one side and a hearty private domain revolving around the homefront on the other.

The Coworker Literature:
Looking in the Wrong Place

What would I learn from the existing literature? Would all of the studies of workplace relationships confirm my hunch about coworker intimacy? And what would they teach me about how it unfolds and develops and about what its implications are? Eagerly I asked a colleague, a sociologist of work, but she knew of no such studies. Thinking that perhaps this was not her particular interest in the sociology of work, I went off to track down the literature myself. Again I came up almost empty-handed, except for Homans's (1950) reanalysis of the men observed in the Hawthorne studies, about which I will have more to say later. The studies of workers doing their jobs made only scant and fleeting reference to coworking close relationships, although I did find a literature on "organizational romances," a topic far narrower than what interested me. Gabarro's (1987) study of four businessmen and their relationships with their various subordinates emphasizes only the task-oriented feature of these working relationships. Self-disclosure is not found in these dyads, nor, in his view, is there any reason why it should be present. After all, we are told flatly, "Working relationships are . . . segmental in nature" (p. 180).

In general, there is something almost Calvinistic about the approach of sociologists to workers at work. It is as if the category "worker" denudes workers from the rest of their lives while they are working, as if all they should be attending to at work is work. Even the early studies (e.g., Roy, 1952) that reveal how informal work groups both control the amount of work that gets done and provide for an ample amount of companionable activity show little interest in the substance of these relationships or in the expressive functions they serve. Simpson (1989) points out that after the 1950s, sociologists abandoned their focus on actual workers as part of informal work groups, and since about 1970 the worker has been seen as a purely economic being: "Emphasis is on the position, not on the flesh-and-blood person who holds it" (p. 579). Similarly Fine (1985) had complained that "despite the prevalence of friendships at work, there has been little discussion of these relationships" (p. 185).

Why have sociologists become so mute about workplace intimacy? Is it due to some Calvinistic notion that hard work is the only moral virtue, so the camaraderie and talk through which people build intimacy becomes a capitulation to the devil of idleness? Is it because sociologists of work and sociologists of the family both implicitly agree with the haven-in-a-heartless-world notion and therefore collude in seeing intimacy as a family matter? Is it because the sociology of work has been male defined, and because females are reputedly more oriented to relationships, they might have been more alert to coworker intimacy if they had been conducting the studies?

Evidence supporting this last possibility arose when I discovered that the most important literature about coworkers had slipped through the net of my search. I had focused my search within sociology and within the multidisciplinary field of personal relationships, thinking I would find other important sources through cross-references. In the meantime, however, feminist anthropologists and social historians published some studies of working-class women on the shop floor (e.g., Benson, 1983; Cooper, 1987; Lamphere, 1987; Tentler, 1979; Westwood, 1985; Zavella, 1987). The scholars I had been reading had either published prior to these superb studies or failed to catch up to this work that resided outside our discipline. My own research projects, as I describe them here, likewise were conceived in ignorance of this literature, and therefore my initial understanding of what I was looking for missed out on the opportunity to be informed by this work. Accordingly the task just now beginning for me is to rethink what I have been doing, with an eye toward bridging my research with the findings of this important feminist work in sister disciplines.

In any case I proceeded on the assumption that if no one is studying intimacy in the workplace (or so I thought) because the workplace is not the place to look for it, then clearly the first task was to show that the phenomenon exists! The opportunity to do so arose when some colleagues alerted me to some items on the 1985 and 1986 General Social Survey (GSS) and to Fischer's (1982) data from his Northern California Communities Study (NCCS).

Some Help From Survey Research

Despite the fact that I had always thought of my professional self as a theorist and qualitative researcher, the GSS and NCCS data provided a painless way of arriving at some empirical generalizations about workplace intimacy. A question from the 1986 GSS asks respondents, "How many close friends would you say you have?" and the next question follows with, "How many of these close friends are people you work with now?" The 1985 GSS asks respondents to name up to five people with whom they "discussed important matters" over the past 6 months, and it then collects information about each named person, including whether he or she is a coworker to the respondent. The NCCS uses the same kind of name-eliciting procedure as the 1985 GSS, but the questions are more elaborate. I selected a question that asks respondents whom they talk with about personal matters or worries, another question asking whose judgment they rely on in making important life decisions, and still another asking whom they visited, invited to their house, or went out with socially in the past three months.

I do not offer any extended summary here of my results (see Marks, 1994). Suffice it to say that my simple working procedure was to find out the percentage of full-time workers who name none, one, two, three, or more coworkers on the various items. I found that 40% to 60% of these working respondents name at least one coworker, depending on the survey and the items selected. I then found no gender differences on any of these items, and no differences by age or by marital status, except on the "getting together socially" item (married and older workers less often get together with coworkers). I did find that intimacy with coworkers on the various "talk" items varies positively with education and occupational prestige. In general, because I assume (provisionally) that having even one coworker to whom a person feels close in these various ways can alter significantly the experience of coming to work and going through the day, I now had an empirical basis for concluding that selective workplace intimacy is indeed a widespread and important phenomenon. I also had to endure the cuteness of some friends and colleagues: "Ha, Stephen," they would smirk, pointing triumphantly to the latest computer printout tucked under my arm, "you're becoming A NUMBER CRUNCHER!"

Feminism and Survey Research

At this point I was not thinking about my research as a specifically feminist project. I was interested in the general phenomenon of close relationships at work, and women's lives were not at the center of my analysis. Then, too, doing secondary analyses of other people's data must to some extent refract one's vision through the lens of the original researchers, and neither the GSS nor the NCCS were inspired by feminist frameworks. This lack does not mean that survey research is inherently less feminist than qualitative, open-ended interviewing of women; a demographic analysis showing that women earn $0.70 to the $1.00 that a man earns can be just as valuable a part of the feminist project as detailed stories of discrimination on the job. The point here is that feminism need not be an all-or-nothing endeavor, and I want to signal two ways in which it was guiding my work.

Gender as a Variable

One question worth asking about any set of findings regarding what "people" do or what men do is whether the claims made are true of women as well. Have women been included in the sample? Do the survey questions adequately tap into women's experience? Although the intimacy items selected from the GSS and NCCS were somewhat lacking in specificity, I thought they were useful enough as a starting point for exploring what both women and men do about intimacy in the workplace. To be sure, running one's variables by gender does not necessarily take one very far in developing a thorough feminist analysis. It is much better to build a vision of the particularities of female experience into the survey design from the ground up. Even failing that vision, however, finding male/female differences can become the starting point of new research that seeks to account for them more fully.

Feminism as Heuristic Strategy

In my case, as already mentioned, I was unable to find any differences between men and women workers in their tendencies toward intimacy with their coworkers. This result thoroughly surprised me because it did not fit with my preconceptions. I had expected that women would show significantly higher frequencies of coworker intimacy than men, at least on the NCCS item dealing with disclosure about "personal matters" and "worries." That preconception did not come from thin air. I try to use various feminist perspectives heuristically—that is, to apply them to new contexts to help focus myself on important themes, issues, and questions. Feminists had established that intimate connectedness with others is a skill built into female development and carried into female relationships (Chodorow, 1978) and into female morality (Gilligan, 1982). To look for this skill in the world of work was a chance to explore it in a new domain. When I found no differences between females and males, my options were either to decide that females and males do not operate differently in their workplace relationships or to conclude that there might, in fact, be differences which the survey questions failed to detect. Although the data provide no way of arbitrating, the beauty of heuristic thinking is that it allows us to think beyond our immediate data and findings. Such thinking is driven by our knowledge of other perspectives and by our imagination, not by any rules of evidence.

Accordingly I left my first venture in quantitative analysis, happy to have demonstrated that the "heartless" world of work is rife with heart. I also had some provocative questions. Even if women's intimacy with coworkers is not different in frequency from that of men, is it the same kind of intimacy? Are the "important matters" (GSS) discussed by women the same or different? Are the talks about "personal matters or worries" (NCCS) the same or different? And what about the style of talk? And the way support is exchanged in these talks? And the nature of the interaction when coworkers get together socially?

No less intriguing is the possibility that there are no fundamental gender differences in the nature of coworker intimacy. Just as Thorne (1986) showed that teachers help create the divisions between girls and boys at school, so perhaps social scientists are doing their part to accentuate the gender differences and thus keep them alive. Even Gilligan's followers have been criticized by other feminists (e.g., Faludi, 1991) for placing women into a kind of relationalistic mold, expecting them to be paragons of caring and empathy and in that way different from men. My own view is that there is no true dilemma here. The fact is that patriarchy and misogyny indeed have created women as separate, as a class of "other"—surely this is the implicit starting point of any feminist analysis. We must start with what women are doing and feeling, move to the larger system of opportunities or constraints that promotes these doings, and, yes, be wary of freezing the doings we find into some naturalistic female condition. In the process, we often will need to begin by ferreting out the gender differences that culture has created.

A Study of Dental Offices

While immersed in my work with the GSS and NCCS, I got the opportunity to build some of my interests in coworker relationships into a new survey. Dennis Kaldenberg, a sociologist at Oregon State University, had a grant to study dental offices in Oregon. He had invited the collaboration of Anisa Zvonkovic, a family scientist, and Anisa pulled me into the project. Although we are still in the thick of a number of analyses, some of the contours of the study and a few sample findings can be mentioned here.

I had excellent reasons for entering this collaboration. Neither the GSS nor NCCS data had large enough clusters of people within any given occupational setting to make possible a separate analysis of coworker intimacy within particular occupational cultures. The best I could do was run my intimacy variables by occupational prestige and by global occupational type, and though suggestive, these analyses could not bring me as close as I wanted to actual workers at work. Here was an opportunity to get closer than I had so far.

The sample seemed tailor-made, not only for exploring coworker relationships in greater detail but also for moving toward a deeper feminist analysis. We surveyed dentists, hygienists, and dental assistants. Virtually all of the hygienists and assistants are women, and because we oversampled female dentists, we can compare offices run by female dentists with offices run by male dentists. We emerged with a sample of 650 individuals—197 male dentists and 74 female dentists, 161 hygienists, and 218 dental assistants. Moreover, in 116 practices all three of the respondents we sampled completed and returned the questionnaire. This triad data will enable us to get quite specific about patterns of self-disclosure and their concomitants within these particular offices.

Several of our research agendas connect rather directly with feminist perspectives, but first I want to think about some limitations of what we are doing. The large presence of women in a sample says little by itself about the feminist merit of a project. Then, too, some would seriously question whether one can learn anything important about women (or anyone else) without hearing their voices. We did not hear them, nor did we allow our respondents their own words, except in a "tell us anything else you would like us to know" type of question at the end of the questionnaire. This was, after all, a traditional survey. We supplied the focus, the topics, the language, and the choices; they supplied responses to questions that may or may not have tapped into their own frames of reference. As with all such research, we traded away the chance to make living, interactive contact with a relatively small number of people, for the chance to make some generalizations about a much larger number. I am not entirely comfortable with this choice. I would rather have engaged a few dozen of these people in a free-flowing conversation about their jobs and their coworkers. Indeed, at those times when the figures on the computer printouts seem enigmatic, I sometimes picture myself in the middle of just such a conversation, probing for additional clarity. But that is just my own bent; I do not offer it as research gospel. Quantitative surveys are a vital part of our enterprise, and there is room for as many angles of vision on phenomena as there are different explorers.

Back to our data and findings. What happens when women work for other women in professions such as dentistry? Do working groups of women create different cultures and coworking relationships from those of working groups of men? O'Leary (1987) suggested that female mentor-mentee relationships are more likely to include "role modeling, acceptance and confirmation, counseling and friendship" (p. 206). In a provocative qualitative study, Statham (1987) found that female managers adopt a style of management and supervision that is at once person invested and task oriented, while male managers are more often autonomy invested and image oriented. We attempted to operationalize Statham's concepts and to put them to the test in Oregon dental offices. In preliminary zero-order correlations, the staff of female dentists are more likely than the staff of male dentists to see their employer's style as person oriented (the dentists themselves perceive no such difference in their respective tendencies). Furthermore, staff are quite responsive to this person-oriented style in the dentist for whom they work: Their job satisfaction is higher, their work anxiety is lower, and their intimacy with coworkers is greater. However, in multiple regressions with job satisfaction as the dependent variable and person investment and the other management styles as independent variables, adding the gender of the dentist to the equation does nothing to strengthen the resulting model. Statham is right about the value of person-oriented management: Its influence on job satisfaction is much greater than that of the other management styles. As yet, however, we find no confirmation that gender differences are at the bottom of this effect.

Our data are not limited to the impact of characteristics of the dentist/manager. We knew we were studying a predominantly female world, given that virtually all hygienists, assistants, and receptionists are females. We made the presumption that, historically, close relationships are elaborate female productions. To study women at work is an opportunity to study these unofficial relational productions, lest we miss an enormous share of the work that gets done in such workplaces. Our findings provide much confirmation of this fact: Dental offices are places where this production of coworker intimacy abounds. No matter how we tap into it, we find the same result. We generated a 9-item closeness scale on which the *average* score is 31 on a scale ranging from a low of 9 to a high of 45, and several of the items are quite stringent (e.g., "We do things together outside the office," "Working with this person is like working with a friend"). We looked at self-disclosure among dentists, hygienists, and assistants by asking respondents whether they have "very personal talks" with each of the other two workers in which they tell them "some details of [their] life that [they] wouldn't share with very many people." Looking, for example, at such disclosures between dentists and assistants, we find that 76.5% of the dentists make them to their assistants, and 84.5% of the assistants make them at least "a few times a year" to the dentist with whom they work (remember that the GSS item concerns "discussing important mattters in the last 6 months").

For those respondents who did claim to have very personal talks with either of two coworkers, we also attempted to learn something about the content of these talks. Fully 75% of all respondents report talking with each of the other two about work, money, coworkers, activities (e.g., what they did over the weekend), family members, and friends. Well over a majority talk to each of the other two about their relationship with a spouse or intimate partner.

Is intimacy among coworkers in these offices principally a female production? The percentages both of male and of female dentists who report having very personal talks with their assistants are very high. But female dentists are significantly more likely than male dentists to have them. When we analyze conversational topics, we find the same mixed result. For all but one topic, the percentages are very high; everyone seems to be talking with everyone else about almost everything! Male and female dentists do not differ in talking with their assistants about friends or money, and assistants are just as likely to talk with male dentists as with female dentists about friends, money, and outside activities. But female dentists are even more likely than male dentists to talk with their assistants about outside activities, and they are much more likely than male dentists ($p < .001$) to make disclosures to their assistants about their relationship with spouse or intimate partner (69% of female dentists vs. 43% of male dentists). Similarly assistants talk more often about this spouse/ partner topic with female dentists than with male dentists (72% with female dentists vs. 54% with male dentists). And on the most intimate topic—"personal things you wouldn't share with your spouse or intimate partner"—gender differences again emerge: 21% of female dentists, compared with only 6% of male dentists, disclose this privileged information to their assistant; and 24% of assistants working for female dentists disclose it to them, compared with 9% working for male dentists.

Some tentative conclusions can be drawn from this selective presentation of findings. First, dentist offices in Oregon are often intimate havens for those who work there; they are not simply places where people do the work for which they are paid. The talk exchanged by many coworkers is not just chitchat; it is also "very personal." Second, coworking relationships must be serving a restorative function at these offices. Judging from the wide range of active conversational topics, we can say these workers are reviewing and presumably evaluating much that is significant about their lives. If the home is sometimes a place where people "check in" with each other about their lives, so are these offices. Third, indications are that the females in these offices are carrying this intimate potential somewhat farther than the males. Concerning the most privileged topics of conversation that we inquired about, we find that females seem more ready to open them up to other females than to males and that males are less likely than females to open them up. Producing intimacy does seem to be part of the work that women do, part of the emotional service that women provide, and it needs to be recognized as significant work, rather than ignored as inconsequential.

Back to the Hawthorne Plant

One of the curious things about the literature on work and workers is that, early on, it was alert to a certain *kind* of expressive coworker relationship. When "primary relations" were rediscovered among workers in the famous Hawthorne studies between 1927 and 1932, the main focus was on their role in the construction of informal norms of work output. There was also some recognition of the joking camaraderie and recreational activity among male workers at work. This much I knew from Homans's reanalysis of the Bank Wiring Observation Room in *The Human Group* (1950), which still had been required reading in my graduate program in sociology in the 1960s. Homans's simple proposition—that the more people share activities and interaction together, the more they like one another—was drawn, after all, from observations of coworkers. But I had never read Roethlisberger and Dickson (1939), the original source.

Poring over their *Management and the Worker* gave me new perspective on the origins of the sociology of work and industry. I learned that the men in the Bank Wiring Room did far more together than generate informal norms of work output. They also conversed freely about numerous topics having nothing to do with work. Some of them routinely ate lunch together. Many of them had become good friends outside the factory. They went to dances, played cards, and went drinking together. One of them invited several of the others to his wedding. I had known already that an observer was in the room throughout this study, but the chapter "Method and Procedure" arrested me with these stunning words: "The observer kept a daily record of significant happenings in the observation room, *of conversations of the employees,* and of his own impressions. *This record, completed, consisted of some three hundred single-spaced typewritten pages*" (p. 406, italics added). Surely, I thought, this typed document must still exist somewhere. Because I knew that in the two other Hawthorne studies an observer also had been present and had kept a "daily history record," I wondered about the status of these records, as well. Whitehead (1938) had offered some thoughtful description and analysis of the women in the Relay Assembly Room, including some verbatim quotes from their conversations, obviously drawn from the observers' records. What else was in these documents, and where might they be preserved?

It took only minor searching to learn that in 1977 the Western Electric Company had made all of these materials available to the Baker Library at Harvard University's Business School, as well as to several other libraries, and that I could borrow the microfiche through interlibrary loan for a fee of $15.00.

The various observers left more than 1,000 pages of very rich, ethnographic, interpersonal coworker data—mainly conversational—that have never been adequately analyzed. Roethlisberger and Dickson (1939), as well as Whitehead (1938), drew on these data very selectively in preparing their books, and there is no evidence that Homans (1950) ever made use of them for his own reanalysis; all of his citations are to Roethlisberger and Dickson's text. Moreover, Homans worked only with that part of the text about the men in the Bank Wiring Room; perhaps this is one reason why the women in the Relay and Mica Room studies never became familiar to the sociological community, despite the fact that some of the observers' data about these women easily rival the richness of the data about the men. I suggest that attention to the caring, companionship, self-disclosure, and mutual support among these Hawthorne women is one of the roads not taken in the sociology of workers.

Now immersed in a number of analyses of Hawthorne, I find that the various observers' records still comprise the most detailed account of coworker interaction among factory workers ever generated and that they offer invaluable leads about the substance and functions of such relationships. The records about the women in the Relay Room are particularly intriguing. Their voices and experiences have never been registered adequately in the legacy of social science. The men who invaded and sought to scrutinize virtually every aspect of these women's lives failed, with the partial exception of Whitehead (1938), to take their qualitative data very seriously; they ignored most of the material that did not bear in some way on the women's productive output. Yet for 5 years these women lived much of their lives together in that room. Their menial jobs did not deaden their vibrant personalities, and in their conversations with one another one can see a clear reflection of the totality of their lives.

When I visit with these women through their conversations, I get to participate in their constant dramas, their continual flow of humor, their stories, their worries, their frivolity, their omnipresent planning for the next grand event, and above all, their intimacy. They have much to say, of course, about every aspect of their jobs and about the various phases of the experiment that brought them together, but they also go way beyond shop talk. Their range of topics reveals the depth and complexity of their relationships with one another. For example, they talk in detail about their family members, especially if one of them is in any kind of difficulty. Here they reveal themselves not only as kin keepers but also as their coworkers' kin keepers: When Theresa's sister is sick and eventually must have an operation, the others ask repeatedly about how she is doing. They also talk about their vacations—where they went, what they did, whom they saw. They talk and joke in some detail about each other's men friends, when they have them. They share their upcoming plans for dates over the weekend, and they recount them afterward. They talk at length about current movies. Theresa initiates conversations about dreams when she remembers them, and sometimes they discuss them. They talk about everything in their sensuous surround. They talk about the moon from the night before; they did this a number of times.

Outside the factory, the four of the five of them who are not married do things together in various combinations and often as a foursome. They go to events sponsored by the Western Electric Girl's Activity Organization. They plan a vacation highlighted by staying together in a cabin. They go roller skating. They arrange theater parties and go to the movies together. They go to the rodeo at the Chicago Stadium, visit each other at their homes, and go on double or triple dates together. Back at work they create a variety of rituals to celebrate their lives together. For example, they institute a birthday ritual—everyone brings lingerie-type presents to the birthday person, whose responsibility is to reciprocate with a half-pound box of Fannie May chocolates to each of the gift-givers.

These qualitative data from Hawthorne offer a different kind of opportunity than the GSS, NCCS, and dentist office surveys discussed earlier. On the one hand, we lose the capacity to generalize to other groups of coworkers; we have no way of knowing whether the patterns in the conversational records are a chance anomaly even within the Hawthorne plant itself. On the other hand, we get to explore some coworker interaction processes in much greater depth. This material is more ethnographic and thus closer to the actual lived experience of these particular coworkers. We become familiar with specific individuals and specific coworker ties; we even come to recognize individual senses of humor and to hear, almost, the voices that speak the conversations we read. We can discern also some considerable differences between male and female coworker relationships—the kinds of differences that slipped through the net of the GSS and NCCS standardized questioning. Perhaps Hawthorne men would have come out the same as Hawthorne women, had either group been asked whether they discuss "important matters" with coworkers, or talk with them about "personal matters or worries," or get together with them socially. With the conversational data, however, the different feel of the relationships among the Relay Room women from those among the Bank Wiring Room men is unmistakable. The "important matters" discussed are different, and so are the style of talk, the range of concerns, and the manner in which support gets exchanged. I next explore some of these differences in the context of some ethical issues that grew salient for me as I became familiar with the conversational material.

The Ethics of Caring in the Research Process

As I work with the data about the Hawthorne women, listen to their voices, and decide what to report, I am very much aware that here I am, yet another man, defining these women. Who am I to "let" them speak? Perhaps this is the paradox of any historical reclamation project about human beings: Someone deprives someone else of the right to be fully heard, and then another person presumes to give the voice back. To muddy the water still further, given the evidence that these women sometimes resented their words being recorded in the first place, how do we ethically justify any further invasion of their privacy?

I confess my lack of confidence about any answers, and indeed I rarely bother to ask these questions. Perhaps I ask them this time because I have gotten to know these women well enough to like them, to care about how they might have felt, what they might have wanted, and to *not* want to add any more to the routine violations of being female subjects in a male-defined series of experiments.

None of these issues came up in my various survey ventures reported earlier. With quantitative survey data, one hears respondents' voices but dimly—one has to imagine them to hear them at all—and so the opportunity to start caring about them is scaled down considerably. This is not a vote against quantitative survey research, but simply a cautionary statement. As Ruddick (1982) has taught us, caring attention is an epistemology that stretches our vision: A sure way to *know* more about a group of people is to *care* more about them. If we find, then, that our caring in the research process is having difficulty getting its proper exercise, we might want to add some distance-closing devices to our methodology.

That said, I should add that it does not always work. Hearing our respondents' voices is no guarantee that we will like what we hear. I have the same kind of conversational data about the men in the Bank Wiring Room that I have about the women. Here are two groups of people—one men, one women—very similar in their average age and in their predominantly never-married status, working as wage laborers in the same factory. But my relationship with the men is uncomfortable. I strain to feel some empathy, some caring for them. I am not attracted to their worlds, and I get little satisfaction from entering into them.

Long before I caught up with the Hawthorne data, I had developed a humanistic perspective about research and writing: As researchers, we should borrow Carl Rogers's (1957) therapeutic principle of "unconditional positive regard" toward clients and extend it to the people we study. We need to treat and write about our respondents with the utmost respect and compassion, particularly when they are doing *us* the favor by allowing us to enter their worlds and to put them into the spotlight.

But this particular spotlight made me uncomfortable. These men elaborate a masculine culture revolving around constant demonstrations of manly prowess. They produce endless varieties of competition, boxing with each other, boasting, gambling, continually seeking to outdo one another in recounting their exploits. They give no indication of liking women or of being interested in their worlds. Females seem to exist only to gratify their needs and to validate their masculine status in the eyes of their fellows. One man brags that his evening out with a woman culminates in a sexual encounter on her davenport, and his emphasis is on how deftly he had managed to spend hardly any money that night. On another occasion two of the men tell the observer of getting fixed up with a woman who's "hot stuff." One of them reminds his friend that his recently married status should disqualify him from taking her out. But the friend is not deterred. "That don't make any difference," he crows. "I'm just as free as I was before. You bring your girl over to stay with the wife some night, and we'll step out."

The men do seem to engage in the kind of side-by-side companionship that the literature on friendship suggests is typical of male culture, compared with the face-to-face intimacy of women. If companionship merely means a waiting-your-own-turn sort of audience for one another, then the men do offer abundant support. But it is much easier to read their activity as competitive display than as intimacy or real support. For example, in the midst of the Great Depression both the men and the women talk frequently about where to find the best consumer values. The women, however, pool their information in a spirit of helpful support. The men merely argue about shrewd consumership; they use their real or imagined knowledge to demonstrate their individual superiority, and the potential benefits of communalizing their information seem to escape them entirely.

I feel no need to lionize the Relay Room women, to use intellectual discourse to put them on a pedestal. They were given to racist slurs against blacks, and there were anti-semitic remarks about going "to fight with the Jews" in buying some article of clothing. One of the women had a grievance against one of the others, and she was clearly mean-spirited in prosecuting her private war. Still, I see much more than merely saving graces in these women, whereas I feel little for the Bank Wiring Room men beyond mild amusement at some of their antics.

The point here is not to choose sides between women and men, but rather to think about caring as an epistemology and about how it relates to the feminist project. As I dug into these data and found myself drawn to these women's lives, I had to struggle with how difficult it was to like the men, to care for them and about them. The struggle was not a matter of some categorical loyalty to my fellow males, but a product of the humanistic ethics I thought should inform my attitude toward the people I study. I certainly could hear the voices of the men well enough, but I did not like what I heard; my capacity to feel much compassion for them grew thin and more abstract. Hence I began to feel in violation of my own research ethics.

I now understand that if feminism is to serve as cultural critique, "unconditional positive regard" can be only a methodological point of departure for studying human beings, not an ethical endpoint, unless we take it to mean nothing more than a readiness to see beyond what is manifest in our data to some deeper humanity that is surely there somewhere, perhaps lying dormant. But feminist social science must start by revealing some barriers to that deeper humanity, at least for women. We need to acknowledge frankly and then use the discomfort that might come up in response to the people we study—use it as an opportunity to clarify and advance the moral sensibilities that have been offended. Because feminism has a certain truth to tell about gender inequity, it offers a direct challenge to the moral vacuum of cultural and ethical relativism. In my own case, feminism has sharpened the focus of my humanistic research ethics. It has pushed me beyond caring as an abstract moral imperative to questions concerning what it is I care about. Analogously, if we choose to study a white-supremacist culture, we might begin with a readiness to see the underlying humanity of its bearers. But as soon as we encounter our own discomfort with the culture they bear, we can choose to respond to it. Racist culture is morally wrong; it is bad for its victims as well as its bearers, and thus caring in this instance means an active renunciation of the behavior we dislike, with an eye toward encouraging those who advocate it to rejoin the ranks of the likable.

Patriarchy and misogyny are likewise bad for their victims as well as their bearers; the feminist vision of gender justice makes this very plain. The men in the Bank Wiring Room not only objectify and diminish women but also reduce their own opportunities to like others and to be likable. Their culture leaves them ill-equipped to bond with women as equals, and it limits their bonding with each other to narrow displays of compulsive masculinity. How adequately could their style of coworker bonding be meeting their real needs if they have to rely on sharing their woes and concerns with the observer, whose *job* it is to put on a friendly face and never take sides in an argument?

I was attracted initially to feminist perspective because it resonated with something in my personal experience; it helped me understand the patriarchal patterns in my family of origin that brought me more distress than comfort, at least as seen through my own eyes. That appeal is still present, but I have added to it an appreciation of the more general ethical guidance that feminism has to offer. It not only teaches me about the nature of caring but also offers me a way to retrieve my caring when people become wrong-headed and forsake the advantages of gender justice. By seeing and then challenging the larger system that valorizes gender injustice, I can honor those victimized by that system and can reclaim my caring for those others who have too much power to perpetuate too many unfortunate choices.

My current work on Hawthorne reflects this more feminist-focused ethical stance. I now see the rich conversations in the little microsettings of the Relay and Bank Wiring Rooms to be female and male mirrors of the surrounding culture. Each group's coworker bonding becomes a matrix for the reproduction of their respective parts of the patriarchal legacy. The women do get closer than the men to unmasking that legacy, perhaps because underprivileged groups virtually always become more aware of the inequities than the groups who construct them. To be sure, the unmarried Hawthorne women obsess regularly about whatever men friends are currently in their lives, and they talk almost daily about getting married, even when they are not involved with particular men. But they also show some shrewdness about assessing their options. They are clearly aware that some married women make a life as homemakers, but they are doubtful that *they* can be those women. And so they often add some wry humor to the topic of getting married. Theresa jokes to the observer: "Hey, congratulate Wanda. She's going to get married tomorrow," and Wanda replies, "Yeah, I'm getting married in the morning and I'm coming back [to work] in the afternoon." In other words, marriage would do nothing to really improve her life, so the thought of doing it becomes a joke. Notice the rhetorical question left unspoken: What could I get out of married life with a man if I couldn't even stay home and be a homemaker? Because this question remains merely implicit, the women cannot move toward questioning the structure of the patriarchal legacy itself, which constrains women's choices to those that males have defined to be in their own interests. The best these women can do is question whether they, as private individuals, can wrest the presumed advantages from that structure. In the meantime the kind of intimacy they have almost daily with each other is probably far richer than what they could get from most of the men in their immediate social surround, if we take the men working nearby in the Bank Wiring Room to be typical of their "field of eligibles."

Elsewhere I am developing the perspective that along with their obsessing about men, these women developed a woman-centered alternative to male-defined existence, contradictory though this may sound. It makes sense to see them as somewhere on Rich's (1980) "lesbian continuum," which includes forms of female intimacy that are not necessarily sexual. I recently learned that two of the five original women in the Relay Assembly Room never married. Did this fact make it possible for them to elaborate a woman-centered existence on a lifelong basis? Fortunately I will have an opportunity to find out, as I have located one of these never-married women, still alive at age 84, plus one of the three who did marry, now 86. Both women have agreed to an interview, and I soon will travel to Chicago to see them. Needless to say, I am thrilled by this opportunity.

Final Thoughts

My journey is far from completed—not my intellectual one (the exploration of coworker relationships), not my feminist one, and certainly not my moral and personal journeys. I have much to learn on all of these fronts, and here I share some thoughts about the process.

My feminist sensibilities seem to be in a constant state of evolution. They started, perhaps, as an egocentric reaction to some autocratic tendencies in my father. Later, with the rekindling of the women's movement in the late 1960s and some intermittent challenges from my partner, I seemed to waver between a bit of awakening and a lot of defensiveness. In the 1970s and into the 1980s, I had an approach-avoidance reaction to feminism; I was drawn to its appeal to equity and justice but was afraid of compromising something—I did not know what. For a long time my feminism was something like an itch: It kept calling for my attention, and I felt great relief when I scratched it, but a part of me fancied greater comfort if it would only go away.

More recently, feminism has relocated well beneath my skin, somewhere closer to my blood. In this overall process, I see a strong connection between what I read, how and what I teach (especially my course on the sociology of gender), how I frame my identity strivings, how I approach whatever struggles I get into with my partner, and how I think about my research. For example, at one point Bly (1990) fueled my lingering desire to hold on to my masculine "difference," to rescue it from the ravages of feminism, as if it were a worthy use of energy to construct a distinctively new masculine character that somehow would be consonant with the new feminist woman. Reading Stoltenberg (1989) convinced me that Bly's project was misguided, perhaps unwittingly misogynist. Affirmative action for women, in the broadest sense, is a moral call rooted in urgencies of fairness and justice, and joining with it means forgetting about how to rebuild masculinity on firmer footing. It means pulling my identity-questing away from the hook of my gender difference altogether, just as I have no interest in hooking myself on my white skin color or on my heterosexuality. As my focus on the "man" in me withers away through benign neglect, I notice that the adult and the human and the moral person in me have more room to unfold and take a direction.

It may seem as if these musings have no bearing on the specifics of my coworker research, but they do. All research is a matter of selective perception. What we select and what we attend to rests on who we are and what we are becoming. Reading feminist texts (especially the ones that are at first hardest to let "in"), trying them out in our teaching, struggling over the issues with our partners and talking with our peers, working on our selves—all of this is potentially transformative, and it cannot help but change our view of females, whether we are men or women. When we then bring our evolving views of females into any research we do for women, that research surely will reflect our larger process, whether we know it or not. The challenge is to become more aware of these linkages and to become more active in directing them.

References

Benson, S. P. (1983). The customers ain't God: The work culture of department store sales-women, 1890-1940. In M. H. Frisch & D. J. Walkowitz (Eds.), *Essays on labor community and American society* (pp. 185-211). Urbana: University of Illinois Press.

Bly, R. (1990). *Iron John: A book about men.* Reading, MA: Addison-Wesley.

Chodorow, N. (1978). *The reproduction of mothering.* Berkeley: University of California Press.

Cooper, P. (1987). *Once a cigar maker: Men, women, and work culture in American cigar factories, 1900-1919.* Urbana: University of Illinois Press.

Davis, J. A. & Smith, T. W. (1988). General Social Surveys, 1972-1988. Machine-readable data file. National Opinion Research Center, Chicago, ed. Storrs, CT: The Roper Center for Public Opinion Research, University of Connecticut, distributor.

Faludi, S. (1991). *Backlash: The undeclared war against American women.* New York: Crown.

Fine, G. A. (1985). Friendship in the workplace. In V. J. Derlega & B. A. Winstead (Eds.), *Friendship and social interaction* (pp. 185-203). New York: Springer Verlag.

Fischer, C. (1982). *To dwell among friends.* Chicago: University of Chicago Press.

Gabarro, J. H. (1987). The development of working relationships. In J. Lorsch (Ed.), *Handbook of organizational behavior* (pp. 172-189). Englewood Cliffs, NJ: Prentice-Hall.

Gans, H. J. (1988). *Middle American individualism: The future of liberal democracy.* New York: Free Press.

Gilligan, C. (1982). *In a different voice.* Cambridge, MA: Harvard University Press.

Hareven, T. (1982). American families in transition: Historical perspectives on change. In A. Skolnick & J. Skolnick (Eds.), *Family in transition* (pp. 73-91). Boston: Little, Brown.

Homans, G. (1950). *The human group.* New York: Harcourt, Brace & World.

Lamphere, L. (1987). *From working daughters to working mothers: Immigrant women in a New England industrial community.* Ithaca, NY: Cornell University Press.

Lasch, C. (1977). *Haven in a heartless world: The family besieged.* New York: Basic Books.

Laslett, B. (1978). Family membership, past and present. *Social Problems, 25,* 476-490.

Marks, S. R. (1986). *Three corners: Exploring marriage and the self.* Lexington, MA: Lexington.

Marks, S. R. (1994). Intimacy in the public realm: The case of coworkers. *Social Forces, 72,* 843-858.

O'Leary, V. E. (1987). Women's relationships with women in the workplace. In B. Guteck, A. Stromberg, & L. Larwood (Eds.), *Women and Work* (Vol. 3, pp. 189-213). Newbury Park, CA: Sage, 189-213.

Peterson, A. (1985). The revolutionary potential of "private": A critique of the family as a revolutionary force. *Acta Sociologica, 28,* 337-348.

Rawlins, W. K. (1992). *Friendship matters.* Hawthorne, NY: Aldine.

Rich, A. (1980). Compulsory heterosexuality and lesbian existence. *Signs, 5,* 631-660.

Rogers, Carl R. (1957). The necessary and sufficient conditions of therapeutic personality change. *Journal of Consulting Psychology, 21,* 95-103.

Roethlisberger, F., & Dickson, W. J. (1939). *Management and the worker.* Cambridge, MA: Harvard University Press.

Roy, D. (1952). Quota restriction and goldbricking in a machine shop. *American Journal of Sociology, 57,* 427-442.

Ruddick, S. (1982). Maternal thinking. In B. Thorne & M. Yalom (Eds.), *Rethinking the family: Some feminist questions* (pp. 76-94). New York: Longman.

Siltanen, J., & Stanworth, M. (1984). The politics of private women and public man. *Theory and Society, 13,* 91-118.

Simpson, I. H. (1989). The sociology of work: Where have the workers gone? *Social Forces, 67,* 563-581.

Statham, A. (1987). The gender model revisited: Differences in the management styles of men and women. *Sex Roles, 16,* 408-409.

Stoltenberg, J. (1989). *Refusing to be a man: Essays on sex and justice.* New York: Penguin.

Tentler, L. W. (1979). *Wage-earning women: Industrial work and family life in the United States, 1900-1930.* New York: Oxford University Press.

Thorne, B. (1986). Girls and boys together . . . but mostly apart: Gender arrangements in elementary schools. In L. Richardson & V. Taylor (Eds.), *Feminist frontiers II: Rethinking sex, gender, and society* (pp. 73-84). New York: McGraw-Hill.

Westwood, S. (1985). *All day, every day: Factory and family in the making of women's lives.* Urbana: University of Illinois Press.

Whitehead, T. N. (1938). *The industrial worker.* Cambridge, MA: Harvard University Press.

Zavella, P. (1987). *Women's work and Chicano families: Cannery workers of the Santa Clara Valley.* Ithaca, NY: Cornell University Press.

8

The Family Division of Labor

All Work Is Not Created Equal

MAUREEN PERRY-JENKINS

Becoming a feminist researcher has been and continues to be a process, as opposed to a single event, that changed my way of thinking. I do recall, however, a moment early in my graduate career when it first became obvious to me that basic underlying assumptions held by a researcher color not only the questions that are asked but also the answers that are uncovered. I was reading a chapter on the division of labor in Robert Blood's (1962) classic book *Marriage.* In his discussion about the impact of wife's employment on marital satisfaction, I came upon the following quotation:

> Wives with light housekeeping responsibilities may be able to work part time without imposing on the husband at all for domestic assistance. Similarly school teaching is uniquely compatible with caring for school-aged children since mothers and children have similar "working" hours and identical vacations. Highly paid wives may be able to employ full-time housekeepers. Those whose talents are unusual may feel that the family's loss is society's gain. (p. 280)

It was clear to me that the guiding assumptions of Blood's work had not led him to ask how or in what ways women's employment affected families, but rather how women's employment was bad for families. As Bronfenbrenner and Crouter (1982) have demonstrated, the research questions that dominate a given historical period usually are based on the guiding values of that time. Thus, when women's employment was viewed negatively, it necessarily held negative implications for families.

Although in the 1990s we have a society more "tolerant" of women's employment than was true in the 1960s, much research continues to be focused on the ways in which women's employment imposes on husbands and children. What are the consequences of not having a full-time cook, cleaner, chauffeur, and caretaker in the home? How have families lost? As Harding (1987) suggests, however, it is in looking at the questions that are *not* asked that one begins to see the bias in defining what is worthy of being asked or what is worthy of scientific explanation. For example, far fewer studies address the issue of how *men's* work hours, work stress, or role overload affect their children's well-being. When researchers do attempt to address pressing questions from a woman's perspective, such as why men do not perform more housework or why women stay in inequitable situations (Ferree, 1990; Hochschild, 1989), it is usually popular reading for about half of the population. The more powerful group often has little interest in the problems or conditions of the less powerful (Goode, 1982; Komarovsky, 1988). If, in the beginning, researchers had been truly intent on understanding how employment affected families, we should have seen the same number of studies focused on the effects of men's employment on the household division of labor as we have seen on the familial effects of women's employment. The fact that we have not witnessed this trend suggests that the study of the division of labor is necessarily a study of gender, gender being the "social construction of maleness and femaleness as oppositional categories with unequal social value" (Ferree, 1990, p. 868). More simply, the unequal division of labor that persists in families headed by heterosexual couples is not a function of innate biological differences between men and women; it is a consequence of how we as a society have come to define what it means to be a "man" or a "woman." This process of socially constructing what it means to be male or female is what West and Zimmerman (1987) refer to as "doing gender." As Hartmann (1987) suggests, "from an economic perspective, the creation of gender can be thought of as the creation of the division of labor between the sexes, the creation of two categories of workers who need each other" (p. 113).

Outstanding books and articles have been written during the past few years that review and add new insight to the literature on the division of paid and unpaid work in families (Berk, 1985; Ferree, 1990; Hochschild, 1989; Spitze, 1988; Thompson & Walker, 1989). My aim in this chapter is not to summarize again what others have already done so well, but rather to examine how feminist principles have informed this literature and, more personally, to reflect on how feminist theory has influenced my own research on family work. First, I discuss how family theory guided my early work, as well as describe how a feminist perspective slowly infiltrated my thinking about the important questions to be asked and how to ask them. Second, I address the personal and political problems I struggled with in applying a feminist perspective to my research. I describe how feminist ideology took me off the traditional "straight and narrow" course to explore issues of gender, power, and entitlement within families and within society at large. I close by examining the specific ways my research has changed as a function of a feminist perspective. The organization of this chapter is based on my own development as I came to understand and assume a feminist perspective in my life and work. Throughout this chapter I discuss the ways in which feminist theory has influenced my research over the years and try, intermittently, to draw some bits of wisdom from the process. You will notice, however, that in many cases, as quickly as I draw conclusions, I just as swiftly question them and head in a new direction. Becoming a feminist researcher has been and continues to be a process for me, one that includes not only periods of continuous growth but also times of discontinuous leaps in thought and perspective.

What Does Social Structure
Have to Do With Who Does the Laundry?

My research career began with a very popular and quite unremarkable research question: Why do men perform less household work than their wives, even when their wives are employed full-time? At the time, this question was intriguing to me, not as a function of my newfound feminist insights, which hardly had emerged yet, but because I was amazed, angered, and indignant about the inequity in family labor. I am sure my feelings stemmed in no small way from my own experiences growing up in a family in which my mother and I cooked and cleaned for my father and four brothers. In fact, I remember distinctly when the unfairness of the division of labor in my parents' home became quite clear to me. I was visiting my family at Thanksgiving, my first trip home since I had begun graduate school. Over dinner I had a long discussion with my older brother about sexism and inequality and was excited to discover that we shared many of the same values and beliefs. As dinner ended, the men, my "enlightened" brother included, headed outside to walk off their dinner while the women began the onerous task of cleaning up. Annoyed by my brother's departure, I accused him of being a hypocrite and pointed out that his behavior was in complete opposition to the views he had just espoused. His response was, "I know, but I really want to take a walk." Feeling betrayed and furious, I returned to graduate school with a revised agenda. I was determined to learn about power, entitlement, and gender as they relate to the division of labor in families.

In my subsequent pursuit of "the truth," I discovered that one of the most consistent and stable findings in the division of labor literature is that married women spend substantial amounts of their time doing household labor. Berk (1985) estimates that, on average, wives contribute about 70% of the total time that all family members spend on household tasks. Of course, estimates vary on the basis of factors such as wives' employment status, age and number of children in the household, women's and men's educational level, and the ways in which household labor is operationalized.

The vast amount of attention focused on men's participation in family work suggests that this phenomenon has remained fairly stable over the years. Despite the research that documents recent increases in men's family work (Pleck, 1983; Ross, Mirowsky, & Huber, 1983), the total increases remain relatively small and the undebatable fact remains: Wives do the majority of family work. The pressing question is Why?

One of the earliest theories proposed to explain the inequity in family work was resource theory (Blood & Wolfe, 1960). In their findings, Blood and Wolfe reported that in couples in which the wives worked outside the home, husbands did more in the home. These researchers offered the following explanation for their results: "Since most household tasks are humdrum and menial in nature, the chief resource required is time. Usually the person with the most time is the wife—providing she is not working outside of the home" (Blood & Wolfe, 1960, p. 73). In sum, Blood and Wolfe concluded that the division of labor between home and the workforce is ultimately the result of husbands' and wives' respective resources. The logical extension of this theory would suggest that as women lose the resource of time when they take on paid employment, the division of labor should begin to equal out. Subsequent research, however, points to a number of discrepant and often opposing sets of findings related to this issue (Berk & Berk, 1979; Ferber, 1982; Walker & Woods, 1976).

From a feminist viewpoint, Ferree's (1987) research has extended and helped clarify the research base on resource theory by looking beyond the behaviors women and men perform to assess how both spouses view the wife's employment. Is the wife's employment seen as a necessity, or is it viewed as a privilege? Ferree found that when a woman's employment is seen as vital for the family, a valued resource, men are likely to perform more household chores. Thus the valued resource is not only time, as Blood and Wolfe speculated, but also the value both husband and wife place on the wife's resources, such as income and occupational status.

In more recent work, Ferree (1990) has proposed that to fully understand behavior and task negotiation at the microlevel of the family, one must not overlook the influence of the larger contexts within which families function. In particular, social power and domination within the institutions of society must be addressed. One may ask, as I did, What does patriarchy and female oppression have to do with the division of labor in families? As Hartmann (1987) would argue, "the organization of production both within and outside the family is shaped by patriarchy and capitalism" (p. 111).

A male-dominated labor market has managed to exclude women from many arenas of skilled employment, as well as to lower the prestige of "feminized" occupations such as nursing and teaching (Reskin, 1988). "Patriarchy's material base is men's control of women's labor, both in the household and in the labor market; the division of labor by gender tends to benefit men" (Hartmann, 1987, p. 114). Hartmann's assessment of how larger institutions influence labor decisions within the family is supported, in part, by research documenting that as women make more money and perform more prestigious jobs, they are more likely to assume provider role duties. In turn, as women take on greater provider role responsibilities, they are also more likely to demand greater equality in terms of household work (Ferree, 1988).

Gender Theory, Sex Role Theory, and Personal Theories

In the early 1980s as I began graduate school, I had yet to be enlightened by the work of Ferree, Hartmann, and other feminist scholars. In my review of family literature at that time, I found that the most popular approach to addressing the issue of inequity in household work was sex role theory. Despite the fact that many feminist scholars (e.g., Connell,

1985; Lopata & Thorne, 1978) were questioning the utility of the "sex role concept," the family literature was ripe with articles addressing sex role attitudes, sex role behavior, women's employment, and the division of labor. I was virtually unaware of the feminist scholarship that had begun to refute the sex role approach. Herein lies one of the biggest factors, early in my career, that hindered my efforts to merge a feminist perspective with my research on the division of labor. Specifically my substantive research interests were written about in family, sociological, and psychological journals, while the majority of feminist literature was not. Komarovsky (1988) suggests that much feminist scholarship has been "ghettoized"—written by women, presented to women, and published in women's journals, a phenomenon that has allowed many social scientists to overlook or ignore its message.

It was not until I read Thorne and Yalom's (1982) book *Rethinking the Family: Some Feminist Questions* in the early 1980s that the utility of a feminist perspective became clear. I was intrigued by the idea of not simply documenting what women are doing, but understanding women's experiences of their lives. Simply knowing that a woman is employed tells us little about what that experience means for her. From a symbolic interactionist perspective, I had come to believe that what truly matters in understanding individuals' behaviors was their interpretation of events in their lives. From the feminist literature I was learning that women's experiences either had been assumed to be the same as men's or had not been considered at all.

An article by Jane Hood (1986) that examined the meaning of the "provider role" for both men and women had a profound influence on my thinking about the division of labor in families. Hood questioned the faulty assumption guiding much of the research on women's employment and the division of labor that concluded that as women entered the labor force and *accepted provider role responsibilities,* men should take on greater family responsibilities. Hood suggested that simply enacting role behaviors, such as women taking on paid employment or men doing household work, did not mean either women or men were accepting the psychological responsibility for the role of provider or homemaker. She proposed that it was critical to assess not only what behaviors wives and husbands were performing both in the workplace and at home but also the meaning they gave to those behaviors.

In defining family roles, Hood emphasized that both wives and husbands work together to negotiate mutual role expectations. Roles are not constructed in isolation, but rather in conjunction with other family members. This idea, which after the fact appeared so obvious, struck me as critically important to understanding the division of labor. I recognized that women's behaviors and roles within the family were a function of not only what they deemed important or worthwhile but also what their husbands deemed worthy as well. If a husband sees housework as a woman's work, it usually becomes her job. It is whatever he *does not* do that the wife must do in terms of family work. In other words, the husband most often has the power to decide to what extent he will become involved in household work, leaving his wife to pick up the slack. On the basis of this rationale, I thought the time had come to understand what factors might explain why men become more or less involved in household work. Specifically I wanted to know how men justified or rationalized their lack of involvement in family work when their wives held down full-time jobs. Once I decided that this was the tack I wanted to take, I became increasingly concerned about my feminist stance. Was I not perpetuating the problem by yet again making men the sole focus of my research? I convinced myself that because the ultimate goal of the study was to understand the roots of inequity in families, my approach was justified. It was not until much later that the wise words of feminist scholars reassured me that research *for* women did not necessarily have to be *about* women.

As I set out to conduct this study about "men's provider-role attitudes," I was forced to address the issue of methodology. I was aware of my efforts to stick to the unwritten rules I had learned about "good" research. Qualitative data were rich, interesting, and informative; however, quantitative research was more valued. I made the safe decision. I conducted a quantitative study with a few good open-ended questions added for spice. The rich and sometimes angry, terse responses that men gave regarding men's and women's roles and responsibilities were used ultimately to fit men into one of three provider-role categories; that was the last I heard from them. It is surprising that in the midst of all the new revelations I was having about feminist research, I remained fully entrenched in traditional methods of studying families. Despite feeling excited and even drawn toward feminist ideology and methods, they remained distinct from my day-to-day style of conducting research. The explanation, very simply, was that I was afraid. Defining my research as feminist meant much more than questioning my methods or adding a "feminist theory" section to a paper's introduction; it meant defining myself as a feminist. It meant addressing patriarchy in my own family, in my relationship with my husband, and in the academic system I was a part of. I was not yet ready for that challenge.

In retrospect, some of the decisions made in designing my study rang true to some gut-level feminist beliefs I held dear. For instance, I reasoned that the only way to understand how men win out in the division of labor battle is to talk to the powerful ones, to the men. Only with knowledge about men's rationale regarding the division of labor could we fight the battle well armed. As the battle metaphor suggests, I was feeling very militant.

In truth, however, little feminist theory or research directly influenced how I conducted my early work. In fact, from a feminist perspective the most controversial decision I was faced with was how to measure household work. I chose to examine tasks that needed to be performed on a fairly regular basis, such as cooking, cleaning, laundry, doing dishes, and making beds. I made a deliberate decision to exclude more "masculine" tasks, such as yard work and car maintenance, for two reasons. First, I would argue (as others have) that activities such as yard work and car maintenance are rarely daily activities and, once completed, the rewards are obvious and relatively long lasting (Berheide, 1984; Berk, 1985). In contrast, completing the laundry or the dishes may offer momentary satisfaction; however, all too soon clothes are dirty again and it is time to start another meal. Second, I was interested in the extent to which men responded to women's increased labor force participation by taking on more of women's tasks; therefore it made sense to examine those tasks primarily performed by women.

This rationale may seem far from earth shattering and anything but controversial. In fact, some committee members believed I was discriminating against men by not including their contribution to family work. In the end I collected data on feminine and masculine chores, analyzed the data for both, and published data on those chores that were performed routinely—the "feminine chores." The "masculine chores" were performed so infrequently that the data could not be analyzed. In the end the numbers proved my point.

At this juncture another important methodological issue should be addressed that relates to the absolute amount of household tasks performed versus the relative proportion of tasks completed. The problem with proportional estimates, as Pleck (1977) has documented, is that husbands' proportion of household labor increases primarily because wives' absolute level of household work decreases. The question of whether husbands actually are performing *more* household tasks as their wives take on outside employment must be addressed by assessing how much actual work is being performed by both spouses. Unfortunately the variability in methods that researchers have used to assess the division of labor makes it difficult to compare across studies and historical time periods to get a true reading of how the division of labor has changed.

Addressing another methodological concern, Huston and Robins (1982) convincingly argue that global assessments of household work that require respondents to do a number of mental calculations about specific activities over time poses serious threats to both reliability and validity. "Event level" data, such as daily diary reports of activities, that require retrospective reports of household tasks completed in the past 24 hours offer advantages over global recall methods. Recalling recent events reduces memory distortions, errors in mental calculations, task substitution, and lumping together of conceptually distinct constructs (Huston & Robins, 1982). Thus I concluded that to fully address my research questions, daily activity data on the type and frequency of household chores performed were necessary.

Unfortunately this was as far as my thinking went on the issue of how to operationalize household work. I worked under a number of assumptions: (a) that household work meant the same thing to men and women, (b) that the consequences of completing household tasks were the same for both, and (c) that household work was an onerous activity offering little reward to women or men. As I discuss in greater detail throughout this chapter, I have since questioned all of these assumptions.

Women's and Men's Provider-Role Attitudes and the Division of Labor in Families

In the study referred to above, we examined linkages between men's provider-role attitudes, their involvement in household work, and marital satisfaction (Perry-Jenkins & Crouter, 1990). Both quantitative and qualitative methods were used in this study of 43 men in dual-earner families. Open-ended questions were used to elicit men's assessments of their provider role both personally and in society at large. As mentioned earlier these data were useful to me only in categorizing men into groups on the basis of provider attitudes. At one level this approach yielded some important results; however, what was lost were the feelings and thoughts these men shared about their marriages and their work.

In addition to the "provider data," standardized questionnaires assessed marital satisfaction. Household task involvement was measured through a telephone interview procedure that was repeated over 4 days.

During each telephone interview, respondents reported on all of the household activities they had performed in the previous 24-hour period.

Findings indicated that men who thought being the economic provider was their most important role did significantly fewer household tasks than men who shared provider responsibilities with their wives. It is important to note that all of the men who participated in this study had wives who were employed full-time outside of the home, pointing to the fact that what appeared to be the same situation "objectively" varied greatly, depending on husbands' interpretations of their role behaviors.

It also was found that the congruence between husbands' provider-role attitudes and their level of involvement in household tasks was related to their reports of marital satisfaction. For example, husbands who viewed providing as their primary role reported higher marital satisfaction if they performed few household tasks. In contrast, husbands who thought they shared providing responsibilities with their wives were more likely to report high marital satisfaction if they performed high levels of household tasks. These findings point to the importance of looking beyond "role behaviors" to understand the meaning that individuals give to those behaviors, for it was men's definitions of their situations that held implications for their family relationships and activities.

In a second study, we examined the implications of women's provider-role attitudes for family life (Perry-Jenkins, Seery, & Crouter, 1992). The central finding of this research was that the symbolic meanings that women attached to their paid work were related to differences in their well-being, marital and mother-child relationships, and division of labor. In terms of psychological well-being, wives who viewed their income as secondary or were ambivalent about their paid work reported more role overload and depression than wives who held more egalitarian views of family roles. These results may be explained, in part, by the fact that husbands of wives who devalued their provider role performed approximately the same number of household tasks as husbands of full-time homemakers (about 20% of all tasks). In terms of wives' household chores, few differences were found in the amount of time employed women spent on housework, regardless of their provider attitudes. I interpreted these findings to mean that, on average, women were spending the maximum amount of time they had available on chores; it was only men who had discretion about their degree of involvement.

The most surprising results emerged when we examined levels of marital satisfaction. Wives who perceived themselves as secondary providers, who reported high levels of depression and overload, and who had husbands who performed the fewest household tasks reported the *highest* levels of marital satisfaction. In contrast, wives who were ambivalent about their provider-role status but who simultaneously acknowledged the importance of their employment reported the lowest levels of marital satisfaction. Thus although women in both groups were experiencing stress from managing work and family tasks, the fallout from this over-load was experienced in the marriages of women ambivalent about their paid work but not for women holding more traditional views. It appears that the more traditional wives, although experiencing role overload and depression, were unlikely to blame their husbands for their struggles be-cause they viewed the home as their exclusive realm. One could speculate that wives holding more traditional notions about gender roles define eq-uity in their marriage quite differently from wives holding more liberal views. As Yogev and Brett (1985) illustrate, husbands' and wives' beliefs about the equity in housework are related to marital satisfaction; how-ever, beliefs about what is equitable often are unrelated to what objec-tively would be considered equal.

In the process of writing up this research and submitting it for publica-tion, an anonymous reviewer questioned our unreserved use of the term *role,* especially because the "provider role" is intimately connected with the "sex role concept." It was then that I first became aware of the inade-quacy of the idea of a sex or gender role. I came to realize that a "gender role" is not one in a series of roles that an individual undertakes in a lifetime. Gender, as West and Zimmerman (1987) suggest, is a "master identity" that, in turn, influences how roles such as husband, wife, worker, and caretaker are constructed. Perhaps even more critical is the idea that gender is not a given; it is not a fixed, static phenomenon that all in-dividuals of one biological sex experience in the same way. Gender is constructed and reconstructed continually through daily interaction. In linking these ideas back to the provider-role concept, it suggests that one's beliefs and attitudes about being a provider are developed within the larger context of how one constructs notions of gender.

The gender perspective would lead one to ask the important question of how women and men come to construct gendered meanings for what could conceivably be construed as nongendered activities—namely, working for pay outside of the home and performing household tasks. Gender theory rejects the notion that it is only through socialization in families that individuals come to learn about gender-specific behaviors (Ferree, 1990). A gender perspective pushes researchers to look beyond interactions within families, to recognize the impact of political and economic institutions that influence families. Race, class, and gender all represent "hierarchical structures of opportunity and oppression" (Ferree, 1990, p. 820), which separately and in interaction with each other affect the family.

Another strength of a gender perspective is the focus on the construction of gender as a dynamic process. If we were to accept the sex role socialization perspective, it suggests that attitudes and behaviors socialized at an early age become stable and enduring personal characteristics. Yet looking back at my personal experiences being raised in a traditional, male-dominated household, one hardly would predict from a socialization perspective that as an adult I would embrace feminism. The more interesting question is how I, and others like me, came to reconstruct the meaning of gender in our lives.

A good example of how a sex role socialization approach may lead us to accept faulty assumptions about the enduring quality of sex role attitudes and behaviors is presented in a study my colleagues and I conducted (McHale, Bartko, Crouter, & Perry-Jenkins, 1990). To summarize, the aim of our investigation was to examine how parents' "gender role attitudes" mediated the relationship between children's involvement in household chores and their psychological adjustment. It was found that when boys' involvement in household work matched their fathers' level of involvement and was in sync with their fathers' "gender role attitudes," they reported better adjustment. An unspoken assumption in this socialization scenario is that early "sex-typed" attitudes and behaviors of these boys will be indicators of their attitudes and behaviors as adults. Gender theorists would argue that, once "socialized," one's behaviors are not internalized and frozen behavioral prescriptions for life. To date, I am unaware of longitudinal research that supports the notion that children's socialized views of appropriate gender attitudes and behavior will influence their beliefs and behaviors in adulthood. Thus the importance of early socialization processes for attitudes and behaviors later in life remains an empirical question.

Who Decides Who Does the Laundry: The Issue of Power

Heidi Hartmann (1987) challenged family scholars to question pervading views of "the family" as "a unified interest group" and to recognize that the family is also a "locus of struggle." For the division of labor, the goal in families may not be to equalize household responsibilities, but rather to assert dominance and control over who does what. It is my contention that the division of labor is of interest to researchers not because we are intrigued with who washes the dishes or mows the lawn per se, but because the division of labor serves as a proxy for that evasive phenomenon called family power.

Research on the division of labor in families necessarily includes the issue of power, whether or not it is explicitly addressed. Unfortunately the research that has attempted to examine the causes and consequences of family power has come up almost empty-handed, as can be attested to by a number of decade reviews (McDonald, 1980; Safilios-Rothschild, 1970). Despite the ethereal nature of the concept of power, its importance in family research must not be minimized. In Thompson and Walker's (1989) list of recommendations for future research on paid and unpaid work, they state, "Research should attend to . . . family work as a source and occasion for power" (p. 864).

In the past, one of the greatest shortcomings of family power research has been the focus on structural and static aspects of power (e.g., money, education, job prestige, "winning and losing") despite the fact that most researchers acknowledge the importance of negotiation and interaction in the "power process." Recent research by Komter (1989) explored "hidden power" in marriage by examining power processes and mechanisms within marital relationships. Komter's analysis highlights the power strategies used by women to achieve equality and by men to maintain the status quo, and it demonstrates why men have thus far been more successful in the hidden battles of marriage. Men can rest on the ideological justifications, in place for generations, that "prove" gender differences exist; women must struggle against old ideology and create new meanings and justification for change. As Komter states,

> Any conscious or unconscious effort to undermine this cornerstone tends to be experienced as deeply threatening because it is so fundamentally tied to the psychosexual and social identities of men and women. And since marriages are created from gendered identities, activities and statuses, one might ask if the partners can ever be equal. (Komter, 1989, p. 214)

Komter suggests that we have far to go in uncovering the "sociocultural and psychic roots of gender inequality."

With the focus in gender theory on "the construction of gender," it is critical that we understand power as it relates to the gender-construction process. Bound into the idea of "doing gender" is the concept of power, for it is perceived degrees of power between women and men in relation-ships, as well as societal dictums regarding what is "powerful," that direct spouses in their negotiations of the division of labor. A focus on the divi-sion of labor offers a fruitful arena for observing how gender and power relations are constructed and maintained.

At this point I want to recognize what may be a faulty assumption that underlies the previous discussion on power. It appears that in many stud-ies about the division of labor, the research questions addressed and the ensuing discussions are based on the assumption that the goal in families is to equalize the division of labor. Once equality is achieved, we will witness more positive outcomes, especially for women. Work by Devault (1991) and Hochschild (1989) suggests, however, that absolute equality may not be a goal for all employed women. In fact, some might argue that if women relinquish many of their household task responsibilities, they will, in part, be giving up an important method of exhibiting love and concern for their family. This surrender would be the case especially in situations in which women do not view providing economically as an expression of love for their family. We are forced, therefore, to examine what notions of equity, equality, and fairness actually mean to women and men in their daily lives.

In her essay on family work, Thompson (1991) points out that although many researchers have documented that the majority of women perform more family tasks than men, only a minority of women view the division of labor in their families as unfair (Benin & Agnostinelli, 1988; Berk, 1985). Thompson proposes that to understand this apparent contradic-tion, we must understand women's sense of fairness about family work. Researchers need to consider (a) valued outcomes, (b) between- versus within-group comparisons, and (c) justification. First, in terms of valued outcomes, Thompson suggests it is the interpersonal outcomes of family work that are valued by women. Specifically the idea that performing household tasks serves as a way of expressing care for family members may be one impetus for women to assume the majority of tasks.

For reference group comparisons, the point is made that women are more likely to compare themselves with other women, and not men. In many cases the woman they use as a referent is "superwoman"—the woman who does it all with little help from her husband. A woman tends to compare her husband's household task involvement with that of other men and often feels "lucky" to get the help she receives. "Women would have a stronger sense of injustice about family work if they made between gender rather than within gender comparisons" (Thompson, 1991, p. 193).

Finally the issue of justification refers to how women and men come to accept the inequity in family work and justify it as fair. Women and men accept men's excuses for lack of involvement more than women's. It is acceptable, and almost amusing, for men to be clumsy, inefficient, slow, or even lazy when it comes to household work; yet none of these excuses are valid for women.

Thompson's work suggests that by understanding why women accept inequity in family work, we then can examine what factors lead women to change meanings and justifications and to push for change. Women and men, in conjunction, shape the meaning of fairness, and only in interaction can they change that meaning.

Thus far I have discussed the ways in which a feminist perspective has (and in many cases has not) influenced my research and the research on the division of labor in general. In the following section, I reflect on the personal and political issues I was forced to address and continue to wrestle with on a daily basis when assuming a feminist perspective.

The Feminist Struggle:
Both Inside and Out

Examining the struggles I face in attempting to incorporate a feminist perspective into my research, I can categorize them into struggles within myself and struggles with my outside world. In many cases the struggles cross boundaries between the personal and the public. As I wrote this section of the chapter, I found myself trying to add depth or value to some of my issues and concerns that may appear to be rather superficial and unenlightened. I take the risk to discuss them because I believe many women have struggled privately with these same issues (and continue to keep them secret) simply because they are rather embarrassing to admit to publicly.

Perhaps the first question I faced personally as I moved toward a feminist way of thinking about my research and my life was, Do I want to be pegged a feminist? I was becoming a feminist when, to many in our society, feminism had become a dirty word, synonymous with trouble-maker, man-hater, and, as I once was called, "a '60s woman in the '90s." Becoming a feminist meant coming to terms with growing up in a household with four brothers and traditional parents, a home in which I played the traditional, Parsonian, "female role" of caretaker, housekeeper, kin keeper, and counselor, a role I often still play. I wondered whether becoming a feminist meant giving up all of those roles, even the ones I liked. How far did I have to go in rejecting the family and society I was raised in to become a feminist?

In terms of my outside world, the concerns I faced in taking on a feminist perspective were reflected in the criticisms others have hailed against feminism. Are feminist questions valid? Why should we study women's experiences separately from men's? Aren't we all individuals? Isn't there such a thing as a "human experience"? Pragmatically the more qualitative, feminist approach to research (that was only my first introduction to one type of feminist research) ran counter to all of my training in quantitative research methods in which reliability and validity were based on large samples, multivariate analyses, and replicable findings.

The answers to many of these questions are still in the making, as I expect they will be for years to come. Becoming a feminist does not mean I can no longer be a caretaker, kin keeper, or nurturer, nor does it relieve me from performing household chores. Being a feminist does give me the freedom and the tools to examine what those behaviors actually mean to me and to question the reasons that I do them. At the same time, being a feminist challenges me to try out new roles and behaviors; it pushes me to feel as comfortable being assertive and powerful as being nurturant and loving. I constantly struggle to make my values and beliefs stronger determinants of how I parent my sons and relate to my husband than the expectations of my parents, friends, brothers, and society. It is a noble goal, but a difficult one to live out. In my irrational efforts to be the best at everything, the perfect wife, mother, and academic, I forget that the men who defined the standards for these roles in our society never had to meet them.

Professionally speaking, being a feminist in academia makes me feel vulnerable. Despite feeling supported and respected by senior faculty, both women and men, I cannot help but wonder how my "feminist activities," such as working on a university family leave policy, participating in campus workshops on women's issues, and supporting women's rights over their bodies, are interpreted by the powers that be.

I worry about losing "objectivity" in my research, even while realizing that no research is value free. I often feel caught in the middle. On the one hand, I worry that I do not measure up to the standard dictated by my profession; on the other hand, I wonder whether I am doing justice to feminist ideology. On another level, I know feminism has pushed me to look beyond the straight and narrow to ask important questions about the status quo. The life stories I have heard from women and men in the course of my research have taught me that women and men do have different experiences of work and family. The so-called "human experience" has been overshadowed largely by the construction of gender in our world.

Despite these doubts and concerns, the question of whether to accept a feminist perspective is, for me, a moot point. Once Pandora's box was opened, I found it could not be closed. As confused and overwhelmed as I was with this new and radical paradigm, I was both excited and relieved. I was excited because it offered a new way to think about and study "the family," and relieved because I finally had found alternative explanations for understanding equity, fairness, and power in relationships. I will continue to plow forward, doing what feels right in my work and life, learning from feminism and recognizing that along the way I will most likely change course many times.

A Feminist Approach
to Tomorrow's Dirty Laundry

The lessons of feminist theory are numerous, and they serve as constant reminders to keep our blinders off and to continually question the "truth." The most important influence the feminist paradigm has had on my work is to make me wary of categories, for it is through constructed dichotomies (whether categories of gender, race, class, etc.) that we lose the richness and "truth" of human experiences. In Harding's (1987) words, "Once we realized that there is no universal man but only culturally different men and women, then 'man's' eternal companion—'woman'—also disappeared. That is, 'women' come only in different classes, races and cultures: there is no 'woman' and no 'woman's experience' " (p. 7).

My current research efforts represent an attempt to move beyond what Ferree (1987) has referred to as "the dual-career model," a model that has focused the dual-earner literature on primarily white, middle-class families. It is critical to question how individuals' beliefs and values regarding paid and unpaid work may differ as a function of gender, social class, and family type. In interviews we currently are conducting with women, children, and men in working-class families, our aim is to understand the meanings, values, and justifications that family members offer for the distribution of paid and unpaid work.

I am interested especially in understanding children's work roles as they are negotiated in families. Children are usually the least powerful members in families, and we know little about how they experience their own work within the home or their parents' work. We have interviewed 115, 8- to 12-year-old children and have talked with them about their experiences in their families. We initially asked them simply to tell us what their family was like and then asked more specific, open-ended questions regarding their feelings and attitudes about their parents' work both in the home and on the job. We asked these same questions of women (and men in the two-parent families). The strength of these data is that we can examine experiences of family life from three perspectives. In addition, because we included two-parent and single-parent families in our sample, we also have the unique opportunity to examine how women, children, and men in two different family contexts experience work and family life. As a feminist researcher, one of my goals is to question traditional conceptualizations of the family and to avoid comparing all types of families to the white, two-parent, middle-class model so often held up as the ideal. Thus a major thrust of my work is not to compare among family types, but rather to look within different types of families to understand what factors and processes lead to the most positive outcomes for all family members.

A second goal of this research has been to examine policies in the workplace that aid women and men in juggling the demands of a job and a family. I strongly believe that my efforts must go beyond studying changes in families and workplaces to include being an active agent in facilitating change. One way I have found to do that is to examine what policies on the job are most useful for women. I have been struck by the number of women in my sample who are unaware of family-friendly policies currently "on the books" of their company. Even in cases where they were aware of the policy, however, misunderstandings and fear limited its usefulness. For example, a number of women I spoke with were afraid of using the voucher system for child care because it had never been fully explained to them. All they knew was that money would be taken out of their paycheck and that if they overestimated the costs, they would lose the money. To address this problem, I currently am working to develop informational seminars about company policies with two of the companies that helped me recruit participants.

In closing, I do not want to leave the reader with the false notion that I have come to a total understanding of feminist principles. As suggested at the outset, my growth as a woman, as a researcher, and as a feminist is an ongoing process. As that process emerges, my ideas, thoughts, and research will reflect the changes. In my view no dichotomy exists that defines one as feminist or not; establishing such categories only furthers patterns of past theoretical approaches that emphasize categories and stratification. There are different ways to be a feminist, just as there are different ways to be workers, mothers, and daughters; all are constructed roles based on our notions of gender. In the worst scenario, a feminist perspective could be used as yet another way to understand reality by only asking one type of question, using one vantage point, and ultimately falling into the same trap that mainstream sociology, psychology, and family studies have so often in the past. At its very best, a feminist perspective continually will push us to question our paradigms, our meanings, our values, and our methods.

References

Benin, M., & Agostinelli, J. (1988). Husbands' and wives' satisfaction with the division of labor. *Journal of Marriage and the Family, 50,* 349-361.

Berheide, C. W. (1984). Women's work in the home: Seems like old times. In B. Hess & M. Sussman (Eds.), *Women and the family: Two decades of change* (pp. 37-55). New York: Hayworth.

Berk, R. A., & Berk, S. F. (1979). *Labor and leisure at home: Content and organization of the household day.* Beverly Hills, CA: Sage.

Berk, S. F. (1985). *The gender factory: The apportionment of work in American households.* New York: Plenum.

Blood, R. O., Jr. (1962). *Marriage.* New York: Free Press.

Blood, R. O., Jr., & Wolfe, K. M. (1960). *Husbands and wives: The dynamics of married living.* New York: Free Press.

Bronfenbrenner, U., & Crouter, A. C. (1982). Work and family through time and space. In S. Kamerman & C. Hayes (Eds.), *Families that work: Children in a changing world* (pp. 39-83). Washington, DC: National Academy of Sciences.

Connell, R. W. (1985). Theorizing gender. *Sociology, 19,* 260-272.

Devault, M. L. (1991). *Feeding the family: The social organization of caring as gendered work.* Chicago: University of Chicago Press.

Ferber, M. A. (1982). Women and work: Issues of the 1980s. *Signs, 8,* 273-295.

Ferree, M. M. (1987). Family and job for working class women: Gender and class systems seen from below. In N. Gerstel & H. Gross (Eds.), *Families and work* (pp. 289-301). Philadelphia: Temple University Press.

Ferree, M. M. (1988). *Negotiating household roles and responsibilities: Resistance, conflict, and change.* Paper presented at the Annual Meeting of the National Council on Family Relations, Philadelphia.

Ferree, M. M. (1990). Beyond separate spheres: Feminism and family research. *Journal of Marriage and the Family, 52*(4), 806-884.

Goode, W. J. (1982). Why men resist. In B. Thorne with M. Yalom (Eds.), *Rethinking the family: Some feminist questions* (pp. 131-150). New York: Longman.

Harding, S. (1987). Introduction: Is there a feminist methodology? In S. Harding (Ed.), *Feminism and methodology* (pp. 1-14). Bloomington: Indiana University Press.

Hartmann, H. (1987). The family as the locus of gender, class, and political struggle: The example of housework. In S. Harding (Ed.), *Feminism and methodology* (pp. 109-134). Bloomington: Indiana University Press.

Hochschild, A., with Machung, A. (1989). *The second shift.* New York: Viking.

Hood, J. C. (1986). The provider role: Its meaning and measurement. *Journal of Marriage and the Family, 48,* 349-359.

Huston, T. L., & Robins, E. (1982). Conceptual and methodological issues in studying close relationships. *Journal of Marriage and the Family, 44,* 1-25.

Komarovsky, M. (1988). The new feminist scholarship: Some precursors and polemics. *Journal of Marriage and the Family, 50*(3), 585-593.

Komter, A. (1989). Hidden power in marriage. *Gender and Society, 3*(2), 187-216.

Lopata, H., & Thorne, B. (1978). On the term "sex roles." *Signs, 3,* 718-721.

McDonald, G. W. (1980). Family power: The assessment of a decade of theory and research, 1970-1979. *Journal of Marriage and the Family, 42,* 841-854.

McHale, S. M., Bartko, W. T., Crouter, A. C., & Perry-Jenkins, M. (1990). Children's housework and psychosocial functioning: The mediating effects of parents' sex-role behaviors and attitudes. *Child Development, 61*(5), 1413-1462.

Perry-Jenkins, M., & Crouter, A. C. (1990). Men's provider-role attitudes: Implications for household work and marital satisfaction. *Journal of Family Issues, 11*(2), 136-156.

Perry-Jenkins, M., Seery, B. L., & Crouter, A. C. (1992). Linkages between women's provider-role attitudes, women's well-being, and family relationships. *Psychology of Women Quarterly, 16,* 311-329.

Pleck, J. (1977). The work-family role system. *Social Problems, 24,* 417-427.

Pleck, J. (1983). Husbands' paid work and family roles: Current research issues. In H. Lopata & J. Pleck (Eds.), *Research in the interweave of social roles: Vol. 3. Families and jobs* (pp. 251-333). Greenwich, CT: JAI.

Reskin, B. (1988). Bringing the men back in: Sex differentiation and the devaluation of women's work. *Gender and Society, 2,* 58-81.

Ross, C., Mirowsky, J., & Huber, J. (1983). Dividing work, sharing work, and in-between. *American Sociological Review, 48,* 809-823.

Safilios-Rothschild, C. (1970). The study of family power structure: A review, 1960-1969. *Journal of Marriage and the Family, 30,* 290-301.

Spitze, G. (1988). Women's employment and family relations: A review. *Journal of Marriage and the Family, 50,* 595-618.

Thompson, L. (1991). Family work: Women's sense of fairness. *Journal of Family Issues, 12*(2), 181-196.

Thompson, L., & Walker, A. (1989). Gender in families: Women and men in marriage, work, and parenthood. *Journal of Marriage and the Family, 51,* 845-871.

Thorne, B., & Yalom, M. (1982). *Rethinking the family: Some feminist questions.* New York: Longman.

Walker, K., & Woods, M. (1976). *Time use: A measure of household production of goods and services.* Washington, DC: American Home Economics Association.

West, C., & Zimmerman, D. (1987). Doing gender. *Gender and Society, 1,* 125-151.

Yogev, S., & Brett, J. (1985). Perceptions of the division of housework and child care in marital satisfaction. *Journal of Marriage and the Family, 47,* 609-618.

9

Reclaiming Public Voice
and the Study of Black Women's Work

SHARON HARLEY

Writing this chapter prompts me to recall recent references to Rosalyn Terborg-Penn and me as "pioneer historians" in the field of Black women's history and to contemplate how my professional development as a historian and a feminist scholar, to a considerable extent, parallels that of African American women's history. My journey as a student of African American women's history began when I was a graduate student first at Antioch College and later in the Department of History at Howard University. My research reclaiming for historical memory the lives of African American women became a site of resistance, a place for me to confront and condemn, intellectually and politically, the racial and gender oppression of women of color.[1]

Multiple Sites of Resistance:
On Becoming a Graduate Student

The academic training I received at the Washington campus of Antioch College, coupled with the political activism of most of the students and faculty, provided me with a critical intellectual and personal understanding of the history of racial oppression in a capitalist society. I came to believe that bringing a Marxist analysis to my research and writing histories that focused on the liberation struggles and resistance of oppressed people would preserve the "revolutionary" fervor important to me at the time.

Enrolling in a doctoral program in the Department of History at Howard University in the early 1970s, I joined a cadre of fellow students, including former Student Non-Violent Coordinating Committee (SNCC) activists Bernice Johnson Reagon, James Early, and Janette Hoston Harris and Northern student activists Rosalyn Terborg-Penn, Evelyn Brooks Higginbotham, and Gerald Gill, with whom I shared a political and scholarly interest in the history of people of African descent. Having come of age at the height of the civil rights and Black power struggles of the late 1960s and 1970s, we were aware, often painfully so, of how the intersection of race, gender, and class affects the lives and perspectives of women, men, and children. In graduate school at Howard University, there were far fewer in-class discussions about the politics of oppression, especially from a Marxist perspective, than there had been at Antioch, although I learned still more about racial oppression in the Americas.

At Howard I learned simultaneously about the history of African Americans in the United States and about the importance of historical evidence, scholarly objectivity, and scientific methodologies. Clearly, in the interest of objectivity and establishing a scholarly reputation, a "good" graduate student was expected to remove self from his or her scholarship. In my desire to be considered a serious student of history, I learned to place a veil of silence over my personal feelings and my humanity in most of my intellectual discourse, especially my written work.

In choosing to become personally voiceless in my written discourse, which paradoxically involved giving public voice to the Black female past, I adopted the expected intellectual demeanor of most graduate students. Suppressing my personal voice in my scholarship seemed to me a small price to pay for the opportunity that graduate school provided me for reclaiming for historical memory African American women and men as agents of struggle and self-determination.

Even then I recognized that calls for "objectivity" can be and often are used to disguise personal motivations, differences in perceived reality, and cultural hegemony by dominant groups. At least one graduate student at Howard that I am aware of employed alternative models of intellectual discourse. Bernice Johnson Reagon, who had been a member of the SNCC Freedom Singers, founded the internationally recognized women's a cappella group Sweet Honey in the Rock. As a graduate student, she consistently evoked her own humanity in her oral and written narratives of the African American past. At that stage in my intellectual and personal journey, I had neither the intellectual courage nor the confidence to assume the personal stance in my written discourse that I did in my oral discourse. Later, as a student and then as a professor, I found that shifting intellectual interests and greater interaction with feminist writings made the veil of silence that had engulfed me less acceptable.

Race, Gender, Labor, and Historical Memory

Naively I began my study of African American working women by focusing, in a seminar paper, on New England female textile workers during the Jacksonian period (proclaimed by some as the "era of the working man"). Ironically this research project revealed one of many historical moments and places in which "woman's" work—in this case, female textile factory work—meant white women's work. Instead of abandoning the project entirely (it was too late in the semester to switch to an entirely new topic), I merely broadened the paper to include an examination of Black working women in the North during the Jacksonian Era. Specifically I looked at how the confluence of racialized and gendered exploitation in a burgeoning capitalist state conspires to exploit both white and Black working women, albeit in vastly different ways (Harley, 1978).

My interest in the lives of Black working women led to a research project on Anna Julia Cooper, a Black educator and woman's rights activist at the turn of the 20th century. Although the time frame and focus differed from those in my earlier work, Cooper and other educated Black professional women lived their lives circumscribed by race, gender, and often class oppression, as did the antebellum "missing" Black female textile workers and Northern Black female wage earners in general. In the Black community of Washington, DC, and especially in the border states and the Southeastern United States, African American women in particular also confronted the issue of skin color difference.

What drew me to Cooper was not so much her experiences as a late-19th-century Black professional woman, but her 1892 feminist treatise entitled *A Voice From the South: By a Black Woman of the South* (Cooper, 1892; Harley, 1978; Hutchinson, 1981). In *A Voice From the South* and other published works, Cooper eloquently articulated Black women's causes and, according to Black feminist sociologist Patricia Hill Collins (1990), joined with other Black women intellectuals in establishing a rich tradition of Black intellectual thought (Collins, 1990; hooks, 1981). As a result of my work on Cooper, I began to incorporate into my study other

Black professional women who were early feminist activists, lecturers, and educators, with an emphasis on the work of Mary Church Terrell.

Yet as interesting as their lives were and as gratifying as it was to me personally to reclaim the public agency of African American women, my continuing, though somewhat diminished, "revolutionary" spirit was not satisfied by focusing exclusively on middle-class women, as if their lives were the only important ones in the Black community and as if they were representative of most women in the race (a claim they regularly constructed).

Taking the next step—writing a labor history of African American women beyond the professional elite—presented enormous challenges but ultimately was more liberating to me as a scholar and a feminist than the earlier work. For the first decade of my research project on the history of Black working women, I was virtually alone even among the cohort of talented Howard University graduate students. There was no community of scholars with interests in race, gender, and labor history that I could turn to for support.

By the end of my graduate career at Howard in the early 1980s, I came to recognize that my research in race, gender, and labor issues required a far more multifaceted approach than I had employed in my previous work. And indeed the study of African American women's labor history proved to be a site of multiple contestations, including such issues as (a) how to incorporate the lives of ordinary Black folk—in particular, Black womenfolk—into a discipline that stressed too often the history of middle-class and upper middle-class Black men: (b) how to present the culture and meaning of women's work in the African American context when there was considerable ambivalence in that community about a woman's place in the labor force; and (c) how to reclaim the Black female past by using the traditional paradigms and evidentiary sources geared mostly toward a linear history of white, middle-class, heterosexual America. In grappling with these questions, issues of where and how to situate myself openly in my work and the interrelationship between wage work and unpaid domestic roles seldom occurred to me.

The Marginalization of Domestic Roles

My focus on Cooper, Terrell, and other middle-class professional Black women in my early work contributes to the marginal position given to the familial responsibilities of Black working women. Prior to the

1920s, school board regulations limited daytime, full-time teaching positions in the District of Columbia public school system to single women (no similar restrictions existed for males); thus in the Washington community the majority of professional women—most of whom were teachers—were unmarried. If the intention of the school board officials in adopting the policy restricting married women from assuming full-time teaching positions was to have them focus full-time on their expected domestic obligations, it did not work. For the most part, college-educated women (whether married or single) publicly championed intellectual and cultural self-enrichment as much as, if not more than, "domestic chores." The more well-to-do among the Black middle-class—Mary Church Terrell, Josephine Bruce, and Helen Cook, to name a few—employed domestics to cook, clean, and provide care for their children (Terrell, 1940/1968). Unmarried middle-class women in general shouldered fewer of the traditional familial responsibilities facing most married women.

On the basis of the records of their very active public lives as educators, club women, and civic activists, I assumed that educated, professional women, regardless of their marital status, led lives remarkably independent of familial responsibilities. As educated women who considered themselves to be "mothers of the world" and not merely "mothers in the home," they decided that their paid work, along with their community work, was more important in their lives than domestic chores. The majority of educated Black women, especially teachers, believed that in both their professional and nonprofessional roles they had a special responsibility to less fortunate members of their race. I explored the interrelationship between Black women's professional and community work in my article "Beyond the Classroom: Organizational Lives of Black Female Educators in the District of Columbia, 1890-1930" (Harley, 1982), but I did not examine the wage work/familial roles dynamic.[2]

In retrospect, I believe that my own upbringing contributed to my tendency to dissociate women's wage work from their domestic roles. Growing up in a household that did not obligate me to any chores, in part because my mother did not work for wages and my father wanted a "traditional" wife who did all of the household chores and his children to do none of them, it was never conveyed to me or to any of my siblings that we had any expected domestic responsibilities or obligations to parents or to other kin.

I now wonder to what extent the traditionally low value attached to the domestic work that women perform in their own homes (Palmer, 1989) influenced my decision to ignore women's domestic responsibilities in my early work on women wage earners. Family work competed with community and professional work for the attention of Black professional women and mine as well. Initially, for all of the reasons cited, the family roles were largely ignored. Consequently it was easy for me on both a personal and an intellectual level to study professional women's work lives and to ignore the relationship between their wage work and familial roles.

One of the first works I read on the subject of the interconnectedness of wage work and familial roles was *Women, Work, and Family* by historians Joan Scott and Louise Tilly (1978). The analysis and the theoretical model were insightful and raised a number of interesting questions for my own work; the focus of the work, however, was European women. As in the past, the question that came to my mind was, how applicable are these findings for understanding race, gender, and labor in the African American community in the United States? It was a significant investigation, but its applicability to African American women's work could not be substantiated without conducting the research myself on the wage/domestic work dynamic.

Shifting Focus: The Wage/Domestic Work Nexus

Expanding my research focus beyond the Jacksonian Era and turn-of-the-century middle-class professional Black women to the "culture" of Black women's work, encompassing a fuller range of Black female occupations and labor experiences, resulted in the domestic/wage paradigm becoming a more central theme in my scholarship. The general impoverishment of the Black community, combined with the strength of the work ethos in Black folk culture, meant that work often preoccupied the time and attention of most African Americans. African American women, like 94-year-old Mrs. S. C. who worked as a dressmaker and occasionally as a White House coatroom checker along with her husband, often combined work for wages, work at home, and work in their church and community. Mrs. S. C. (personal communication, June 2, 1977) revealed that she was busy attending church women's clubs, teaching Sunday school, and "working at home too, housekeeping and things like that." Later she added: "You know, when you're busy like that and you put in your days from 9 to 5, you don't have time for much more. You talk and you cook and you keep your house going." The reality was that Black women, irrespective of marital status, frequently had to work for wages, but such work did not preclude individual members of the Black community from articulating what they believed was the ideal role for married Black women and from expressing opposition to married women's paid employment. The general public criticism of wage-earning wives and mothers propagated in middle-class white America became part of the public and private discourse in urban Black communities throughout the early 20th century. Male attitudes toward wage-earning married women reveal the dichotomy between the ideal and the real in the African American community.

Some middle-class men and women disingenuously proclaimed that racial progress required Black mothers and wives to be full-time home-makers. In the early 20th century, Giles B. Jackson and D. Webster Davis, authors of *The Industrial History of the Negro Race* (1908), were not alone in claiming that "the race needs wives who stay at home, being supported by their husbands, and then they can spend time in the training of their children" (p. 131). Ironically, opposition to married women's wage work in the Black community was generally strongest toward families who needed the income of a wage-earning wife or mother the most.

Even in the poorest Black families, husbands and fathers, not wives and mothers, were considered the primary breadwinners regardless of the duration of their paid employment. In fact, Black men, though seasonally unemployed, usually earned higher wages than Black women (Harley, 1992). Conversely wives and mothers were considered the primary child care providers, cooks, and household cleaners in their own homes, whether or not they worked for wages outside the home.

A reading of Zora Neale Hurston's autobiography, *Dust Tracks on the Road* (1942/1969), helped me more fully appreciate the pride that certain Black men took in not having their wives "work" for wages. Hurston informs us of her father's proclivity to boast to his male friends that "he had never let his wife hit a lick of work for anybody in her life" (p. 5). Hurston's mother's absence from the paid labor force was more than compensated for, however, by the hard work required in giving birth to and raising a large number of children. Not surprisingly, her father also boasted of the large number of his offspring.

In general, Black wage-earning women responded to public and private criticisms by downplaying, both publicly and privately, the nature and significance of their work as "wage" work, emphasizing instead the service aspect of their paid employment. For example, teachers located the value of their wage work in the "racial uplift" domain, rather than in the economic benefits. It appeared important to many middle-class, educated Black women to tie their professional (wage) work as teachers with traditional expectations about women's proper roles in either the family or the community. As "mothers of the world," Black educated women proclaimed that they brought to the public domain, including the workplace, the same instincts and virtues traditionally deemed essential to a positive home life. In doing so, they combined their traditional "private" roles with their public roles. In their attempt to perpetuate a single image of themselves as magnanimous public servants or racial uplifters, teachers seldom either considered themselves or referred to themselves publicly as wage earners. Educating the children of poor, unlettered African Americans was considered part of their moral and social obligations as educated women. Teaching was defined less often in these terms by male teachers (Bowser, 1920; Harley, 1982).

For Black domestics, employment provided the resources for them to be "helpmates" to their husbands and providers for their parents or children, real and fictive. Whether married or single, fulfilling familial responsibilities was central to the Black domestic's wage work. For both groups the acceptance of their wage work outside the home required them to attach a worthy cause to it, such as racial uplift, familial assistance, or community support.

As a result of this desire to abide by conventional notions of women's proper roles and low status in the occupational structure, the majority of Black wage-earning women, especially mothers and wives, usually did not believe that their presence or their position in the labor force alone was an accurate reflection of who they were or how they should be viewed by members of the Black community.[3] For the masses of Black women, opportunities for social status existed outside the labor market—in their family, community, and organizational and church lives, though not totally unrelated to their income-producing activities. It was the nickels and dimes of low-income working women and men that supported most churches and schools in African American communities (Higginbotham, 1993).

In turn, some Black men tended to de-emphasize their wives' employment outside the home. Others responded with expressions of pride (like Hurston's father) in having wives who were full-time homemakers, boasting of having "nonworking" wives. The ways in which these tensions were played out in individual families and households varied, depending on the dynamics within each individual household, the nature of the work, the familial background and education of both the wife and the husband, and the social position of the family.

Professional married women encountered less opposition in the community or in their homes, although they likely encountered it in the workplace when they competed with Black men for employment. This dissimilar response to professional women, compared with other groups of wage-earning women, was based, in part, on their higher status in the occupational hierarchy. Moreover, the presence of educated, professional, married women in the labor force was seldom viewed as a reflection of either familial instability or a husband's inability to care for his wife and family.

In light of the precarious financial condition of most households in the Black community, however, the appeal to Black wives and mothers to remain in the home and be cared for by their husbands was unrealistic for the majority of African American families. Few Blacks, even among the middle class, failed to recognize that racial oppression and discrimination in the labor market and in society at large often forced men, women, and children in a given family to earn a salary. Implicit in even the Jackson and Davis (1908) denunciation of married Black women and mothers in the paid labor force was the idea that when husbands could not earn enough to provide fully for their families, then it was permissible for Black wives and mothers to engage in income-producing activities. Thus it appears that economic survival, not a Black cultural ethos favoring married women's wage labor, was the most significant explanatory factor for married Black women's presence in the labor force.

Within the context of an economic reality characterized by unemployment and low wages and a communal ethos that emphasized the "dignity" of work, mutuality, and familial obligation, women still couched their wage work in terms of more acceptable roles for women—as "helpmates" and "racial uplifters." In doing so, they sought to safeguard, indeed enhance, their status in the African American community at the turn of the 20th century. Consequently a 75-year-old former child nurse whom I interviewed when a graduate student in June 1977 worked "because it helped him [her husband] . . . it helped us both to make a successful home at that time" (Mrs. L. R. K., personal communication, June 2, 1977).

The research of feminist scholars studying contemporary Black women's wage and domestic work and the recent publications of anthropologists reaffirms the tradition of work, reciprocity, and independent spirit that resonates in the early 20th-century Black female community. As one 73-year-old woman who started working when she was 9 years old and still did "a little day's work, you know, because I am poor" proclaimed in an interview with anthropologist John Langston Gwaltney (1980): "We [Black women] can do for ourselves and we will do so in a minute" (p. 149).

In sum, Black people in general operate out of a dual set of social and cultural expectations perpetuated by systems of capitalism and racial patriarchy on one hand, and the strength of core Black cultural values on the other hand. As I explored the culture of women's work, I became more clearly aware of how Black folk negotiate the socially constructed gendered expectations of the dominant middle-class society that simultaneously denies them an opportunity to "live up to" most of these expectations. During the late 19th century and the opening decades of the 20th century, African American women created both "public" and "private" spaces in which working women were not defined by their wage work.

Professional Women Have
Familial Obligations Too

Despite my omission of educated middle-class women's domestic roles in my initial research on professional women in the African American community, educated Black women often needed to work for wages as much as the masses of uneducated Black women and for some of the same reasons: to fulfill personal and familial financial obligations. A female teacher in the District of Columbia public school system informed Mrs. Raymond B. Morgan, a member of the local board of education, in October 1923 that she supported Morgan's opposition to the motion to reenact the ban against married female teachers. Questioning why women who made enormous sacrifices for a professional career should be penalized for marrying, the anonymous correspondent declared that professional women's "personal obligations—to relatives, for example—do not cease with their marriage and, therefore, [they] have legitimate reasons for continuing to work." Besides, she warned, "in view of the high cost of living, the proposed motion would lead to secret marriages, fewer families, and fewer vacancies."[4] Under the guise of financial and familial stability, middle-class professional African American women spoke less openly about personal and familial obligations to kin, whereas among the masses of Black womenfolk, the fulfillment of obligations to kin was considered a legitimate, even noble, purpose for female wage labor.

Anna J. Cooper, a widow, was teaching at the M Street School and was a doctoral student at Columbia University when, at the age of 55, she became mother to five great-nephews and -nieces. Cooper relocated the children (ranging in age from 6 months to 12 years), whose mother had recently passed, from their home in Raleigh, North Carolina, to Washington, D.C. Concerned about the monumental task of raising such young children, Cooper's friends and colleagues attempted to deter her from becoming their legal guardian. To both provide for the children and fulfill her professional and academic responsibilities, Cooper eventually sent them to boarding schools (Hutchinson, 1981).

The seeming lack of independence and "divided duty" experienced by married, middle-class white women prompted Susan B. Anthony to question why the great antilynching crusader and woman's rights advocate Ida B. Wells Barnett would marry. When Wells Barnett, in turn, asked her whether she believed women should marry, Anthony responded: "Oh, yes, but not women like you who had a special call for special work. I too might have married but it would have meant dropping the work to which I had set my hand" (Duster, 1970, p. 255). With her marriage in 1895 and the birth of her first child in 1896, Wells Barnett, aided by an occasional child's nurse, maintained an active public life. However, as she bore more children, the sense of the "divided duty" between public activism and familial responsibilities prompted Wells Barnett to curtail her public and professional life (Duster, 1970).

In the personal correspondence and manuscript collections of educated, middle-class African American women, information about women's domestic lives and familial responsibilities languishes in comparison to material highlighting their community and professional work. There are few extant personal diaries of these women that can be gleaned for information about familial life. Rare is the diary like *Give Us Each Day: The Diary of Alice Dunbar Nelson* (edited by feminist scholar Gloria T. Hull, 1984) that lay bare the innermost details of an African American woman's "private" life and feelings. For instance, after a particularly busy day on May 25, 1929, Nelson pens the following note: "Nearly cracked when I got home a wreck, and Bobbo [Robert J. Nelson, her husband] asked me if there was anything to eat in the ice-box" (Hull, 1984, p. 319). A year later Alice noted: "Life is one continual procession of visitors, one unending routine of collecting and washing glasses and emptying ash-trays" (p. 393).

The tensions between the private and public demands of educated, professional women are quite apparent in Dunbar Nelson's diary and, at times, in Mary Church Terrell's autobiography, *A Colored Woman in a White World* (1940/1968). Despite her husband's public affirmation of her active public life, she, and not he, was primarily responsible for preparing meals, cleaning the house, and raising their two daughters. Even though she was assisted occasionally by her mother and a series of live-in domestics, Terrell openly admitted her dislike for and discomfort with the domestic chores she was expected to perform and expressed a sense of frustration with having to choose between fixing dinner (which she especially loathed because she was not good at it), spending time with her children, and working as a civic activist, writer, and public lecturer. In her autobiography Terrell offered the following explanation for not signing a contract to write a book about lynching:

> Even if I had possessed both the ability and the courage, I should have had to surmount many obstacles to find the time, the opportunity for concentration and the peace of mind necessary to write such a book. I had to discharge my duty to my family, to the public schools in my capacity as a member of the Board of Education, and not infrequently I filled lecture engagements. (Terrell, 1940/1968, p. 235)

The dilemma that Terrell faced—having to juggle public and career ambitions with domestic responsibilities—paled in comparison with the work and domestic responsibilities of the vast majority of women confined to low-paid, demanding domestic service and agricultural work in the United States. The childrearing and domestic responsibilities of live-in domestics were compounded by extended periods of absence from their families. The economic and social experience of African American women was such that domestic service positions were not limited to the most uneducated individuals in the Black community; college-educated women labored in domestic service positions in the absence of other employment opportunities.

However, educated African American women who never married, such as Lucy Moten, a 1897 graduate of the medical school at Howard University, presumably had fewer domestic responsibilities than married women, especially married women with children. Although neither marriage nor gender-based domestic responsibilities deterred Moten's career as they might have deterred Terrell's and those of other mothers and married women, gender was no less a factor in the pursuit of her career. The lack of hospital residencies and appointments limited Moten's ability to pursue medicine as a full-time career. Instead, with medical degree in hand, she dedicated 25 years of her life to serving as principal of the Miner Normal School of the District of Columbia, a well-known teacher training program for African Americans (Moldow, 1987).

Of course, there was then no fast track for unmarried career women, partly because all women, regardless of their educational training and interest, were expected to marry. In his 1908 essay "Surplus Negro Women" addressing the problem of the uneven sex ratio in the Black communities in Washington, D.C., and Baltimore, Maryland, noted Black sociologist Kelly Miller labeled unmarried women in these cities "hopeless females, for whom there are neither present nor prospective husbands" (Harley, 1988, p. 166).

The sentiment expressed in this statement reflects the social contradictions around the family/work nexus today as much as in the early 20th century. The culture of women's work in the turn-of-the-20th-century Washington Black community that I study reveals a close link between women's market work and their unpaid domestic and community roles in the Black community. The self-perceptions and public expressions of this tie may vary across class and gender lines, but this relationship is an important aspect of the fabric of Black community life.

An examination of the role that family plays in the employability of women (or men, for that matter) offers a different twist on the tendency to examine the family/work nexus by concentrating solely on the relationship between wage and nonwage domestic work. During the late 19th and early 20th centuries, race, gender, class, and even skin color combined to determine professional job opportunities for African American women in the nation's capital. An essential ingredient of class determination in the African American community has been and continues to be familial background, for which education may or may not compensate. Thus the educated daughters of washerwomen faced greater obstacles in their quest for professional employment—primarily teaching positions in the local "colored" school system—than did the daughters of the social elite.

Women's work, both paid and unpaid, offers a major site for analyzing the conflicting nature of gendered and class expectations in African American communities. Conflicting socially constructed gendered expectations of women in the Black community reflect the uneasy amalgamation of traditional Black cultural values with middle-class, white American gendered expectations.

The Wage/Domestic Nexus
and Self-Transformation

Addressing the wage/nonwage nexus in the lives of women in the Black community opened a new and largely uncharted terrain for me, a world filled with the new and exciting scholarly work of Black and white feminist scholars, many of whom are not historians. The challenges posed by conducting research on working women, particularly women of color, range from limited and scattered sources to male-dominated bourgeois notions of work. These challenges, however, foster considerable inter-action among the feminist scholars studying issues of class, race, and gender in the Black community. The work of Black feminist sociologists, particularly Bonnie Thornton Dill (1979, 1980, 1988), Cheryl Townsend Gilkes (1980, 1982, 1988), Patricia Hill Collins (1986a, 1986b, 1991), and Elizabeth Higginbotham (Higginbotham & Watts, 1988), and other scholars and writers (Christian, 1985; Washington, 1980, 1987) and novel-ists (Hurston, 1937/1969; Marshall, 1959), feminist critics (hooks, 1981, 1984, 1989; Lorde, 1984), and anthropologists (Gwaltney, 1980; Mullings, 1986) introduced me to new paradigms and innovative approaches for studying Black women's lives and varied ways of reconstructing their daily lives. Exposure to this growing body of interdisciplinary scholar-ship contributed to a critical watershed in my own development as a femi-nist scholar.

As impressive as the few historical studies of African American women were in the mid-1980s, they rarely dealt with the daily fabric of African American women's lives, particularly their familial roles and nonwage work. The works of the above-named feminist sociologists, anthropolo-gist, feminist critics, and writers appear to better reflect the spirit, feel-ings, beliefs, and experiences of what anthropologist Gwaltney refers to as the average, ordinary, "drylongso" African American (1980). In the absence of significant historical scholarship on the topic of attitudes about wage work at the time, their research findings, albeit for a different period, have been important in both influencing and corroborating many of my research conclusions. Such corroboration is important to the work of scholars, especially to feminist scholars of color, as they explore un-charted waters, often without the comfort of having a supportive intellec-tual community.

As a graduate student, I first became acquainted with the use of oral interviews as an important technique to collect data about the life experi-ences and perspectives of "ordinary" and not-so-ordinary women. So in the late 1970s I interviewed more than 100 women (most African Ameri-cans) who had worked in Washington, DC, prior to the 1930s. These women helped "set the record straight" and in the process often "set me straight" about the work lives of poor "colored" women in Washington, DC. The exchange that ensued during the course of these interviews made it possible for me to begin unraveling the culture and meaning of women's work in ways that written records generally did not permit. Yet I never trusted this information-gathering process enough to make it a significant source for my scholarship.

The works of Dill, Gilkes, Gwaltney, and other scholars that I encountered in the mid and late 1980s employ oral interviews and life histories extensively to reveal the daily lives and attitudes of Black women and men (Dill, 1980; Gilkes, 1980; Gwaltney, 1980). Inspired by the insightfulness of their work, I became more comfortable with the use of oral interviews as a data-gathering technique.

According greater credence to this research methodology has been crucial to my development as an African American feminist historian. As I moved from an almost exclusive reliance on the traditional historical methodologies emphasizing manuscript and textual analysis to investigating Black women's material culture, literary and nonliterary texts, and "good talk," I discovered additional, frequently unexplored sites for understanding Black female experiences and perspectives (Carby, 1990).

Within the last decade, an increasing number of Black and white feminist historians have begun studying various facets of Black women's work (Brown, 1990; Brooks Barett [Higginbotham], 1978, 1984; Clark-Lewis, 1987; Harley, 1988, 1990, 1991; Palmer, 1989; Terborg-Penn, 1985). Locating African American women in the history of wage work in the United States received a major boost in 1985 with the publication of two scholarly works: Jacqueline Jones's *Labor of Love, Labor of Sorrow* and Dolores Janiewski's *Sisterhood Denied: Race, Gender, and Class in a New South Community*. More recently, writing about the feminization of the Black Baptist church, historian Evelyn Brooks Higginbotham (1993) presents invaluable information about the meaning of women's work and the duality of their wage work and domestic roles in the African American community.

The existence of a collective of Black feminist historians is extremely gratifying on several levels. For the first time, an opportunity exists to have insights and perspectives about wage-earning African American women either affirmed or disputed by scholars working on that particular topic. Without the work of Black feminist scholars, one often is forced to continue to draw conclusions or make comparisons based on research findings in which Black working women are either absent or occupy a small, marginalized place—a process that can be both intellectually and personally frustrating. For feminist scholars working alone in not-too-friendly waters, the affirmation of one's own research findings and analytical framework by other feminist scholars is extremely important in warding off the quagmire of self-doubt and apprehension that exists when breaking new ground in an academic world that cherishes the old and traditional. Unfortunately marginalization of both feminist thought and Black women continues within the white-dominated academic community.

I believe that a new generation of feminist historians will offer feminist writers and scholars who are not historians a fuller understanding of the history of Black women's actions and thoughts and a historical context in which to place the development of Black feminist thought and other issues related to gender and the Black experience. I hope that ultimately my work and that of others who constitute this new generation of feminist historians in combining feminist theoretical models with historical data will shorten the invisible divide that seems to exist between the so-called "theorists" and "nontheorists" within the feminist community.

Finally I believe that a merger of the two strains of feminist scholarship—theoretical and evidentiary—represents the ideal manner in which to understand the dynamics of Black women's wage and unpaid domestic work. Reading the works of Dill and Gilkes on the work/family nexus of African American women early on forced me to begin integrating my historical data with feminist theories and research methodologies. Most feminist theoreticians immersed in metatheory have generally not been concerned with examining historical documents before offering critiques of Black women's lives and thoughts. To some extent the heavily theoretical aspects of some feminist scholarship, rarely possessing any historical specificity, has made it both less accessible to many people, including other feminist scholars, and certainly less valuable for some historians who believe that documentation and historical data should be the underpinning of theoretical constructs. A historical study of Black women's wage work and familial experiences should inform feminist theoretical constructs and paradigms no less than feminist paradigms inform historical analyses.

Theorizing based more on the daily lived experiences and expressions of Black women than on the major events and movements of the few "representative" (bourgeois) African American women has provided me with a clearer understanding and appreciation of Black women's work culture. At present I join a host of other, mainly feminist scholars who share anthropologist Gwaltney's vision of having their writing "be an acceptable vehicle for the transmission of [the] views" of ordinary Black women- and menfolk. Harriet Jones, a young Black woman whose personal narrative appears in Gwaltney's book *Drylongso*, made the following remarks about the representation of Black folk in published works and the media:

> Since I don't see myself or most people I know in most things I see or read about Black people, I can't be bothered with that. I wish you could read something or see a movie that would show the people just, well, as my grandmother would say, drylongso. You know, like most of us really are most of the time— together enough to do what we have to do to be decent people. (p. xxiv)

While acknowledging the feminist scholars and writers whose works have contributed to my development as a feminist scholar, legions of often anonymous Black women and men whose daily lives and ideas about living and survival with dignity often form the basis of contemporary Black feminist theoretical constructs must be formally recognized. From the personal narratives that form the basis of Gwaltney's (1980) self-portrait of Black America, he asserts: "It is evident that Black people are building theory on every conceivable level. . . . These people not only know the troubles they've seen, but have profound insight into the meaning of those vicissitudes" (p. xxvi). Similarly literary critic and cultural theorist Houston A. Baker, Jr., proclaims, "WE ARE ALWAYS embroiled with theory—even when the word itself is absent" (Baker, 1991, p. 1). Gwaltney added: "Black Americans are, of course, capable of the same kind of abstract thinking that is practiced by all human cultures, but sane people in a conquest environment are necessarily preoccupied with the realities of social existence." "Prudent" scholars cannot analyze the social realities of Black Americans without incorporating the wisdom and perspectives of the Black masses in their analysis.

My early development as a feminist scholar began as an attempt to document and reclaim women's lives for historical record: women such as Jacksonian Era textile workers, and Black professional women such as Cooper and Terrell. Not surprisingly this approach has been characteristic of most of the early work in the field of Black women's history. Almost by necessity the development of more sophisticated theoretical constructs and theories came later.

My expansion into the new and largely uncharted terrain—the historical nexus of Black women's market and nonwage domestic work—has revealed as much about the gendered and class ideals of African Americans as the relationship between wage work and familial responsibilities. Indeed, after a more careful reading of the historical sources, the interlocking between labor market work and familial responsibilities of

African American women is far less obscure than I originally had envisioned. Members of the African American community have been quite vocal about the domestic lives and work roles of women and men in the Black community.

Self-Identity and Historical Memory: Yet Another Stage

Another central milestone in my development as a feminist scholar occurred with the introduction of the primacy of self-representation in my scholarly discourse (hooks, 1989). Audre Lorde, Angela Davis, bell hooks, and other feminist writers characterize this "coming to voice" as an act of resistance. In speaking we engage in a process of self-transformation whereby we move from being objects to subjects. For as hooks argues, it is "only as subjects we can speak" (1989, p. 12).

While engaged in writing this chapter, I began to give serious consideration to my own voicelessness in my scholarship and to confront the significance and meaning of locating self in one's writings. Recognizing that it is fundamentally impossible to completely divorce the self from a research project does not make any easier the task of openly situating myself in my writing about Black women's work. In *Talking Back: Thinking Feminist, Thinking Black* (1989), bell hooks attributes her slow pace in writing the book to her reluctance and uneasiness with "revealing the personal. It has to do with writing—with what it means to say things in print" (p. 1). After nearly two decades of avoiding personal references to myself in my written work, lifting the veil of silence surrounding my development as a feminist scholar and my research on women's wage and familial work has been more challenging than I ever would have imagined.

The self-recovery and coming to voice in the study of the culture of women's work in African American communities and in writing this chapter has allowed me to transform my quiet revolutionary spirit into a public voice that is self-liberating and that will contribute to the collective liberation of my readers. Finally by combining the writing of the history of African American working women with finding my public voice, I occupy a public space that extends the feminist discourse to people who now can know that the "I" in my written discourse means "we." Just as feminist scholar Hazel Carby concludes in " 'It Jus Be's Dat Way

Sometime': The Sexual Politics of Women's Blues," we hear the " 'we' when the [women blues singers] say 'I' " (1990, p. 248).

Notes

1. In writing this chapter, I have borrowed from ideas introduced in two earlier publications: "For the Good of Family and Race: Gender, Work, and Domestic Roles in the Black Community, 1880-1930" in *Signs, 15* (1990). Reprinted in M. P. Malson, E. Mudimbe-Boyi, J. F. O'Barr, & M. Wyer (Eds.), *Black women in America: Social science perspectives* (pp. 159-172). Chicago: University of Chicago Press; and "When Your Work Is Not Who You Are: The Development of Working-Class Consciousness Among Afro-American Women" in *Gender, Class, Race and Reform in the Progressive Era* (Lexington: University Press of Kentucky, 1991).

2. Similarly sociologist Cheryl Townsend Gilkes has examined the nature and level of the community work of other groups of women in the Black community (1980, 1982, 1988).

3. Nannie Helen Burroughs, founder and president of the National Training School for Women and Girls, pioneered the campaign to garner greater respectability for the domestic service work that preoccupied most Black working women (Higginbotham, 1993).

4. See letter "An earnest teacher" (anonymous) to Mrs. Raymond B. Morgan, 23 October, 1923, Mary Church Terrell Papers, Box 4, Moorland Springarm Research Center, Howard University, Washington, DC.

References

Baker, Jr., H. (1991). *Workings of the spirit: The poetics of Afro-American women's writing.* Chicago: University of Chicago Press.

Bowser, R. D. (1920). What role is the educated Negro woman to play in uplifting her race? In D. W. Culp (Ed.), *Twentieth century Negro literature: Or, a cyclopedia of thought on the vital topics relating to the American Negro* (pp. 177-182). Toronto: J. L. Nichols.

Brooks Barett [Higginbotham], E. (1978). Nannie Helen Burroughs and the education of Black women. In S. Harley & R. Terborg-Penn (Eds.), *The Afro-American woman: Struggles and images* (pp. 97-108). Port Washington, NY: Kennikat.

Brown, E. B. (1989). Womanist consciousness: Maggie Lena Walker and the independent order of Saint Luke. In M. R. Malson, E. Mudimbe-Boyi, J. F. O'Barr, & M. Wyer (Eds.), *Black women in America: Social science perspectives* (pp. 173-196). Chicago: University of Chicago Press.

Carby, H. V. (1990). "It jus be's dat way sometime": The sexual politics of women's blues. In E. C. DuBois & V. L. Ruiz (Eds.), *Unequal sisters: A multi-cultural reader in U.S. women's history* (pp. 238-249). New York: Routledge, Chapman & Hall.

Christian, B. (1985). *Black feminist criticism: Perspectives on Black women writers.* New York: Pergamon.

Clark-Lewis, E. (1987). "This work had a end": African-American domestic workers in Washington, D.C., 1910-1940. In C. Groneman & M. B. Norton (Eds.), *To toil the livelong day: America's women at work, 1780-1980* (pp. 196-212). Ithaca, NY: Cornell University Press.

Collins, P. H. (1986a). The Afro-American work family/nexus: An exploratory analysis. *Western Journal of Black Studies, 10*(3), 148-158.

Collins, P. H. (1986b). Learning from the outsider within: The sociological significance of Black feminist thought. *Social Problems, 33*(6), 14-32.

Collins, P. H. (1991). *Black feminist thought: Knowledge, consciousness, and the politics of empowerment.* New York: Routledge, Chapman & Hall.

Cooper, A. J. (1892). *A voice from the South; By a Black woman of the South.* Xenia, OH: Aldine.

Dill, B. T. (1979). The dialectics of Black womanhood. *Signs, 4*(3), 543-555.

Dill, B. T. (1980). The means to put my children through: Child-rearing goals and strategies among Black female domestic servants. In L. F. Rodgers-Rose (Ed.), *The Black woman* (pp. 107-123). Beverly Hills, CA: Sage.

Dill, B. T. (1988). "Making your job good yourself": Domestic service and the construction of personal dignity. In A. Bookman & S. Morgen (Eds.), *Women and the politics of empowerment* (pp. 33-52). Philadelphia: Temple University Press.

Duster, A. M. (Ed.). (1970). *Crusade for justice: The autobiography of Ida B. Wells.* Chicago: University of Chicago Press.

Gilkes, C. T. (1980). "Holding back the ocean with a broom": Black women and community work. In L. F. Rodgers-Rose (Ed.), *The Black woman* (pp. 217-232). Beverly Hills, CA: Sage.

Gilkes, C. T. (1982). Successful rebellious professionals: The Black woman's professional identity and community commitment. *Psychology of Women Quarterly, 6*(3), 289-311.

Gilkes, C. T. (1988). Building in many places: Multiple commitments and ideologies in Black women's community work. In A. Bookman & S. Morgen (Eds.), *Women and the politics of empowerment* (pp. 53-76). Philadelphia: Temple University Press.

Gwaltney, J. L. (1980). *Drylongso: A self-portrait of Black America.* New York: Random House.

Harley, S. (1978). Anna Julia Cooper: A voice for Black women. In S. Harley & R. Terborg-Penn (Eds.), *The Afro-American woman: Struggles and images* (pp. 87-96). Port Washington, NY: Kennikat.

Harley, S. (1982). Beyond the classroom: Organizational lives of Black female educators in the District of Columbia, 1890-1930. *Journal of Negro Education, 51*, 254-265.

Harley, S. (1988). Mary Church Terrell: Genteel militant. In L. Litwack & A. Meier (Eds.), *Black leaders of the nineteenth century* (pp. 307-321). Urbana: University of Illinois Press.

Harley, S. (1990). For the good of the family and race: Gender, work, and domestic roles in the Black community. *Signs 15*(2); reprinted in M. R. Malson, E. Mudimbe-Boyi, J. F. O'Barr, & M. Wyer (Eds.), *Black women in America: Social science perspectives* (pp. 159-172). Chicago: University of Chicago Press.

Harley, S. (1991). When your work is not who you are: The development of a working-class consciousness among Afro-American women. In N. Frankel & N. S. Dye (Eds.), *Gender, class, race and reform in the Progressive Era* (pp. 42-55). Lexington: University Press of Kentucky.

Higginbotham, E., & Watts, S. (1988). The new scholarship on Afro-American women. *Women's Studies Quarterly, 16*(1-2), 12-21.

Higginbotham, E. B. (1993). *Righteous discontent: The woman's movement in the Black Baptist church, 1880-1920.* Cambridge, MA: Harvard University Press.

hooks, b. (1981). *Ain't I a woman: Black women and feminism.* Boston: South End.

hooks, b. (1984). *From margin to center.* Boston: South End.

hooks, b. (1989). *Talking back: Thinking feminist, thinking Black.* Boston: South End.

Hull, G. T. (Ed.). (1984). *Give us each day: The diary of Alice Dunbar Nelson.* New York: Norton.

Hurston, Z. N. (1969). *Dust tracks on the road.* New York: Arno. (Original work published 1942)

Hurston, Z. N. (1969). *Their eyes were watching God.* Greenwich, CT: Fawcett. (Original work published 1937)

Hutchinson, L. D. (1981). *Anna J. Cooper: A voice from the South.* Washington, DC: Smithsonian Institution Press.

Jackson, G. B., & Davis, D. W. (1908). *The industrial history of the Negro race.* Richmond, VA: Virginia Press.

Janiewski, D. (1985). *Sisterhood denied: Race, class, and gender in a New South community.* Philadelphia: Temple University Press.

Jones, J. (1985). *Labor of love, labor of sorrow: Black women, work, and the family from slavery to the present.* New York: Basic Books.

Lorde, A. (1984). *Sister outsider.* Trumansberg, NY: Crossing.

Marshall, P. (1959). *Brown girl, brownstones.* New York: Avon.

Moldow, G. (1987). *Women doctors in gilded-age Washington: Race, gender, and professionalization.* Urbana: University of Illinois Press.

Mullings, L. (1986). Anthropological perspectives on the Afro-American family. *American Journal of Social Psychiatry, 6*(1), 11-16.

Palmer, P. (1989). *Domesticity and dirt: Housewives and domestic servants in the United States, 1920-1945.* Philadelphia: Temple University Press.

Scott, J., & Tilly, L. (1978). *Women, work, and family.* New York: Holt, Rinehart & Winston.

Terborg-Penn, R. (1985). Survival strategies among African-American women workers: Continuing process. In R. Milkman (Ed.), *Women, work, and protest* (pp. 139-155). Boston: Routledge & Kegan Paul.

Terrell, M. C. (1968). *A colored woman in a white world.* Washington, DC: National Association of Colored Women's Clubs. (Original work published 1940)

Washington, M. H. (1980). *Midnight birds.* Garden City, NY: Anchor.

Washington, M. H. (Ed.). (1987). *Invented lives: Narratives of Black women, 1860-1960.* Garden City, NY: Anchor.

PART III

The Experience of Violence in Close Relationships

10

Reflections of a Feminist
Family Violence Researcher

KERSTI YLLÖ

The physical and sexual abuse of women is probably the most politically and emotionally charged topic within family studies. It is not surprising, then, that our impressive progress in understanding wife abuse has nevertheless been marked by numerous controversies. Although a great deal of important research has been conducted by mainstream social scientists, this is an area of study in which feminist scholarship has been critically important. The issue of wife abuse was brought to public consciousness by the women's movement. The shelter movement has begun to offer women alternatives to violence, and feminist activists and researchers have contributed importantly to our understanding of the problem. Yet our work has only begun, and there are controversies in the field and a division between those who bring feminist perspectives to bear on the problem of battering and those who do not.

The tensions between those who regard themselves first and foremost as family researchers and practitioners and those who see themselves as feminists (researchers and activists) are longstanding, to a certain extent inevitable, and often useful in the development of the field. I believe, however, that the tensions, hostilities, and sometimes open conflicts also can be counterproductive, especially when the many sides stop talking and listening to one another.

AUTHOR'S NOTE: This chapter is a revised and expanded version of "Political and Methodological Debates in Wife Abuse Research" in K. Yllö and M. Bograd (Eds.), *Feminist Perspectives on Wife Abuse,* Sage, 1988.

Because virtually everyone who studies wife abuse and other violence against women wants to see an end to such abuse, we might regard all of this work as feminist in some sense. However, this is clearly not the case. Leaving aside the openly antiwoman analyses of wife battering (usually provided by psychoanalysts; see Hilberman, 1980), we see extensive research by nonfeminists (though not necessarily antifeminists), most of whom focus on families and wife abuse as a part of that system of interaction. Because much of this work does not take gender or power into account as a central factor, the focus is not feminist. Further, the methods used (usually quantitative surveys or psychological tests) have been questioned as patriarchal.

These debates are particularly salient to me because for the 15 years I have studied wife abuse, I have been both a family sociologist and a feminist. As a doctoral student and postdoctoral fellow with Murray Straus at the Family Violence Research Program at the University of New Hampshire, I was well trained in mainstream methodology and a family-focused analysis of wife abuse. As a feminist interested in feminist theory and radical critiques of methodology, as well as in the practical consequences of our research for the lives of battered women, I also have stepped outside of family studies. Family studies (specifically family sociology) is the field in which I am trained and which houses my scholarly work. However, I do not feel that it is my home. My passion (in research and in life) is feminism. When I present or publish my work in family studies, I often think I must proceed carefully, lest my feminist consciousness be seen as just a political bias (as if other perspectives are nonpolitical). In contrast, I feel at home at feminist conferences and with feminist publications. I have more in common with feminist scholars studying a wide array of topics than I do with many family scholars focusing on the same issues of violence by intimates. So although I am in family studies, I am also outside it, and the debates in the area of wife abuse are often a dialogue I carry on with myself. Marcia Westkott (1979) comments eloquently on the nature of such debate for feminist scholars:

> These dialogues are not debates between outsiders and insiders; they are, rather, critical confrontations among those who have been educated and trained within particular disciplines. The feminist debate arises because some of these insiders who are women are also outsiders. When women realize that we are simultaneously immersed in and estranged from both our own particular discipline and the Western intellectual tradition generally, a personal ten-

sion develops that informs the critical dialogue. . . . In some fundamental way, we, as critics, oppose ourselves. (p. 422)

Westkott's theme of opposition and tension has been echoed by many feminist researchers. Cook and Fonow (1990) point to the feminist "double vision" or "double consciousness" as central to our work and broader understanding of the social world. This double vision (being inside and outside) is a valuable standpoint that feminism affords us. In using the concept, however, we should recognize that it is not an original feminist formulation. In his discussion of the methods used in his study *The Dark Ghetto,* Kenneth Clark (1964) talks about a double vision as a black man in this culture. He refers to W. E. B. DuBois's vision as a guide in studying life in the ghetto. With due recognition of our intellectual heritage and the understanding that all women or all feminists cannot be compressed into one vision, I think we can make good heuristic use of the notion of a double vision. The tensions and contradictions that duality engenders are a powerful source of energy and insight for our work.

The purpose of this chapter is to explore some of the debates between mainstream scholars and clinicians and feminist researchers and activists. In this chapter I do not attempt to give an overview of all points of contention, but emphasize a few key issues. Further, I discuss them in the context of my own research and development as a feminist scholar. First I take up the methodological challenges posed by feminism. Then I look at current theoretical debates about the nature of domestic violence and its implications for clinical practice.

In discussing these issues, I refer to three research projects that I have undertaken regarding wife abuse. In many ways the first two studies represent the quantitative and qualitative methodological approaches that often are regarded as opposed. The first, a quantitative analysis of secondary data on family violence, has been criticized as patriarchal in its methodology. The second, involving in-depth interviews with women who were victims of physical abuse and rape in their marriages, often is regarded as a more feminist approach. As I try to make clear, I believe that the labeling of these two studies as "nonfeminist" versus "feminist" in method is counterproductive. We need not create a simple dichotomy where a complex distinction exists. The deeper issues of epistemology—how we know what we know—need to be explored in order to understand these debates more fully. I refer to these two studies because, as Feyerabend (1978) has argued, "to discuss methodology apart from concrete research is like discussing the role of keys without careful attention to the nature of locks" (p. 42). The third study I discuss is my current research on how family therapy conceptualizes and treats domestic violence. In discussing this project, I shift focus from methodology to theory and clinical practice.

The Personal and the Professional Are Political

Before I turn to the three studies, I want to provide some background about how I came to be a feminist family violence researcher. I am often asked why I study a subject as grim as wife abuse, and I often think the questioners are probing not about my professional development, but about my personal experience. They seem disappointed to learn that I am one of the fortunate women who has not experienced battering firsthand.

I came to study wife abuse for a number of fortuitous reasons. As an undergraduate in the early 1970s, I took the first women's studies course ever offered at my college. More than 100 students showed up at a class designed for 20. Books such as Robin Morgan's *Sisterhood Is Powerful* (1970) and Germaine Greer's *The Female Eunuch* (1972) provided me with a new lens through which to view the world. I was stunned by the clarity of vision that was possible. What before seemed to be a murky assortment of troublesome issues (e.g., passivity, pornography, poor pay) became at once more understandable and more disturbing. At the same time, I found family sociology intriguing, especially when I began to pose feminist questions to the more traditional faculty and texts. Graduate school seemed to be the ideal place to pursue these matters. (The cocktail waitressing I had been doing, though lucrative, offered little opportunity for focused feminist criticism.)

At the University of New Hampshire, my efforts to grow as a feminist scholar and teacher were strongly supported by Murray Straus, who has been the object of much feminist criticism. Although we disagreed on some key points (violence by wives being the most prominent), Straus was quite open to feminist analysis of the patriarchal nature of marriage and other social institutions. Most importantly, he had very high expectations of me in my work and aspirations. So despite some discouragement by other faculty (one senior professor told me "women are a fad"), graduate school was a very positive experience.

I arrived at what seems now to be my life's work rather serendipitously. Although I had an intense interest in family and power relations, I had not considered the issue of domestic violence until I began to work with Straus. Thanks to pre- and postdoctoral fellowships supported by the National Institute of Mental Health, I became involved with the research being conducted by Straus's Family Violence Research Program. Wife abuse seemed to be the ideal focus for my concerns about family, gender, and power. As the next sections of this chapter show, this has remained my focus even as my theoretical and methodological thinking has evolved.

During graduate school my husband was my POSSLQ (person of the opposite sex sharing living quarters, to use the U.S. Census Bureau's term for cohabitors). I was fortunate to find a supportive, feminist partner who could put up with a never-ending analysis of the patriarchal nature of marriage. I was deeply committed to our relationship, but I had serious doubts about marriage—which I thought of at the time as an institution, rather than as a relationship. We married mainly to make our families and the school board for which my husband worked happy. I never have regretted our decision to marry, and we have struggled to create an egalitarian relationship. Now that we have two children, the challenges are even greater. Yet there is no question that having this supportive home base has given me great freedom to pursue my academic work and activism.

The feminist dictum that the "personal is political" continues to provide insight for me. Whether the issue is childrearing, publishing, classroom dynamics, or curriculum development, looking through a feminist lens helps me see more clearly. Although I often do not like what I see, I find strength in the fact that feminism offers me not only a special lens on the world but also a vision for changing it.

Methodological Debates

The Status of Women and Wife Beating

My first major research project—my dissertation—was a study of how women's status in society affects levels of violence within the family. I had grown frustrated by the proliferation of studies that focused only on individual psychology or marital dyads: So much of the research regarded marriage within a social vacuum, ignoring the patriarchal structure of society. My feminist perspective led me to explore the structure of male power. A real problem for me was how to operationalize gender inequality at the societal as well as individual level.

My approach to this feminist question was quantitative and methodologically mainstream. Using census and other secondary data, I constructed a Status of Women Index by which I ranked American states regarding the economic, political, educational, and legal status of women. A typical item in the index was "proportion of women in technical/managerial occupations." I correlated the index with state rates of wife beating drawn from the nationally representative survey on family violence conducted by Straus, Gelles, and Steinmetz (1980).

My central finding was that inequality at the state level did indeed affect rates of battering, but not in the linear way I had hypothesized. Wife abuse did not simply decline as women's status improved. Rather, the relationship was curvilinear. Wife battering was high in low-status states and declined as women's status improved. However, rates of abuse increased in those states in which women's status was highest relative to men's (see Yllö, 1983, 1984a, 1984b for fuller discussion of these findings). The evidence seemed to indicate that rapid social change toward equality may bring a violent backlash by husbands. The implication I drew is not that we need to slow the pace of change, but that we need to direct our attention and resources to those who are paying most dearly the price of the change.

I was stunned when my paper reporting these findings was rejected from a respected feminist journal. The problem was not with the nature of my concerns or conclusions, but with my methodology, which, I was told, was "inherently patriarchal." Quantitative studies could contribute no feminist insights, the editor wrote. This rejection inspired me to begin exploring feminist critiques of science and methodology, an exploration that is still ongoing.

Rape in Marriage

At about the same time, as a postdoctoral fellow, I began to work with David Finkelhor on the issue of marital rape. As we explored the intersection of my work on wife battering and his on child sexual abuse, we discovered an enormous gap in the research. Marital rape was legally nonexistent and virtually absent in all of the work on family violence, sexuality, and rape.

As we began our research into the experiences of women who had been raped, Diana Russell conducted her landmark survey on sexual assault, including wife rape (see Russell, 1982, for a discussion of the most thorough survey to date). David and I decided against a survey and focused our study on a qualitative description of the experience of rape in marriage. We were concerned with the "sanitary stereotype" of marital rape (the best known example being Rhett Butler carrying a struggling Scarlett up the stairs, with Scarlett beaming happily the next morning). We were concerned that journalists and legislators were asserting that wife rape was simply not very serious. "But if you can't rape your wife, who can you rape?" asked State Senator Bob Wilson in the debate about criminalizing marital rape in California.

We decided to interview women who had been raped by their husbands and find out what happened and what impact it had on them. Through family planning agencies, feminist health centers, and battered women's shelters, we contacted women who had indicated in intake interviews that a partner had used force or threat of force to try to have sex with them. I conducted most of the 50 unstructured, in-depth interviews with women ranging in age from 17 to 60. These 50 case studies were the qualitative database for this study. We chose to talk with women about their experiences because of the exploratory nature of the research. Although it is true that an inductive, experiential approach often is equated with a feminist approach, we did not initially choose our method for those reasons.

The findings of this research are detailed in *License to Rape: Sexual Abuse of Wives* (Finkelhor & Yllö, 1985). By listening to the women's experiences, we discovered three basic types of rape in marriage. The first, which we call *battering rape,* occurs in marriages that have a high overall level of violence. The women are battered, and the rapes are an additional element of the beating and humiliation. The second type, *force-only rape,* occurs in marriages that are otherwise nonviolent. The husband's desire for control seems to lead him to use sexual coercion. He uses only as much force as necessary to coerce his wife to comply. Power, rather than anger, appears to be central to force-only rapes. The third type, *obsessive rape,* is most openly sadistic. Sexual violence is central to the husband's arousal. The husband is not a batterer who adds rape to the assault, but rather, he is obsessed with sex, usually uses violent pornography, and inflicts pain as a part of sex. Although these husbands can be termed sadists, it is important to note that the wives were not masochists.

Although the women's experiences with marital rape varied greatly in terms of physical pain and injury, all of the women reported being greatly traumatized. Although the impact is different from that of stranger rape, it is not less serious (as Russell, 1982, has shown statistically). The violation of trust was the most profound psychological consequence. These women spent much time, often many years, in trying to escape their marriages and then to let themselves trust and develop intimate relationships with men once more (though many have not reached that point and do not believe they ever will).

In this study (in comparison with my first) I heard the voices of the women "subjects" themselves. What they told me was a sort of data quite different from the data from my earlier computer printouts, and it provided a picture of the women's experience that numbers could never portray. As Reinharz (1992) points out, interviewing is an approach that reduces researcher control and increases connection to research subjects. It is the prevailing method of feminist researchers at present.

Feminist Critiques

I have no doubt that my interviews with marital rape survivors provided rich, contextual data about the women's experiences, but I cannot conclude that intensive interviewing should be *the* method of feminist researchers. In the sections that follow, I raise questions about both quantitative and qualitative approaches to the study of woman abuse.

The quantitative approach at the core of the positivist paradigm carries the greatest prestige and respect in the area of family studies, as in all of the social sciences. Much of this status can be traced to the privileged position of science and masculinity in our culture. As Keller (1978) argues, it appears to be the most rational and objective, providing "hard" data. It is the most highly regarded method in an intellectual tradition and society in which anything linked to the feminine is devalued.

Consequently statistical data generated by the Conflict Tactics Scales (CTS), developed by Straus and his colleagues (Straus et al., 1980) and now widely used, are taken most seriously. These scales measure abuse by counting individual acts of violence by husbands and wives, without regard to the severity of injury or the issue of self defense. Undoubtedly the most controversial finding produced in this way is that "1.8 million wives are physically abused by their husbands each year (3.8%) while nearly two million husbands are physically abused by their wives (4.6%)" (Gelles & Straus, 1979, p. 550). Straus et al. were surprised by these results and have spent many years explaining that they did not consider the context of the violent acts, that most of the women's violence was certainly in self-defense, and that they did not measure the consequences of the acts, which surely resulted in greater injury to the women. Although they have stated that wife abuse, not husband abuse, is the pressing problem, the damage was done. Those few simple numbers and the notion of the "battered husband syndrome" (Steinmetz, 1977-1978) have been a powerful influence on policy makers and the public.

What is most disturbing is that the criticisms of the CTS seem to have gone unheeded. Gelles and Straus (1986) recently published the findings of the 10-year follow-up national survey. Their scales were unrevised, and the new finding is that "women are about as violent within the family as men. This highly controversial finding from the 1975 study is confirmed by the 1985 study" (p. 470).

The debate about violence *by* women and "husband abuse" seems to be intensifying, rather than abating. The Gelles and Straus findings have been the basis of even more extreme arguments. On the one hand, McNeely and Robinson-Simpson (1987), for example, argue that the abuse of husbands is a more serious problem than the abuse of wives. On the other hand, the feminist response grows stronger. Saunders (1988), DeKeseredy and Hinch (1991), and Dobash, Dobash, Wilson, and Daly (1992), among others, provide powerful critiques of the Conflict Tactics Scales and the empirical data the scales generate, as well as the theoretical assumptions underpinning "husband abuse research." Further, beyond the academic debate, the daily experience of practitioners belies the notion that marital violence is gender neutral. The national network of shelters is overwhelmed by battered women. Steinmetz's (1977-1978) argument that vast numbers of battered husbands are just hidden from the helping professions and the criminal justice system because of shame and stigma is implausible and unsupported by evidence.

Despite the theoretical and empirical critiques by feminist researchers and the contrary experiences of practitioners, the quantitative work based on the CTS still predominates in the family violence field. Although Straus and many other quantitative researchers are critics of the patriarchal institutions, such as economic discrimination and the criminal justice system (Straus, 1974, 1980), that entrap battered women, they do not question the patriarchal nature of social science and the status of their methods within it. I believe, however, that it is only when we consider these issues at the level of epistemology that the criticisms of the "hard" data become clearer and more substantive. The problem is not just quantification per se (although the CTS certainly could be made a better measure). It is also in the status of quantitative research as the most objective (best) way to "know" about a subject.

Objectivity and Social Commitment

An important feminist critique concerns the idea of scientific objectivity, which supposedly requires a divorce between rationality and research and any emotional or social commitments (Fee, 1981). This objectivity is a significant problem when one's topic of study is wife abuse. The majority (if not all) of the researchers who study family violence do not hold to the strictest interpretation of objectivity—that is, that their research is entirely value free and that they, as researchers, have no social or political commitments. No, these are people who generally abhor violence and see their work as contributing to the ending of violence. There seems to be little reluctance among these researchers to discuss the practical and policy implications of their work, whether it be before congressional committees or at murder trials.

Nevertheless there are important differences on this question of objectivity and commitment. Although mainstream researchers may recognize their own values, they attempt to separate these from the practice of research, which they see themselves conducting objectively (by trying to eliminate bias technically). Certainly something can be said for eliminating technical biases. It is in this area that the critiques of "sex bias" in methods have been helpful. Yet a vague and often unarticulated allegiance to the positivist notion of objectivity remains: that the research simply uncovers what is "out there." In contrast, many feminist researchers regard their work as being not only *about* women but also *for* women. The explicit goal is to end violence against women by challenging the patriarchal society of which it is a part. For us, wife abuse is not part of the separate, observable, empirical world out there. Its existence is connected intimately to our own lives as women, whether we personally have been victimized or not. The distance between knower and known diminishes and, in many cases, disappears.

An added aspect of doing research for women involves accountability for how findings are used by others. How data are interpreted, where results are presented and published, and how they may be misused are all important concerns. Feminists do not release findings into the marketplace of ideas, assuming that truth will win out. Caution must be taken to prevent damaging use of information.

The stated commitment to work for women is another element of the subjectivity that is contrasted with the objectivity of the empiricists. I have attended many national conferences at which feminists have been labeled "true believers" or "ideologues" and their work devalued as a result. Somehow the mainstream researchers' commitments to vague goals such as "social justice" and "nonviolence" are not seen as subjective or problematic, whereas feminist goals to end patriarchy are. That the challenge to patriarchy grows out of more radical political theory than does the goal of social justice, part of liberal ideology, could be the subject of a whole separate paper. The point here is that politics and methods are connected in myriad ways. The evaluation of a particular ideology and its connection to research depends greatly on the prevailing power relations in the social sciences and society at large.

Often the issue of politics and research, subtly present throughout the research process, becomes an overt concern with respect to publishing decisions. When David and I were trying to find a publisher for *License to Rape* (Finkelhor & Yllö, 1985), we were anxious to get an advance that would help fund our research, because granting agencies had not been supportive. Our literary agent called with a modest but solid offer from Playboy Press! "Liberal" Playboy wanted to publicize sexual abuse. Publishing a marital rape study through Playboy was out of the question for me. However, I also had to face the possibility that the study would not be completed or published at all. We were saved by a comparable offer from a reputable publisher a few weeks later.

Another struggle involving a publisher occurred in connection with *Feminist Perspectives on Wife Abuse* (Yllö & Bograd, 1988). Our publisher, Sage, had a strong, scholarly reputation, but had marketing concerns about using the term "Feminist Perspectives" in the book title. The publisher suggested using "New Perspectives"; the word *feminist* seemed too strong, too political, perhaps even biased. After some discussion, Sage agreed to go with our original title and, I believe, the book has done better than it would have with a more neutral, seemingly objective, title.

Such political debates are unavoidable in feminist research. And I would argue that we do not want to avoid them. A litmus test for political correctness should not be required at each controversial point. The challenge is to deal with the issues openly and fairly and to make decisions we can live with while recognizing their political dimensions.

"Experts" and "Nonexperts"

A further dimension of the concept of objectivity and empiricism is the distance between "experts" and "nonexperts," reflecting again the separation of thought from feeling (and masculine rationality from female emotionality). One of the deepest cleavages in the field is between mainstream researchers and activists in the battered women's movement. I believe that a crucial component of this division lies in the different ways the two groups "know" about abuse and how those different forms of knowledge are evaluated and acknowledged.

Adherence to the scientific method and the claim of objectivity by mainstream researchers sets up a system in which the flow of knowledge is unidirectional. Researchers gather and analyze data and then draw implications for policy and practitioners. Although nothing is wrong with this process per se, the problem is the trickle of knowledge in the other direction. The analyses of shelter workers and formerly battered women often are regarded as nonscientific, subjective, political, and therefore biased. In other words, they are not comparable to analyses based on "hard" data. Activists sense a fundamental disrespect for their analyses. Sure, their work in the trenches is appreciated and researchers support the development of more shelters. But the theoretical analyses, which grow inductively from experience, often are regarded with suspicion, if not contempt.

To build a better and more productive relationship between researchers and activists, we must challenge positivist assumptions about experts and nonexperts. To regard someone who spends every day working with abused women and helping them negotiate the bureaucracies of welfare, housing, and criminal justice as a nonexpert is patently wrong. Assigning that expertise to some lower, subjective status robs us of important knowledge.

In my own experience, these issues have been played out in numerous small ways—in relationships with colleagues, in research decisions, and in the words I choose in lectures. I have consciously tried to collaborate with mainstream researchers, clinicians, and feminist activists without turning into a chameleon. I have tried to remain grounded in my feminist views while openly communicating with researchers and clinicians who do not share my perspective. I also have tried to explain the views of researchers to activists, who are often quite skeptical of the kinds of rules, procedures, and assumptions about knowledge that academics make. Although these efforts are laudable in principle, they have been far more difficult in practice.

A few years ago, for example, I helped organize a meeting of battered women's activists for a discussion of the ethics of research. I was working with David Finkelhor on a research agenda for the field of family violence (Finkelhor, Hotaling, & Yllö, 1988), and I wanted to be sure that activist voices were heard. Yet when the 2-day meeting was held at my institution, Wheaton College, I was not allowed to attend. After all, I was a researcher. Although I understood the activists' distrust and decision, I was still disappointed.

On another occasion I again was caught between traditional research assumptions and feminist ones. I was part of a research team that included several eminent Harvard Medical School epidemiologists. We debated how to proceed with interviewing women who had just given birth, regarding violence during their pregnancies. My position that interviewers needed to be well trained about domestic violence so that they could interview empathetically was challenged as bias-producing and unscientific. Interviewers should be blind to the issue of violence, it was argued. The feminist activists on the research team were appalled by this view. It fell to me to explain the validity of a feminist approach to the scientists, as well as to explain the legitimacy of their concerns about bias to the activists. I sometimes think my role is first and foremost that of a translator.

Efforts to improve the relationship between researchers and activists will be most successful if researchers examine their own assumptions about what counts as evidence or knowledge. We should involve practitioners in our research, not out of guilt or gratitude for the hard work they do, but out of a recognition that they have important insights to contribute. Further, with their input, more of our research can be useful to those providing services to abused women.

The Subject/Object Dichotomy

The separation between subject and object of research, between knower and known, is central to positivism and generally is assumed in the social sciences. This distance is regarded as essential for the conduct of objective research. Yet feminist critics point out that it does not deliver what it promises because observation is inherently value laden. The operationalization of concepts and their measurement are not neutral processes. For example, Straus et al. (1980) define violence in terms of the intent to cause harm, yet the Conflict Tactic Scales do not operationalize the concept to include the dimension of intent. Consequently it is impossible to distinguish between men's attacks and women's attempts at self-defense; the numbers show equivalent rates of violence by males and females. Statistical analyses, too, are infused with the researchers' values.

The question of which variables to consider and how many controls to introduce are not political decisions. If a result is disturbing to a researcher, he or she may well do more or different analyses. This augmentation is not evidence of dishonesty, but an example of the impossibility of true human objectivity.

The split between subject and object has other implications. We have seen that the separation of knower and known by methodological screens does not eliminate the subjectivity of the researcher. Moreover, this distancing objectifies the people we are studying. This objectification is a crucial problem when we are studying women who have been the objects of violence.

Quantitative methods have a special capacity for dehumanizing the people we study. My research on wife abuse and the status of women was relatively painless for me because the women's suffering had been reduced to a score on an index with an unemotional numerical label. I think the disconnection enabled by numbers and computers is problematic, though I do not go as far as some critics of the whole enterprise. Russell and Rebecca Dobash are the most outspoken critics of mainstream violence research. They have argued that positivism promised "methodological tickets to scientific respectability but delivered intellectual blinkers and mindless adherence to sterile sophistication" (Dobash & Dobash, 1983, p. 263).

In my experience, shifting from statistical analysis to qualitative analysis does not necessarily resolve the problem. Although the personal approach I used in interviewing marital rape survivors clearly reduced the cognitive and affective distance between the survivors and me, it did not free me from the problem of objectification. The raw data of taped interviews undergo several transformations before they are published in articles or books. We edit, revise, and analyze. We forget the individual women after dozens of interviews become case studies to be word processed. The computer allows us to organize and recombine the women's words to make our points. The danger, as we process women's words, is that we no longer hear their voices.

I was acutely struck by how words objectify experience when I was editing the third draft of *License to Rape* (Finkelhor & Yllö, 1985). The copy editor had picked through the book line by line, and I was responding to her queries and making needed changes. In the section where some of the most brutal rapes are described, the editor was concerned that we were being redundant. She wanted me to find different ways of saying "he tried to rip out her vagina." I went to a thesaurus. How about "yank" or "tear"? At that point I recognized the distance between subject and object and the stripping of context, and I realized that avoiding numbers did not avoid the problem. I do not think it is possible to do research and avoid all objectification. As a researcher I am separate from the women whom I interviewed. I did not experience their rapes; I can only write about them. I believe that what is important is not the elimination of objectification (which I see as impossible), but rather a recognition of the problems that it poses.

Coming to this conclusion was difficult because I was moved by the radical critiques of methodology. It is hard to hear that you, as a researcher, are exploiting abused women all over again. However, I am not just a feminist, but a feminist *researcher,* and my commitment to creating knowledge is a strong one. The difficulty is in doing research that is not merely nonexploitive, but directly empowering to women.

In challenging androcentric knowledge, I believe that quantitative studies can and do provide us with valuable knowledge. It is quite possible to recognize the limitations of positivism and quantification, to see oneself as a feminist doing research for women and still conduct large-scale statistical surveys. In fact, given the power of statistical analysis, I would argue that it is our responsibility as feminists to undertake this work. I can think of no better example of feminist quantitative research than Russell's survey on sexual assault (1982, 1984). Her data profoundly question the sexist assumption/theory that rape, both inside and outside the family, is a rare occurrence. She also provides statistical evidence on the impact of rape and shows that marital rape is as traumatic as stranger rape (despite the Rhett and Scarlett stereotype). These are examples of important feminist questions that cannot be answered if we rely only on historical, case study, and interview methodologies.

As Harding (1986) points out, relativist approaches challenge the claim of "scientific objectivity." "But," she questions, "does our recognition of the fact that science has always been a social product—that its projects and claims to knowledge bear the fingerprints of its human producers—require the exaltation of relativist subjectivity on the part of feminism?" (p. 137). Fee (1981) reminds us that if we cannot reject theories on the basis of evidence, then creationism is as valid an explanation as evolution. In the absence of standards for evidence, the decision between patriarchal and feminist explanations of wife abuse would come down to political power (and we know which would win on those terms). Harding

(1986) argues that a leap to relativism is not necessary and that it "misgrasps" feminist critiques. Feminist theory and research regard traditional thought as "subjective in its distortion by androcentrism—a claim that feminists are willing to defend on traditional objectivist grounds" (p. 138).

At the end of this lengthy discussion of critiques and controversies, I do not want to end with merely a simple call for the "triangulation of methods," a strategy entirely consistent with the positivist paradigm despite its usefulness. Instead I hope we can work toward an approach to the study of wife abuse that recognizes and challenges the limits of unexamined positivism and the claims of objectivity. At the same time, however, we need to consider what parts of the scientific method are of value. Fee (1981) argues that the idea of creating knowledge through a constant practical interaction with the world and the expectation that all assumptions and findings will be subjected to critical evaluation are aspects of science to be preserved and defended (p. 383). It is not possible at this point to envision fully the transformation that science—and social science—might undergo in response to feminist and other radical critiques. (A friend once gave me a T-shirt with the words "I dream of feminist science.") Although I am committed to the transformation of science, I believe that transformation occurs in small steps. Such work will require more self-reflection and criticism of our assumptions about knowledge, the issue of objectivity, our relations with activists, and our own politics. In trying to meet these challenges, we can do better, less myopic research on wife abuse.

In my own work, I continue to keep these methodological and political issues in mind. But in practice I cannot focus foremost on them as I gather data, analyze, and write. After all, critiques of epistemology and concerns about the subject/object split are quite abstract. Most of my writing, by contrast, is quite focused and, recently, practice oriented. This is not in contradiction to the concerns I have outlined above. It is just the reality of doing sociological research. So at the same time that I struggle with the tensions between research and activism (being inside and outside my discipline simultaneously), I also shift levels of analysis from the theoretical to the practical. What I have come to see over the years is that there is joy in the struggle. These tensions are not destructive. They are more like counterbalances that keep me in balance and keep my work moving forward. In the following section, I shift from methodological concerns to my most recent project, which takes up a very practical issue: therapeutic responses to domestic violence.

Therapeutic Debates

The therapeutic debates regarding domestic violence are wide ranging, and a full overview of them is beyond the scope of this chapter. I do, however, want to discuss one of the important recent theoretical debates that is closely connected to therapeutic practice. Specifically, in this final section, I focus on my current study: an exploration of family systems theory and conjoint therapy as they pertain to domestic violence. This is a new area for me and one I find very challenging, for the debate revolves around the core feminist theoretical principle that in order to understand the family and the abuse within it, we must take gender and power into account (Yllö & Bograd, 1988). Further, it is a theoretical debate with immediate practical implications for how we treat perpetrators and victims of violence.

Before I discuss the issues posed by family systems theory and therapy, I need to explain my shift in research focus. When I have spoken on this topic, I have been asked more than once, "What is a family sociologist (who is a researcher rather than a clinician) doing in this area?" My interest in treatment approaches to domestic violence was piqued when I spent a sabbatical year at the Family Development Clinic at Boston Children's Hospital. I accepted a fellowship there not in order to be trained clinically, but because of my interest in observing and understanding the clinical world. This interest is part of my wider desire to bring together researchers, activists, and clinicians, feminists and nonfeminists. I believed I needed exposure to the doctors, nurses, and social workers who daily struggle with the ugly realities of family violence.

My year at the clinic was quite valuable, and I became involved in a number of new collaborative projects, including one on family therapy. I learned a great deal about the complex field of family violence. I enjoy the challenges of trying to work at the intersection of academic research, clinical work, and feminist activism. However, as one colleague noted when I made that comment to her: "When you are standing in the middle of an intersection, it's easy to get run over." Fortunately, to date, there have been no collisions, just the ongoing opportunity to experience the "critical confrontations" to which Westkott (1979) referred.

During several clinical interviews at the Family Development Clinic, it became clear that battered women often seek couples' counseling early on in an effort to save their marriages. We got the impression, however, that the violence was not dealt with in conjoint treatment and that sometimes the therapy exacerbated the abuse. From discussion with a feminist social worker on our clinical team, the idea for a research project took form. We decided that a more systematic study of conjoint treatment was in order. Our concern was that key assumptions and practices within family therapy were obscuring violence and endangering battered women. In collaboration with two men who counsel batterers, we embarked on a multiyear study of family therapy as it confronts domestic violence.

As noted family therapist Paul Dell (1989) points out, family therapy has been slow to address violence in the family. Yet there has been increased interest in family therapists and in domestic violence among couples in the last several years, and the debates in the emerging clinical literature indicate that this interest is a major controversy. Beyond the problem that violence is still largely overlooked in therapy is a real question of why it occurs and what to do when it is discovered. In grossly oversimplified terms, the theoretical question is whether domestic violence is a problem of men battering women as a tactic of coercive control, or whether it is a couple problem best understood as a transactional phenomenon.

Let me be clear: I tend to view it more as the former, but I think this dichotomy is far too simplistic. I am struggling to develop a fuller picture of battering—one in which the stark outlines of gender and coercive control are shaded in by insights from more systemic work (in this area the work of Goldner and Penn, 1991, is promising). As one feminist researcher put it, on the one hand we have a political movement in search of a therapeutic practice (E. Stark, personal communication, March 1989). On the other hand we have a therapeutic school struggling to deal with a newly exposed family problem. It seems to me that a dialogue between the different perspectives is absolutely essential if we are to develop better means of addressing violence in families.

In family systems theory and in family therapy, one theme is that the couple and the immediate family are taken as the unit of analysis and treatment. The focus is on this system and the dynamic relationships within it. In challenging the traditional psychotherapeutic focus on an individual patient, family therapy focuses on the family as patient. Therapists concern themselves with the processes within the family boundary; the individual actors within the family and the social and political context of the family are rendered invisible through this lens.

When violence against the wife is ongoing, this focus is especially problematic. The actions of an individual that may be life threatening are dismissed as only "one punctuated sequence" (Lane & Russell, 1987) among many. Further, by choosing to disregard the family as a sociopolitical institution, therapists particularize family problems so that a particular family's dysfunction appears to be located in its own process and structure. As James and McIntyre (1983) point out, family therapists "replicate the very mistake they accuse individual therapists of making: they approach the problem as if the nuclear family is 'child' to the wider society 'parent,' and insist on seeing the 'child' out of the family context" (p. 123).

The crucial theoretical point is that the sociohistorical context of contemporary families cannot be ignored if we are to make sense of any gender relationships within them. Our families are the legacy of the "familia," Latin for the totality of women, children, and slaves owned by a man. Although legal ownership of a woman is no longer an issue (at least in this culture), her subordination to her husband is. The sexual division of labor in families is alive and well despite some increased "help" by husbands. Women still earn about $0.70 for every $1.00 that men earn, so their freedom to choose alternatives to marriage is limited. None of this is news; yet much of family therapy proceeds as if these facts were irrelevant to understanding what goes on in a given family.

The second important theme in much of family systems theory and practice is the neutrality of the therapist. Although neutrality has much to recommend it in general family treatment, Dan Willbach writes in an article on ethics and family therapy, "It is important to realize that neutrality is a technique and not a goal" (1989, p. 43). He argues that when a therapist discovers violence, the overt goal should become its cessation. Further, he maintains that neutrality should not be used in these cases, but rather the therapist should use his or her ethical judgment in identifying individual responsibility for the violence (p. 44).

The notion of individual responsibility for violence goes against the grain of systemic family therapy. As Lane and Russell (1987) indicate, each person's view is regarded as valid. Moreover, each view of reality is seen as personally constructed. As Searight and Openlander (1987) describe the "new epistemology" or constructivist perspective, "one's view of reality is always qualified; each person's central nervous system computes a unique and subjectively held reality" (p. 55).

Although I agree that individual views of reality are constructed, I would argue that they are *socially*, as well as *personally*, constructed. Numerous feminist critics (Bograd, 1984; James & McIntyre, 1983; Taggart, 1985; Willbach, 1989) have pointed out that worldviews are not constructed in isolation. They are patterned along key social factors such as gender, age, race, ethnicity, and social class. The cultural construction of worldviews is a particularly salient point when we are concerned with relations between men and women in families. It is difficult to think of a relationship that carries more baggage filled with sexist stereotypes.

When a batterer says he hit his wife because she undermined him by going out and getting a job, should we simply accept this as a valid personal worldview? Should the problem then be identified as that of an "overadequate" wife (Bograd, 1984)? If he says he knocked her down because he cannot stand her nagging, do we "punctuate the sequence" as verbal aggression causing physical aggression—another example of "mutual circular process"? Does this "punctuation" blame the victim?

Dell takes up the issue of mutual circular process in an important article entitled "Violence and the Systemic View: The Problem of Power" (1989). He draws our attention to Bateson's retraction of the victim-victimizer concept of the double-bind because it was an inaccurate *lineal* portrayal of a *mutual-circular* interactional process. "With this retraction," writes Dell, "the lineal violence of families was effectively swept under the rug for family therapists for about 25 years" (p. 2).

Willbach (1989), like Dell, maintains that violence must be seen as lineal. He writes:

> The victim in some important sense cannot choose to react to an act of violence. Physical injury occurs to the victim according to invariant laws of physics. If you get punched in the nose hard enough, your nose breaks, no matter what you would like your reaction to be. (p. 45)

Willbach suggests that idealist perspectives that focus on people's beliefs and worldviews are seductive for therapists because they offer more hope for creating change. He continues:

> If the problem is one of "world view" instead of power structure, then all we have to do is change people's minds instead of grappling with some of the bases for victimizers' domination in the material realm, such as the control of economic resources or the use of violence. (p. 45)

It is clear from this brief review of family systems thinking that we are quite critical of current practice in the field. Instead of simply offering a feminist rebuttal to their approach, we wanted to go further. We thought we needed a deeper, empirical assessment of what was going on—for our own understanding and to convince others of our views.

We have just completed the second wave of a panel study of marriage and family therapists. In 1989 and again in 1992 we surveyed a representative sample of members of the American Association of Marriage and Family Therapists. We also are interviewing former battered women, former batterers, and therapists for a more qualitative picture of current practice.

The longitudinal study of marriage and family therapists was designed to assess their level of awareness of domestic violence and to explore their understanding of it. We were disturbed to discover that in our first wave survey, nearly two thirds of the respondents indicated that marital violence was *not* a significant problem in their practice. The remaining one third indicated they actually treated few cases. These data alone suggest a serious problem within the field. Because of the theoretical assumptions of systemic thinking, many therapists are not "seeing" battered women even when the women are in the therapists' offices. If therapists do not recognize the severity and prevalence of domestic violence and ask about it directly, they miss it, and the victims are the losers in the therapeutic transaction.

Although we have not fully analyzed our data or completed our written work, we already are embroiled in difficult debates. In my observation these debates are even more intense and divisive than those between mainstream researchers and activists. Feminist challenges to marital and family therapy have been met with rage and outrage at major meetings (see Sprenkle, 1992). On the one hand, feminists have been labeled "fundamentalists" (Erickson, 1992) whose very critique is abusive. On the other hand, feminists have used disturbing metaphors to describe family therapists and accused the field of colluding with male violence by diffusing responsibility for violent acts (Avis, 1992) and by failing to recognize and assist abused women when they appear in therapy with their husbands (Kaufman, 1992).

Although it may be difficult to understand the anger, turmoil, and tension generated by a challenge to rethink the way therapy is done, it is important to remember that the charge that a form of therapy actually may be harmful is more threatening than challenging researchers in the same way. After all, the therapist's prime commitment is to help and heal in a way that the researcher's commitment is not. In addition, the field of family therapy, with its commitment to systemic, nonlinear analysis, has long prided itself on being the progressive challenge to psychoanalysis and individual treatment models. To now be described as continuing treatment inadequacies rather than as eliminating them strikes at the heart of family therapy's sense of itself.

I think the theoretical debates around systemic and feminist conceptualizations of domestic violence will continue to grow in the next several years as more and more family therapists begin to deal with domestic violence. In contributing to this debate, my hope is to learn from clinicians, to challenge assumptions and practices I see as dangerous, and to move toward a fuller understanding of domestic violence and the means by which we can end it. As with earlier debates between mainstream researchers and feminists, the current controversies can be productive if we do not allow ourselves to become too polarized by them.

Conclusions

In reflecting on the development of my research and thinking as a feminist in family studies, I return again and again to Westkott's (1979) point that we, as critics, oppose ourselves. I can get as carried away as the next academic by abstract discussions of epistemology, methodology, social structure, and "mutual-circular process." However, my scholarly voice is challenged continually by my activist voice, which asks, So what? How does this apply to real women's lives? As we debate theory and method, millions of women are being battered, and many are being murdered by their intimate partners. Although this opposition of voices and the tension it creates is often problematic, I find it an important source of insight and energy. It has fueled my work since graduate school and, so far, it shows no signs of diminishing.

References

Avis, J. M. (1992). Where are all the family therapists? Abuse and violence within families and family therapy's response. *Journal of Marital and Family Therapy, 18*(3), 225-232.

Bograd, M. (1984). Family systems approaches to wife battering: A feminist critique. *American Journal of Orthopsychiatry, 54,* 558-568.

Clark, K. (1964). *The dark ghetto.* New York: Harper & Row.

Cook, J. A., & Fonow, M. M. (1990). Knowledge and women's interests: Issues of epistemology and methodology in feminist sociological research. In J. M. Nielson (Ed.), *Feminist research methods* (pp. 69-93). Boulder, CO: Westview.

DeKeseredy, W., & Hinch, R. (1991). *Woman abuse: A sociological perspective.* Toronto: Thompson Educational Services.

Dell, P. (1989). Violence and the systemic view: The problem of power. *Family Process, 28,* 1-14.

Dobash, R. E., & Dobash, R. P. (1983). The context-specific approach. In D. Finkelhor, R. Gelles, G. T. Hotaling, & M. Strauss (Eds.), *The dark side of families: Current family violence research* (pp. 261-276). Beverly Hills, CA: Sage.

Dobash, R. E., Dobash, R. P., Wilson, M., & Daly, M. (1992). The myth of sexual symmetry in marital violence. *Journal of Social Problems, 3,* 70-91.

Erickson, B. M. (1992). Feminist fundamentalism: Reactions to Avis, Kaufman, and Bograd. *Journal of Marital and Family Therapy, 18*(3), 263-267.

Fee, F. (1981). Is feminism a threat to scientific objectivity? *International Journal of Women's Studies, 4,* 378-392.

Feyerabend, P. K. (1978). From incompetent professionalism to professionalized incompetence. *Philosophy of the Social Sciences, 8,* 37-53.

Finkelhor, D., with G. Hotaling & K. Yllö. (1988). *Stopping family violence: A research agenda for the coming decade.* Newbury Park, CA: Sage.

Finkelhor, D., & Yllö, K. (1985). *License to rape: Sexual abuse of wives.* New York: Free Press.

Gelles, R., & Straus, M. A. (1979). Determinants of violence in the family: Toward a theoretical integration. In W. Burr et al. (Eds.), *Contemporary theories about the family* (Vol. 1, pp. 549-591). New York: Free Press.

Gelles, R., & Straus, M. A. (1986). Societal change and change in family violence as revealed by two national surveys. *Journal of Marriage and the Family, 48,* 465-479.

Goldner, V., & Penn, P. (1991). Love and violence: Gender paradoxes in volatile attachments. *Family Process, 29,* 343-364.

Greer, G. (1972). *The female eunuch.* New York: Bantam.

Harding, S. (1986). *The science question in feminism.* Ithaca, NY: Cornell University Press.

Hilberman, E. (1980). Overview: The wife-beater's wife reconsidered. *American Journal of Psychiatry, 137,* 1336-1347.

James, K., & McIntyre, D. (1983). The reproduction of families: The social role of family therapy. *Journal of Marriage and Family Therapy, 9,* 119-129.

Kaufman, G. (1992). The mysterious disappearance of battered women in family therapists' offices: Male privilege colluding with male violence. *Journal of Marital and Family Therapy, 18*(3), 233-243.

Keller, E. F. (1978). Gender and science. *Psychoanalysis and Contemporary Thought, 1,* 409-433.

Lane, G., & Russell, T. (1987). Neutrality vs. social control: A systemic approach to violent couples. *Family Therapy Networker, 11,* 52-59.

Morgan, R. (1970). *Sisterhood is powerful.* New York: Random House.

Reinharz, S. (1992). *Feminist methods in social research.* New York: Oxford University Press.

Russell, D. (1982). *Rape in marriage.* New York: Macmillan.

Russell, D. (1984). *Sexual exploitation.* Newbury Park, CA: Sage.

Saunders, D. G. (1988). Wife abuse, husband abuse, or mutual combat? In *Feminist perspectives on wife abuse* (pp. 90-113). Newbury Park, CA: Sage.

Searight, H. R., & Openlander, P. (1987). The new epistemology: Clarification and clinical application. *Journal of Strategic and Systemic Therapies, 6,* 52-66.

Sprenkle, D. H. (Ed.). (1992). Violence: The dark side of the family [Special section]. *Journal of Marital and Family Therapy, 18*(3).

Steinmetz, S. (1977-1978). The battered husband syndrome. *Victimology, 2,* 499-509.

Straus, M. A. (1974). Leveling civility and violence in the family. *Journal of Marriage and the Family, 36,* 13-29.

Straus, M. A. (1980). Sexual inequality and wife-beating. In M. A. Straus & G. Hotaling (Eds.), *The social causes of husband-wife violence* (pp. 86-93). Minneapolis: University of Minnesota Press.

Straus, M. A., Gelles, R., & Steinmetz, S. (1980). *Behind closed doors: Violence in the American family.* Garden City, NY: Doubleday.

Taggart, M. (1985). The feminist critique in epistemological perspective: Questions of context in family therapy. *Journal of Marriage and Family Therapy, 11,* 113-126.

Westkott, M. (1979). Feminist criticism of the social sciences. *Harvard Educational Review, 49,* 422-430.

Willbach, D. (1989). Ethics and family therapy: The case management of family violence. *Journal of Marriage and Family Therapy, 15,* 43-52.

Yllö, K. (1983). Sexual equality and violence against wives in American states. *Journal of Comparative Family Studies, 1,* 67-86.

Yllö, K. (1984a). The impact of structural inequality and sexist family norms on rates of wife-beating. *Journal of International and Comparative Social Welfare, 1,* 1-29.

Yllö, K. (1984b). The status of women, marital equality, and violence against wives: A contextual analysis. *Journal of Family Issues, 3,* 307-320.

Yllö, K., & Bograd, M. (Eds.). (1988). *Feminist perspectives on wife abuse.* Newbury Park, CA: Sage.

11

Women Who Use Aggression
in Close Relationships

BETH C. EMERY
SALLY A. LLOYD

Feminist perspectives on wife abuse have appeared in the literature since the problem of battering first was identified. Feminists brought the issue to the forefront of the national agenda in the late 1970s and worked tirelessly as advocates for battered women in the shelter movement (Yllö, 1988). Despite the fact that feminists initiated inquiry into the problem, the majority of research conducted on battered women during the last 20 years has a decidedly empiricist and nonfeminist or even antifeminist flavor.

As a result of the different theoretical perspectives taken on the examination of wife abuse, several controversies have arisen in the literature. Perhaps the most visible of these controversies has been the view that women are just as violent as men and that a "battered husband syndrome" exists. Some scholars argue that in terms of acts of aggression, women perform as many as, or more, acts of physical aggression against their male partners than vice versa (McNeely & Robinson-Simpson, 1987; Steinmetz & Lucca, 1988). These scholars are criticized for ignoring issues of context, injury, control, and women's lack of power relative to men (Bograd, 1990; Saunders, 1988a). As feminists we were intrigued by this controversy and quickly became aware that the issue could be framed differently—moving from the issue of whether women can be labeled as "equally violent" as men to the point of asking women why they used aggression in intimate relationships. In an effort to move from a comparison of men and women to understanding women, we embarked on a qualitative study of why women hit in dating relationships.

When asked to contribute a chapter to this volume, we were excited by the unique opportunity to describe our development as feminist researchers and the pathway that our first explicitly feminist research project has taken. Indeed, as we have presented this work at conferences and to journal editors, we have ail too often been encouraged to downplay the explicitly feminist aspect of the work and to force our qualitative presentation of results into traditional statistical models. In this chapter we discuss not only our research project on the question of why women hit in dating relationships but also our personal journeys as we attempt to integrate feminist principles into our work.

A recent article by Linda Thompson (1992) provides an excellent framework for this personal and project autobiography. Thompson discusses feminist research methods for family studies, outlining three fundamental aspects of research inquiry: agenda, epistemology, and ethics. We discuss each of these aspects in light of the feminist literature and subsequent implications for the development of a feminist methodology that is used as an organizing framework for our chapter.

A Feminist Agenda

One's agenda is a fundamental consideration of feminist methodology. The selection of topic is considered crucial in defining research as feminist (Peplau & Conrad, 1989; Stanley & Wise, 1990). Research can be either on or for women, with the former focus to document and adjust for sexism, and the latter striving to empower women (Thompson, 1992). Later in this section we address how the development of our research dovetails with two components of Thompson's (1992) definition of a feminist research agenda for women—research that connects women's experiences to the larger social context and that challenges the formulation of prevailing questions and theories about the experiences of women. First, however, we digress into an account of how we have evolved toward feminist research from decidedly traditional training in the social sciences. Thus this portion of our description of our feminist agenda is decidedly personal.

Our Personal Journeys

Kersti Yllö (1988), in describing the methodological debates in research on wife abuse, focuses on "women scholars who found themselves at odds with their own training" (p. 36). We both believe that this statement eloquently captures a critical juncture in our development as feminist researchers: the experience of dissonance wherein methodologies, strict reliance on quantification, the development of objectivity, and one's clear understanding of what is scientific evidence are questioned as the "best" scientific method. The two of us came to this point of questioning by different routes. To both of us the most important issue is that we do collaborate and agree on the feminist perspective that shapes this research. We would be remiss, however, if we did not acknowledge both sets of experiences as they have influenced our personal and professional careers.

For Beth Emery, the path was one of a convergence of personal values with professional development that was catalyzed by support from feminist colleagues. She recounts: I did not fully realize the extent to which a feminist perspective influenced my teaching and research until we began this study. In retrospect I was raised both personally and professionally as a feminist. I cannot remember a specific time when I became a feminist, but rather experienced a gradual awareness of my feminist stance in response to challenges to my beliefs about and commitment to women's issues and experiences. Through colleagues, friends and readings, I have come to realize this is not an uncommon process. I have struggled with a definition of feminism for many years and have come to regard this as a very personal journey of consciousness and contradictions centering on a variety of women's issues (gender equity and power; women's value and experiences, empowerment, and advocacy). It is value laden and emotional.

As an example of this evolutionary process, I offer the following experience. Recently a woman whom I did not know well asked whether I was a feminist. I hesitated and then said, "Yes. What woman can afford not to be?" She looked thoughtful and then launched into her topic. For days my initial reaction of discomfort and amusement puzzled me until I realized that *no one* has ever asked me that question before! My colleagues' and friends' understanding and acceptance of me and my beliefs have occurred over time, as has my development as a feminist. Too, I was uncomfortable with a simple yes because it was so completely inadequate. What did she mean by "feminist"? She required simple, categorical information, while I needed a philosophical discussion! This innocent question impressed on me the scope of my own feminist experience, as well as the nearly impossible yet necessary task of consolidating my thoughts on the subject into some sort of coherent and concise response.

My professional training has served to support my feminist development in two ways. First, it is rooted in my home economics background which, compared with the traditional androcentric scientific approach, is an applied discipline—a preventionist approach to the problems and issues that face families and women in their daily lives.[1] Second, I am an educator and approach all tasks from that perspective. In other words, research is a means to an end for me in that the topic and the results must be of benefit for the researched themselves and, I hope, society. If not to improve the human condition, of what use is our research?

My interest in the topic of dating aggression developed in graduate school when working with Sally Lloyd, Rod Cate, June Henton, and Jim Koval, and with ties back to my high school teaching experiences as well. In graduate school I learned the research process and collegiality. In teaching high school I learned concern for the relationships of young adults. As an educator my focus was developing students' potential, yet almost as an aside I came to realize the importance and implications of the dating relationships by which they defined themselves. These relationships were not always positive. One vivid memory is of a 15-year-old student who was physically abused by her boyfriend. She refused to leave him and even defended his actions, as did her friends. At the time I was dumbfounded and outraged. Now I recognize that hers was the first of many experiences I was to hear that contained the common themes of self- and victim-blaming so prevalent in women's stories and experiences. Later, as I began to conduct research, my persistent feeling, due in part to this early experience, was that the numbers we manipulated in order to identify the phenomenon of relationship aggression were a poor and incomplete representation of the haunted eyes of women I had talked with and known. I became uncomfortable with my previous research, as well as with much of what I had been exposed to.

These feelings existed, in part, because I had no vocabulary with which to support or express my uneasiness with not only methodology but also the selection of topics and the exclusion of women's experiences from the data and subsequent interpretations. I have discovered that many share this discontent. For example, Jesse Bernard (1987) speaks of the necessity of paradigm shifts from "social euphemisms," which require or, at best, allow, social scientists to ignore the intensity of human experiences. She purports that a term such as *domestic violence* is too bland to cover the experiences of battered wives and abused children (p. 210). It would seem, then, that an inappropriate vocabulary may be as much a part of the problem as is the lack of vocabulary with which to portray women's experiences and perspectives. The development of an adequate vocabulary is one of the major tasks facing feminists today.

When Sally Lloyd and I decided to approach the issue of women's use of aggression from a qualitative perspective, I was excited. I saw that this perspective was in keeping with my own feminist values regarding the topic, as well as ethically fitting the questions we thought needed answers. I could integrate some of myself into this research and in doing so create a sense of continuity that previously had been missing for me. To me this research decision signified my professional homecoming.

I have learned much since my entry into academe, primarily from other women, not necessarily feminists, and from feminists who are not necessarily women. It has been both exhilarating and painful. From these experiences I have come to realize the enormity of what is to be learned and still to be done. Hence the most important challenge of being a feminist is one's commitment to an ongoing process and to change.

For Sally Lloyd, the path was different; however, similar to Beth's, the role of colleagues in helping formulate a feminist research agenda has been invaluable. She recounts: Throughout undergraduate and graduate school, I was fascinated by mathematics. I was one of only a handful of students who loved statistics and methods courses. I was smugly certain of the intrinsic reliability of the findings of a research project that was methodologically sound and analyzed with sophistication. The ideas that the questions one asks, the chosen method for studying those questions and operationalizing the variables, and the choice of statistical analysis were political and fundamental philosophical issues never entered my head. Although these notions were undoubtedly a part of the research methods courses I took, they were treated with passing notice and went unheeded by one immersed in the power of numbers, facts, and the scientific method.

Thus, after I completed graduate school and embarked on a career in academia, I began with the certainty that I knew how to conduct research the "right" way (oh, the self-righteousness of youth). In graduate school I had become interested in the issue of the abuse of women by their male partners in both marriage and courtship. I was fortunate to be involved with a great team of researchers in two of the earliest studies of courtship aggression (see Cate, Henton, Koval, Christopher, & Lloyd, 1982; Henton, Cate, Koval, Lloyd, & Christopher, 1983). My interest in this topic continued into my academic career. Although I was very much aware of the different approaches to the issues of "courtship/marital violence" and "wife/woman abuse,"—with the former being empiricist, "objective," and a-contextual, and the latter being decidedly feminist and contextual—I strove to remain out of the fray. Frankly, being numbers oriented, I found it difficult to ignore the fact that when queried with scales such as the Conflict Tactics Scale, women reported rates of aggression equal to those of men. Yet at the same time, I also believed that the underlying dynamic behind those numbers was one of male aggression and female victimization. Rather than rethink how I asked the question or my methodology and measurement, I chose to beg the question by downplaying gender differences and relying instead on a rather generic discussion of courtship/marital violence.

Within my academic career, I have maintained a strong emphasis on community service. This service has included several key experiences working with battered women. I assisted battered women in filing protective orders against their abusive spouses, an experience that opened my eyes to the pain of these women's lives and to the nonsupportiveness of the court system. If I, as a well-educated professional, found the experience of going to a judge and asking for his or her signature on an ex parte protective order intimidating, I could only imagine what it must be like for the wife who has been beaten both physically and psychologically. I quickly learned how to work the system: I learned to go first to the judges who understood the problem of wife abuse and who were supportive. I also learned about courage—the courage it takes to leave an abusive situation, knowing that you have nowhere to live, no financial support, and no family to turn to, and full of worry and concern for the well-being of your children. Other community service with sexually abused children as a guardian ad litem and on the Utah Domestic Violence Advisory Council gave me experience with political action on behalf of victimized women and children.

As a result of these experiences and my association with feminist advocates, I became interested in the application of feminism in my teaching, although I did not yet apply it to my research agenda. Topics such as poverty, power and control in relationships, family violence, and wage equity were all enhanced by a feminist perspective. Discussion with colleagues both at my university and at conferences was increasing my awareness of the body of feminist literature that questioned traditional conceptualizations of women's experiences. Having been entirely unexposed to a feminist perspective in graduate school, I found myself 5 or 6 years later seeking out feminist readings that could inform my teaching of courses on marriage and family. This seeking-out process was rather haphazard, as I started out pretty much on my own in schooling myself in feminist literature. Fortunately, at about this time, a feminism and family studies section was formed within the National Council on Family Relations; this section introduced me to a wide variety of colleagues who were addressing similar issues. In addition, my friend Beth Emery provided me with a wealth of feminist readings, for she has always been several years ahead of me in working on her feminist teaching and research agenda.

My feminist reading eventually began to spill over into my research agenda. Primarily I began to see that my attempt to beg the question of men's versus women's rates of aggression was really not possible. At the same time, I experienced a growing discontent with strictly quantitative methods, for I began to view such methods as inadequate to answer the question I most sought to have answered—*why.* I became convinced that letting women speak in their own voices as they describe their experiences could make a major contribution to our understanding of the dynamics of aggression in relationships—namely, to our understanding of the why.

Thus I have been moving from ignoring gender in my work on violence, to acknowledging women's victimization, to devising research studies that are explicitly feminist from their inception. This is an evolutionary process, and one that certainly is not complete; as a result all of my research does not yet reflect a strong feminist perspective. And I still feel very much a neophyte with respect to the literature on feminism and feminist epistemology. The evolution will be a lifelong one, I believe.

We hope the above digression into our personal journeys toward a feminist perspective has been helpful in identifying how we first arrived at a feminist research agenda. Having described our personal journeys toward a generalized feminist agenda, we now turn to a discussion of the specifics of how our work on why women hit reflects the themes of the feminist research agenda identified by Thompson (1992) and how our topic challenges prevailing conceptualizations of the experiences of women.

Placing Women's Use of Aggression
Within a Larger Social Context

About 4 years ago we embarked on our first explicitly feminist research project. We decided to tackle the issue of why women use physical aggression in heterosexual dating relationships from a new perspective: using qualitative methods while employing a feminist perspective to interpret our findings.

We are interested in the issue of women's use of aggression in intimate or dating relationships for several reasons. First, given our basic interest in premarital relationship development and its influence on future relationship patterns, it seemed crucial to understand the use of aggression in dating relationships. Because we know that aggression often predates the marriage ceremony many times, preventing its use before the constraints of children, legal ties, and relationship history come into play may be the most effective method of breaking the cycle of violence.[2]

Second, we had been fascinated by the controversy in the literature over this issue, although it was limited primarily to the marital violence literature. When Suzanne Steinmetz published an article in 1977-1978 on the battered husband syndrome, a controversy that had been brewing for some time erupted into print. This controversy centered around questions concerning women's use of aggression in marriage and other intimate relationships. Researchers quickly were pigeon-holed into one of two extremes of thought. On the one hand were empiricist studies that examined the rates of males' versus females' use of aggression without reference to issues of context, initiation, or self-defense. Studies of premarital and marital violence would note that "women are just as violent as men," with the caveat that women are more likely to be injured and less likely to cause injury (McNeely & Robinson-Simpson, 1987). On the other hand were activists and feminists who decried the use of numbers taken out of context and their potential negative impact on badly needed services for battered women (Breines & Gordon, 1983; Yllö, 1988).

The early stages of this controversy centered on the issue of whether a true "battered husband" *syndrome* existed. Steinmetz (1977-1978) estimated there were 250,000 battered husbands across the United States, a number she thought deserved attention as a social problem. Other authors concluded, however, that the problem of "husband battering" was minuscule, compared with the assault on wives. Analyses of both police records and data from the National Crime Survey revealed that wives are the victims of domestic assault in upwards of 94% of all cases, whereas husbands are victims in fewer than 6% of cases (McLeod, 1984; Pagelow, 1984; Schwartz, 1987). The overall injury ratio remains approximately 1:18 men to women (Schwartz, 1987).

Although the argument over the extent of the battered husband syndrome may have started as an academic issue, the misuse of information on battered husbands hurled the controversy into the political realm. Steinmetz's (1977-1978) estimate of 250,000 battered husbands became inflated by the media to 12 million (Pagelow, 1984). Policy making was affected, in some cases causing the denial/withdrawal of funds to shelters for battered women on the basis of the backlash argument of discrimination against men (Pagelow, 1984; Yllö, 1988).

The battered husband syndrome controversy eventually died down, but the issue of women's use of aggression continued to cause heated debate. Feminists roundly criticized studies that reported incidence rates of women's use of aggression without providing a context for their interpretation (e.g., see McNeely & Robinson-Simpson, 1987; the reactions by Saunders, 1988a; and the letters to the editor by Darling, Gondolf, Jackson, and Singer in the March-April 1988 issue of *Social Work*). Arguments about the relative importance of gender in understanding aggression in close relationships continue to surface (e.g., see Bograd, 1990; McNeely, 1990).

We believe that feminist critiques of the violence literature have made a major contribution to our understanding of aggression in courtship and marriage through their emphasis on gender and context. Neither a man's nor a woman's use of physical aggression in a close relationship can be understood strictly in terms of "numbers" or "rates"; rather, both immediate and distal contexts must be examined. The immediate context includes the other dynamics of the relationship that contribute to the use of aggression, as well as the different motivations and consequences of aggression for men versus women. For example, a male's use of aggression may be only one of many tactics of control of his partner's behavior (Stets, 1988). A woman's use of aggression may not occur until she has experienced repeated aggression from her partner (Bograd, 1990). The motivation of men to use aggression may be to control the actions of the woman (Stets, 1988), whereas women may be motivated to use aggression largely in self-defense (Makepeace, 1986). Men appear to use the most lethal forms of aggression, such as homicide, in the ultimate attempt to control and dominate, whereas women use lethal aggression in an attempt to escape lifetime battering (Bograd, 1990).

At a more distal level of analysis, the patriarchal context within which our relationships are embedded must be acknowledged (Dobash & Dobash, 1979). Lloyd (1991) emphasizes that this context contains different relationship themes for men and for women. For men the theme is one of "control of relationships," a theme that gives them permission to enact that control by almost any means, including aggression. For women the theme is one of "connection and intimacy." This theme encourages them to remain even in relationships that contain highly negative behavior such as physical aggression. Unfortunately this theme all too often encompasses a belief of "relationships at any cost"—and the cost may well exceed psychological and physical injury and result even in death. This distal context is complicated further by the fact that institutions that possibly could intervene in the problem of physical abuse of women are so imbued with the same ideology that they are rendered ineffective at best, and part of the problem at worst (Stark & Flitcraft, 1983).

Due to our awareness of the controversy and argument surrounding women's use of physical aggression, our feminist agenda for the topic of why women hit in dating relationships first began with a desire to place this phenomenon into a larger social context that clearly recognizes gender inequities and male domination both at the proximal and distal levels.

Challenging Current Conceptualizations
of Women's Use of Physical Aggression

Challenging current conceptualizations of women's use of physical aggression in intimate relationships has two aspects. First, the assumption that one can treat the rates of males' and females' use of aggression in relationships as somehow "equal" phenomena must be seriously questioned. Due to context, differences in motivations and dynamics, and differences in power, material resources, and consequences of men's and women's use of aggression, the use of aggression is a different phenomenon for men and for women; however, men and women must be held equally responsible for their decisions to behave aggressively.

Second, part of the reason we have labeled the issue of why women hit as controversial is the fact that raising this issue causes some discomfort among feminists/advocates, ourselves included. This discomfort may stem from the very real fears that women subsequently will be "blamed" for their male partners' use of aggression and from the fact that in an environment of backlash against feminism (Faludi, 1991), women's use of aggression may be used to downplay the problem of battering and to deny services to these women. Thus as researchers we worry that in acknowledging women's use of aggression, the plight of women as victims will be diminished or efforts to change undermined.

These fears are real. Yet we decided to proceed with investigating women's use of aggression because downplaying its incidence or arguing solely that such aggression is merely self-defensive in the face of evidence that notes some aggression is initiated by women will not advance our understanding of why women use aggression. We believe that this type of response is limiting, as well as having a down side, as noted by Breines and Gordon (1983):

> It has been unfortunate that most responses to Steinmetz were limited to denying the findings, challenging the reporting of statistics, and demanding additional contextual factors. They have not questioned the terms of the inquiry. This kind of limited thinking leads to a trap, for it implies that women ought to be and usually are nonviolent, and that this virtue is what entitles them to our sympathy. (pp. 512-513)

Harding (1987b) discusses this issue. She speaks to the limitations of research that focuses primarily on women as victims of male domination and control. Although such studies have forever challenged the public view of women's experiences of violence, rape, incest, and pornography, there are problems with viewing women exclusively as victims:

> Victimologies have their limitations too. They tend to create the false impression that women have *only* been victims, that they have never successfully fought back, that women cannot be effective social agents on behalf of themselves or others. But the work of other feminist scholars and researchers tells us otherwise. Women have always resisted male domination. (p. 5)

We argue that the continued debates about women's use of aggression in intimate relationships will be settled only by refocusing the debate toward an understanding of *why* women hit. The question, What is the *extent* of women's use of aggression? focuses the debate away from understanding the context. And although many feminist researchers already have begun to emphasize the importance of context, we hoped to expand their work by changing the focus of the debate toward an understanding of how a woman's use of physical aggression in a relationship might be understood as a response both to the conditions of her relationship and the conditions of larger society.

This refocusing of the debate has both conceptual and methodological implications, the latter being discussed later in this chapter. Conceptually the fact that women use aggression must be explicitly acknowledged, with the understanding that this fact in no way relieves the male batterer from his responsibility for his aggression or society from its victimization of battered women through lack of responsiveness to their plight. This acknowledgment then allows us to consider whether women's use of aggression is an active response to male domination in the relationship and/or societally. As Harding (1987b) notes, it allows us to see women as responding to male domination, rather than as being strictly passive. Ultimately, however, a reframing of women's use of aggression as an active response to male domination should not be viewed as condoning aggression in males or females or as removing either party's responsibility for choosing to behave aggressively.

Feminist Epistemology

Epistemology is a philosophy of knowledge that examines the nature, origin, limits, and methods of obtaining knowledge. In this section we deal with questions concerning how we come to know what we know. Although there is no one definitive feminist epistemology, we nevertheless attempt to identify concepts essential to the development of our work on why women hit in dating relationships. Borrowing from Thompson's (1992) outline, we include the following issues of interest: combining feminist ideology with empirical science, the connection between researcher and researched, and women as a source of knowledge. We then turn to a brief description of the methodology, analysis, and results of our study of why women hit in dating relationships.

Feminist Ideology and Empirical Science

First, we reiterate that our choice of topic and method of study was an attempt to deal with issues that we strongly believed needed to be addressed. Therefore the traditional tenets of research methods—that of the objective researcher and value-free inquiry—seemed impossible to maintain. We do not advocate, however, overlooking contradictory evidence or discouraging examination or criticism of our findings, for these are the basis of enlightened discourse. But complete objectivity is impossible, as no research can be unaffected by the dynamics of politics, history, culture, or values (Harding, 1991).[3] Our feminist ideology requires that we examine issues within a social and political context, thus rendering objectivity and value-neutrality moot (Stanley & Wise, 1990). In the case of our research, we acknowledge our subjectivity in our politicized interpretation of the results within the overall context of male domination and patriarchy.

With regard to the values of the researcher, many feminists (e.g., Harding, 1987b; Kelly, 1988) speak to the importance of researchers placing themselves within the context of their research. By identifying their inherent subjectivity and making their cultural and experiential biases known, objectivity, rather than objectivism, of the research is increased. We recognize our biases in that we are white, middle-class women—at once part of an oppressed group, yet privileged by our race, class, and education—examining an issue that creates debate within our science and among feminists. Our research is affected by the beliefs and experiences of our culture and gender. Specifically our place within our research comes from a belief in the individual's worth and a theoretical divergence from previous research in the area.

Second, much of the previous research on relationship aggression reveals a lack of sensitivity to women's experiences, although there are notable exceptions. We agree wholeheartedly with Harding (1987b), who asserts that the questions asked or not asked are as crucial as the answers. Even when questions have been asked of women themselves, the answers are put forth on their behalf primarily through androcentric interpretations. An unfortunate example of such interpretation appears in a chapter by Feld and Straus (1990). In their longitudinal study of wife assault in marriage, these authors concluded that their findings suggest "assaults by the wife increase the probability of severe assaults by the husband" (p. 501). Although Feld and Straus (1990) offer several methodological explanations for this finding, they fail to acknowledge that a deeper exploration of why some wives use severe tactics of aggression in their marriages may lead to very different conclusions. The fact that their two time points are separated by 12 months and that they offer no exploration of how the dynamics of the marriage might have changed over this time period is telling in and of itself. Instead the simple explanation that if she behaves aggressively, she will suffer for it later is offered. We believe that an in-depth conversation with some of the women who participated in this longitudinal study may reveal a different explanation for changes in aggression over time. If we want answers to important questions such as why women hit their intimate partners, what better way to find out than simply to ask them?

Surprisingly few research studies have directly asked women to explain their use of physical aggression (Holzworth-Munroe, 1988). Makepeace (1986) provided premarital partners with a list of motives for their use of aggression; women listed self-defense and the intent to harm their partners as the most common motivations. Follingstad, Wright,

Lloyd, and Sebastian (1991) found that women noted (a) to show anger, (b) in retaliation for being hurt emotionally, (c) an inability to express self verbally, (d) getting control over the other person, and (e) protecting oneself as their motivations for using aggression. Saunders's (1988b) study of battered women noted that self-defense and/or fighting back were the primary reasons women gave for their use of aggression. By using a structured approach that constrains the response of the women, however, these researchers have only begun to tap the question of why. We hope to expand their work by identifying the complexity of women's use of physical aggression and capturing the essence of women as active agents in their own lives.

Connection Between Researcher and Researched

How is knowledge generated? We believe it is essential to acknowledge here the synergism created by the understanding of the subject matter and what is learned about the respondents. Be it procedural (e.g., through interviewing and, hence, talking and listening) or personal experience, the researcher develops a link, sometimes an intuitive one, with the researched and the subject matter (Kelly, 1988; Reinharz, 1992). It is through this awareness of both self and knowledge that we come to know the social reality we seek (Thompson, 1992).

Paralleling these ideas, we designed our study by using a modified grounded theory approach (Glaser & Strauss, 1967; Strauss & Corbin, 1990), which stresses theory development from a systematic analysis of the data without a priori hypotheses. We do use feminist theory to direct our examination of the data, hence the term *modified*. In addition, we used open-ended interviews to allow dialogue between researcher and subject that provided a diversity and richness of response. This use enabled us to analyze the data for common themes and new concepts regarding women's use of aggression. And perhaps most importantly, acknowledgment of the connection between researcher and researched allowed us to acknowledge how we were changed and moved by our subjects' willingness to share their stories with us.

Women as a Source of Knowledge

The final epistemological issue regarding our research centers on "women's experience as a source and justification of knowledge" (Thompson, 1992, p. 11). Women and their experiences are of value in and of themselves and as a correction of the historical and conventional view of science that has emphasized primarily the interests and experiences of males. Through our use of interviews, women were allowed to speak in their own voices, which gave them authority based in their own experiences. Each woman was asked how often aggression had occurred and to explain why her partner hit her, why she hit her partner, the dynamics of the aggression in that relationship, and the effects of that aggression on her life. All of the respondents talked at length about their experiences, with very few additional questions or probes from the interviewer. The interviewers did not comment on the content of the interview during the interview process, thereby allowing each respondent to describe her own behavior without undue influence from the interviewer.

Not only are women empowered in this process, but they also provide more realistic accounts of the social problem at hand. The feminist concept of "double vision of reality" (Walker, Martin, & Thompson, 1988) purports that women, conscious of their membership in an oppressed group, have a more accurate and complete view of the world than do men. The powerful—in this case, men—seek to maintain their myopic views of social reality, while the less powerful—women and minorities—have a clearer vision of the world because they see both the dominant and their own, minority perspectives. Such qualitative study of women's use of violence, then, may provide the clearest perspective on the context and dynamics of aggression yet.

Choosing a Method and an Analysis Strategy
for the Study of Why Women Hit

The use of qualitative versus quantitative methods in feminist research can be a controversial issue. It is not our intention to advocate one method as more feminist than the other, because any research can be sexist or feminist regardless of the methodology employed (Peplau & Conrad, 1989). Rather, we would urge that serious thought be given to the suitability of the data collection and the analysis of the research question itself. On the surface this statement may seem trivial, but the conventional view of science, as well as the criteria of many of the prestigious journals in the social sciences, may blind us to the use of anything other than quantitative methods. This prejudice within the academic community is a frustrating force. We have found our use of qualitative methods and feminist theory to be a detriment to publishing our research or obtaining even small faculty grants. Feminist concepts such as the connection between researcher and researched were denigrated, and it even was suggested they be cut from manuscripts to ensure publication. Although editing is a common occurrence, when the foundations and motivation for doing particular research are unacceptable to a reviewer, it becomes a discouraging and frustrating process.

Following the advice of Bograd (1988) and Holzworth-Munroe (1988), we chose to use qualitative, in-depth interviews to help us find answers to the question of why women behave aggressively in dating relationships. We thought such a methodology could provide a rich, diverse source of information and could best answer the question we were investigating. Quantitative methods, such as a checklist of reasons why the woman might have hit her partner, reveal the biases and limitations of the researcher (Holzworth-Munroe, 1988), and not necessarily the experience and knowledge of the subject. In studying the question of women's use of aggression, Holzworth-Munroe (1988) encourages the use of an unsolicited attribution technique to avoid leading the respondent. Although qualitative interviews have limitations of their own (e.g., small sample size, lack of generalizability), they do convey flexibility and acceptance of knowledge through experience.

We interviewed 17 women who responded to a flyer requesting interviews with women who had been involved in abusive dating relationships. The women who volunteered to be interviewed were white, middle-class, predominantly single, and ranged in age from 19 to 28 years. All had been involved in an abusive, heterosexual dating relationship, ranging from 9 months to 4 years duration, with the average being 28 months. Sixteen of these women were no longer in the abusive relationship.

The interviews were tape-recorded and subsequently transcribed for analysis. The process of data coding was based on the qualitative approaches described by Allen (1989), Glaser and Strauss (1967), and Strauss and Corbin (1990). The grounded theory approach involves an open coding procedure (Strauss & Corbin, 1990) that differs significantly from traditional quantitative content analysis procedures. Open coding entails an iterative process of data examination, cross comparison for similarities and differences, and questioning one's assumptions about the phenomenon being studied. The final analysis of the data is limited to those categories "that exist in the actual data collected—not what you think might be out there but haven't come across" (Strauss & Corbin, 1990, p. 112). Furthermore this approach emphasizes the importance of context in analyzing and understanding the data. Thus, unlike content analysis, simple utterances or sentences are not analyzed outside of the broader context of the entire transcript.

The first step of our qualitative analysis was for both of us to scan independently the written transcripts of the interviews, making preliminary notes on the categories present in the data. Second, we compared notations and theme categories, focusing primarily on the similarities and differences we noted among the categories. At this point the process became an iterative one, with each of us comparing, contrasting, and questioning the degree to which category labels reflected what was actually present in the transcripts. Third, categories were refined by making associative connections and collapsing fine-grained categories into broader themes. The final step was to verify the themes by a reexamination of each transcript. Overall, the grounded theory approach to qualitative data analysis entails a constant interplay between proposing and verifying themes in the data. Using a team approach in this analysis necessitates extensive discussion, some debate, and ultimately a shared conceptual analysis (Glaser & Strauss, 1967).

Results of Our Study

We found that 10 of the 17 interviewees had used physical aggression in their relationships. In 9 of the 10 cases, the male partner usually initiated the aggressive incident; the aggression the men perpetrated was both more frequent and more severe than the aggression enacted by the women.

The results of this study lead us to conclude that the motivation underlying women's use of violence is complex. Self-defense is too simplistic an explanation. In reality it is why women do *not* hit that is simple. Of the seven women in this study who did not use violence, one believed there were better ways than violence to control a situation, and the remaining six cited fear as the primary reason they did not use violence. In answer to the question "Why didn't you ever hit [your partner] back?" One woman stated:

> Because I was scared that if I hit him back, he'd hit me three times harder than he did. If he gets into one of those moods, the best thing to do is let him do whatever he wants to and just get away from him.

Another typical response:

I was scared to. I knew it would take a really violent act to take care of him and I wasn't capable of it.

Finally one woman expressed a common feeling:

I wanted to [hit him back] but I was always afraid to . . . He was 6'4", weighed 250 lbs. He was huge.

Although the issue of these women's avoidance of violence seems straightforward enough, the explanation of women's use of violence is a more complicated one. Throughout the interviews two major themes emerged in answer to the question why women hit back. It seemed that women who responded to violence with violence were doing so (a) in an attempt to establish a balance of control in the relationship and (b) out of frustration or anger.

Establishing a Balance of Control in the Relationship

In analyzing the experiences of the women in this study, it became apparent that one theme on why they were violent was an attempt to gain control over the immediate situation and/or some power in their relationship. This theme contains a distinct element of self-defense; however, the women's descriptions of their reasons went beyond the notion of defense to include broader themes such as stopping the abuse, regaining control of the situation, and establishing a balance of power in their lives and relationships. For example, one woman noted that she hit back

to prove to him that he was not going to beat me up, that he was not going to hurt me, because I was going to hurt him right back. To let him know what he was doing to me. . . . It was my way, too, of saying, "Hey, I'm not this little girl you think you're going to control, because I'm not going to let you." And so I'd hit him back, trying to get away from him.

Another woman noted that her violence is a response to her partner's attempts to be the dominant person in the relationship:

I think that he thinks that because he's the guy I should listen and do what he says. Which I don't agree with. Just like the time he thought that it was all right to aggravate me [tease, pinch, hit playfully], and when I told him to quit it, he just wasn't taking me seriously. And he thought that because he was the guy, he should be able to do whatever he wanted to do. . . . I was just trying to pay him back for hitting me.

Although these anecdotes contain some threads of self-defense (e.g., "trying to get him away from me"), the women do not speak in terms of self-defense per se. Rather, their explanations are more complex, containing elements of resistance to being dominated, as well as responding to the violent behavior of the partner. Categorizing these reasons merely as "self-defense" fails to capture the multiple meanings their own violent behavior has for these women. They are reacting to the immediate violent behavior, yet they are responding also to the cumulative conditions of their relationships. These conditions were described with an overall theme of male control—control over friends, appearance, manner, career, and so on:

> He talked down to me a lot. It was like, you know, he wanted me to be the little girl I'd been when he'd started dating me. A little girl that said, "O.K., whatever," and gave in to whatever he said without fighting about it, and who said "O.K., you know everything and I know nothing." . . . He told me I was selfish, stubborn, immature, and I couldn't handle life without him. He wouldn't let me wear skirts, and I had to button everything all the way up . . . I wore my hair a certain way. . . . He was always trying to tell me what to do.

These explanations underscore the feminist view that violence must be understood within the context of power relationships (Breines & Gordon, 1983). In fact, it would seem that the women in this study are suffering from a "double whammy" effect with regard to their own powerlessness. First, men as a class hold power over women (Bograd, 1990; Saunders, 1988b), a fact most females come to recognize by adulthood. Second, in addition to this power differential at the societal level, it has been brought home to these women that they are *again* powerless at the relationship level, as a result of their partners' use of violence toward them. Not only are they members of a powerless social group as compared with males, but now they also have been stripped of their "personal" power and influence within a relationship with specific males. The result is a violent reaction that can be interpreted as an attempt to prevent the partners' domination of them and the relationship.

Frustration and Anger

The second theme recurrent in the interviews dealt with the women's feelings of frustration and anger with their partners and/or the immediate situation. The frustration usually resulted from the partner's lack of responsiveness. A typical example:

I'll say, "We really need to talk about this," and he acts like I'm not there. I'll say, "I can't sleep if we're fighting. We gotta work things out," and he'll say, "I don't care." That's the button that he pushes—"Just do what you want. I don't care." That's the bottom line, and that's when I'll turn his face to me and say, "Look at me and talk," and he just turns away and watches TV and he shuts me out and that's when I hit him and say, "You *will* listen to me, *you will*" because I have been pushed to the point where he will not talk to me and I cannot stand it [the situation] anymore, so I throw things and I beat him, trying to make him stop.

Another woman related:

It wasn't anything really big [what they were arguing over], but he would accuse me of stuff and then I would tell him how ridiculous he was being and he would throw a frying pan at me. . . . And that's when I threw it right back at him. And he was just really hateful and malicious in his verbal stuff, and I'm really sensitive to stuff like that and I couldn't think . . . I couldn't think of what to say back at him and so that's when I would throw back a pencil or something.

The phrase "I couldn't think of what to say back at him" illustrates frustration at a limited repertoire of strategies for responding to verbal and physical abuse.

In other instances anger was the motivating factor for the use of violence. For these women violence seemed a culmination of a series of aggravations and anger. This woman talked about the circumstances under which she hit her boyfriend. This anecdote also contains the element of domination in the attempt to lay blame on the woman:

I was MAD! . . . I would just get so aggravated and frustrated because he would just turn everything around and blame it on me. And I knew it wasn't my fault, but he would just keep on, keep on, and on, and on, and on.

Responding to aggression with aggression may not be the most effective strategy for putting a stop to male aggression (e.g., see Bowker, 1983). In our patriarchal culture, however, women are accorded only a limited repertoire of relational strategies for influencing their partners, most of which place them in a very helpless or passive stance (e.g., crying, hinting, trying to persuade). The fact that some women respond to aggression or frustration with aggression may be indicative of an attempt to break free from the strictures of "how women should behave" and of an attempt to eliminate oppression from their lives.

On the surface it may appear that what we have identified as females' motivations for their use of aggression is exactly the same as that described by males—that is, frustration and regaining some control. Although they may seem similar, these motivations operate in different ways and cannot be isolated or removed from the overall context of the relationship. For example, males who describe establishing control as their reason for behaving aggressively discuss this theme in terms of the need to dominate the female, attempts to coerce the female into adopting the male's rules for the relationship, or fear of the female gaining independence (Dutton, 1988, p. 38). We are not aware of any analyses of males' motivations including a discussion of how gaining control is a *response* to the extreme attempts of their female partners to control their lives. Also a male's use of physical aggression due to anger and frustration stems from the belief that his partner should be doing what she was told and is not, or that these are the only emotions allowed to or appropriate for him (Greenblatt, 1983). Thus men and women may use some of the same terminology in describing why they behave aggressively, but a careful and contextualized analysis reveals very different dynamics.

The limitations of this study should be acknowledged. Our results are not generalizable, due to the small sample size, method of recruitment, and homogeneous nature of the sample. By using volunteers, we interviewed a unique set of women who were comfortable in disclosing their experiences and feelings. They also may have been working through some of the trauma of their abuse. In addition, these interviews represent retrospection about past events. A degree of accuracy is assumed in recalling the events and feelings that surrounded the violence. However, recall may not be perfect and also may be affected by to the degree to which each interviewee has thought about and attempted to make sense of her experiences. In addition, the majority of these women were no longer in the abusive relationship, another fact that may affect perceptions of past events. This study, then, is based on the belief that perceptions of relationship processes are themselves valid and interesting data for scrutiny. Future studies will have to explicate perceptions of aggression in intact relationships.

Feminist Ethics

Many times it is difficult to separate epistemological and ethical issues. Feminist ethics greatly influence one's motivation for and implementation of research, for example. Several concerns must be faced in any type of research. The first concern deals with the purpose of the research, or whose interests are being served—the researcher's (for the betterment of the individual researcher's career or the advancement of an androcentric science) or the subject's (Thompson, 1992). From a feminist perspective, the former is exploitative in nature, while the latter is a form of empowerment.

We hope that traditional science might benefit from this research on why women hit in dating relationships. Scientific work has been greatly shaped by androcentric biases (Harding, 1987a). The questions we asked and the subsequent findings do not support the dominant patriarchal system of control, whether within society or science. Rather, we hope our findings empower women and men who are concerned about and/or involved in dysfunctional, abusive relationships by demystifying women's use of aggression. Many people accept and buy into explanations of relationship aggression that are "victim-blaming" in nature. Victim-blaming is a reality of the powerful because it does not challenge the prevailing patriarchal attitudes that condone the abuse and domination of women, children, and the elderly in this society. We hope this research has taken us one step farther toward changing that reality.

When we ask what effect this research may have on the women who participate in such a study, the diversity of possible answers is unsettling. In keeping with feminism as a social and political movement, our goal is to increase our understanding of women and their use of aggression and, in doing so, to provide information that will help improve the conditions of women at risk for abuse. But is that really what happens, or do we unwittingly create problems for individual women through our inquiry?

It seems that the women themselves gave us a partial answer to this concern when they voluntarily discussed their perceptions of the research with us. For many of the women interviewed, this was the first time they had talked about the abuse with anyone other than a close friend or spouse. The data collection itself was important to them and obviously beneficial in a therapeutic sense. One such woman stated:

> Like I said, I never really thought about it as abuse, until after we came to your class and did this [the interview]. And then I read that article and I said, "Oh, my God!" When I think of abuse, I think of somebody, you know, beating somebody up. Having black eyes and stuff. But it's not.

Most of the women expressed an intense interest in what would happen with the results of our study. They seemed pleased to know that their words and experiences would be published but were adamant in urging the interviewers personally to reach a larger, more immediate audience, to tell others what had happened to them.

Some women expressed an urgency and even a sense of pride in that, by participating in this research, they could help prevent abuse or provide the impetus for another woman to leave an abusive relationship. Their responses typify a relief at finally speaking out, as well as at the onset of an awareness of their own power resulting from their experiences. As such, the implications of their responses to the interview are powerful.

A second concern of importance is that of preserving the authority of the subject. We have discussed the fact that we thought it essential to our understanding of why women hit back to allow them to speak in their own voices, thereby valuing their experiences and perceptions. The subjects retained responsibility for their lives and behaviors through these narratives, rather than being reduced to a noninclusive set of questions and numbers. Also we have included anecdotes from the transcripts that further allow for direct contact with subjects' responses and the opportunity for the reader's own interpretations.

Although we have discussed common themes as they emerged from the data, we hope we have shown the diversity of the women's experiences as well. A relatively homogeneous group ethnically, distinct differences, nonetheless, were found among these women. For example, it is evident that they were at different places in processing their experiences. Some reported feeling stronger and more self-confident for having survived this relationship. Others noted they were wary of involvement with men, for fear that the aggression would recur in a new relationship. Many reported being on the lookout for abusive tendencies in the men they dated, some even to the extent of terminating a relationship at the first sign of domination or control from the partner. Many factors may account for this diversity in response, including maturity, age, and length of time out of the relationship. Unfortunately our data do not allow for extended analysis of these factors.

It became clear to us that the subjects were active participants in the research process. They provided us with direction and impetus for the use of our results. Therefore we must acknowledge the impact this research project has had on us both personally and professionally. We agree with Yllö (1988) that it is difficult to remain untouched by the experiences these women describe. To this day, it is still possible to see the faces of the women we interviewed, hear their words, and, more importantly, feel their pain. Thompson (1992) puts forth the notion of research characterized by compassion. Perhaps we should not strive so hard for emotional distance, but rather embrace the feelings created by this study. It may never be possible to forget these women, and we have come to believe that we should not try. Their collective voice has provided the energy and motivation for our work when it would have been easier to quit or change course. We have grown tremendously in our understanding of our discipline, feminism, and selves. That growth has fostered a sense of responsibility as feminists to continue our inquiries, to rethink our science, and to maintain our commitment to and caring for the individual voice. To do so is to empower not only the women of our research but also others who also are asking difficult questions about close relationships.

We assert that advocacy must become a part of our priorities as professionals. The effort may occur through education, the creation of domestic violence shelters, counseling and support groups, law enforcement, the provision of new insights into families and relationships, or friendship. Whatever it may be, the choice of involvement is part of the feminist experience.

We dedicate this work to the wonderful women who found the courage to speak about the difficult with us. With that act, they changed our lives. We are grateful.

Notes

1. We believe that the origins of the home economics discipline, when placed within the broader social context of the 19th and early 20th centuries, are very much in the feminist tradition. The concerns of the early home economists parallel those of home economists, sociologists, social workers, psychologists, and feminists today. They fought to improve conditions for women and children primarily in the private sector (the family) through work against poverty, poor sanitary conditions, inadequate health care, alcoholism, and abuse. These home economists held the view that women were oppressed and that women and their families were greatly influenced by their environment (patriarchal cultures and society). In addition, they were strong advocates for women in terms of improving and upgrading the traditional work of women through education and the creation of an academic discipline. However, the controversy over the compatibility of feminism and home economics will not be settled in this chapter.

2. Due to the paucity of research on women's use of aggression, we draw on literature that describes both marriage and courtship in building the background for this study.

3. Yllö (1988) makes an interesting comment on the issue of objectivity and research on wife abuse. She notes that most researchers of the topic acknowledge that their research is value laden, to the extent that social justice and an end to violence in the home are the ultimate aims of their work. Oddly enough, however, mainstream researchers who acknowledge such goals still are seen as objective, whereas feminist researchers who acknowledge

their analysis of wife battering in the context of patriarchy are seen as subjective (as having lost their objectivity).

References

Allen, K. R. (1989). *Single women/family ties: Life histories of older women.* Newbury Park, CA: Sage.

Bernard, J. (1987). Re-viewing the impact of women's studies on sociology. In C. Farnham (Ed.), *The impact of feminist research in the academy* (pp. 193-216). Bloomington: Indiana University Press.

Bograd, M. (1988). Feminist perspectives on wife abuse: An introduction. In K. Yllö & M. Bograd (Eds.), *Feminist perspectives on wife abuse* (pp. 11-27). Newbury Park, CA: Sage.

Bograd, M. (1990). Why we need gender to understand human violence. *Journal of Interpersonal Violence, 5,* 132-135.

Bowker, L. H. (1983). *Beating wife beating.* Lexington, MA: Lexington.

Breines, W., & Gordon, L. (1983). The new scholarship on family violence. *Signs, 8,* 491-531.

Cate, R. M., Henton, J. M., Koval, J. E., Christopher, F. S., & Lloyd, S. A. (1982). Premarital abuse: A social psychological perspective. *Journal of Family Issues, 3,* 79-90.

Darling, A. (1988). Letter to the editor. *Social Work, 33,* 189.

Dobash, R. E., & Dobash, R. P. (1979). *Violence against wives: A case against the patriarchy.* New York: Free Press.

Dutton, D. G. (1988). *The domestic assault of women.* Boston: Allyn & Bacon.

Faludi, S. (1991). *Backlash: The undeclared war against American women.* New York: Crown.

Feld, S. L., & Straus, M. A. (1990). Escalation and desistance from wife assault in marriage. In M. A. Straus & R. J. Gelles (Eds.), *Physical violence in American families* (pp. 489-505). New Brunswick, NJ: Transaction Books.

Follingstad, D. R., Wright, S., Lloyd, S., & Sebastian, J. A. (1991). Sex differences in motivations and effects in dating violence. *Family Relations, 40,* 51-57.

Glaser, B. G., & Strauss, A. L. (1967). *The discovery of grounded theory: Strategies for qualitative research.* Hawthorne, NY: Aldine.

Gondolf, E. W. (1988). Letter to the editor. *Social Work, 33,* 190.

Greenblatt, C. S. (1983). A hit is a hit is a hit . . . or is it? Approval and tolerance of the use of physical force by spouses. In D. Finkelhor, R. Gelles, G. T. Hotaling, & M. Straus (Eds.), *The dark side of families: Current family violence research* (pp. 235-260). Beverly Hills, CA: Sage.

Harding, S. (1987a). Epistemological questions. In S. Harding (Ed.), *Feminism and methodology* (pp. 181-190). Bloomington: Indiana University Press.

Harding, S. (1987b). Is there a feminist method? In S. Harding (Ed.), *Feminism and methodology* (pp. 1-14). Bloomington: Indiana University Press.

Harding, S. (1991). *Whose science? Whose knowledge?* Ithaca, NY: Cornell University Press.

Henton, J. M., Cate, R. M., Koval, J. E., Lloyd, S. A., & Christopher, F. S. (1983). Romance and violence in dating relationships. *Journal of Family Issues, 4,* 467-582.

Holzworth-Munroe, A. (1988). Causal attributions in marital violence: Theoretical and methodological issues. *Clinical Psychology Review, 8,* 331-334.

Jackson, J. (1988). Letter to the editor. *Social Work, 33,* 189-190.

Kelly, L. (1988). *Surviving sexual violence.* Minneapolis: University of Minnesota Press.

Lloyd, S. A. (1991). The dark side of courtship. *Family Relations, 40,* 14-20.

Makepeace, J. (1986). Gender differences in courtship violence victimization. *Family Relations, 35,* 383-388.

McLeod, M. (1984). Women against men: An examination of domestic violence based on an analysis of official data and national victimization data. *Justice Quarterly, 1,* 171-194.

McNeely, R. L. (1990). Domestic violence is a human issue. *Journal of Interpersonal Violence, 5,* 129-132.

McNeely, R. L., & Robinson-Simpson, G. (1987). The truth about domestic violence: A falsely framed issue. *Social Work, 32,* 201-205.

Pagelow, M. D. (1984). *Family violence.* New York: Praeger.

Peplau, L. A., & Conrad, E. (1989). Beyond nonsexist research: The perils of feminist methodology in psychology. *Psychology of Women Quarterly, 13,* 379-400.

Reinharz, S. (1992). *Feminist methods in social research.* New York: Oxford University Press.

Saunders, D. G. (1988a). Other "truths" about domestic violence: A reply to McNeely & Robinson-Simpson. *Social Work, 33,* 179-183.

Saunders, D. G. (1988b). Wife abuse, husband abuse, or mutual combat. In K. Yllö & M. Bograd (Eds.), *Feminist perspectives on wife abuse* (pp. 90-113). Newbury Park, CA: Sage.

Schwartz, M. D. (1987). Gender and injury in spousal assault. *Sociological Focus, 20,* 61-75.

Singer, T. L. (1988). Letter to the editor. *Social Work, 33,* 189.

Stanley, L., & Wise, S. (1990). Method, methodology, and epistemology in feminist research processes. In L. Stanley (Ed.), *Feminist praxis* (pp. 20-60). New York: Routledge.

Stark, E., & Flitcraft, A. (1983). What factors shape professional and social responses? Social knowledge, social policy, and the abuse of women: The case against patriarchal benevolence. In D. Finkelhor, R. Gelles, G. T. Hotaling, & M. Straus (Eds.), *The dark side of families: Current family violence research* (pp. 330-348). Beverly Hills, CA: Sage.

Steinmetz, S. (1977-1978). The battered husband syndrome. *Victimology, 2,* 499-509.

Steinmetz, S., & Lucca, J. (1988). Husband battering. In V. Van Hasselt, R. Morrison, A. Bellack, & M. Hersen (Eds.), *Handbook of family violence* (pp. 233-245). New York: Plenum.

Stets, J. E. (1988). *Domestic violence and control.* New York: Springer Verlag.

Strauss, A., & Corbin, J. (1990). *Basics of qualitative research.* Newbury Park, CA: Sage.

Thompson, L. (1992). Feminist methodology for family studies. *Journal of Marriage and the Family, 54,* 3-18.

Walker, A. J., Martin, S. S. K., & Thompson, L. (1988). Feminist programs for families. *Family Relations, 37,* 17-22.

Yllö, K. (1988). Political and methodological debates in wife abuse research. In K. Yllö & M. Bograd (Eds.), *Feminist perspectives on wife abuse* (pp. 28-50). Newbury Park, CA: Sage.

12

Feminist Journeys

Final Reflections

DONNA L. SOLLIE
LEIGH A. LESLIE

This is a book of personal journeys. Mary Catherine Bateson, in her book *Composing a Life* (1989), states that we each have personal narratives that reflect "that act of creation that engages us all—the composition of our lives" (p. 1). We asked the contributors in this book to describe the composition of two aspects of their lives: the interweavings of their personal beliefs as feminists with their professional paths as academics. Their journeys are voyages of discovery, following their own visions and seeking answers to their own questions. These questions often are concerned with essential aspects of women's experiences, including their intimate relationships, and oriented toward enhancing women's lives. The contributors found it difficult to separate their personal convictions about equality and justice from the research they wanted to pursue. Their research journeys, inextricably bound to their personal journeys, reflect these concerns and led them into research that is very clearly *for women*.

For most of the contributors, our request to integrate their personal and professional journeys was an unusual one. Such an approach does not fit with the traditional social scientific model of maintaining distance and objectivity in designing and conducting research projects and focusing on more straightforward, "factual" accounts of specific research studies. Thinking about and describing these journeys was an exhilarating but sometimes frustrating experience for the contributors, and for us, as editors of this book. Going beyond the bounds of the traditional scientific model can be freeing, yet unfamiliar. In the first chapter, we identified a number of issues that face feminist researchers: What does it mean to be a feminist researcher? How should our commitment to improving the status of women influence our empirical work? Can one be both a feminist and an empiricist? Must we discard all of the lessons learned as graduate students and beginning scholars and start over? Are there guidelines or models that would facilitate our evolution as feminist researchers? How do we ascertain whether our work as feminists is "good enough"? Although there are no definitive answers to all of these questions, the journeys portrayed in this book provide an array of responses to the issues that feminist academics in the fields of family and close relationships have faced.

In this chapter we address three issues. The first focuses on the impact that taking a feminist perspective has had on the scholarly pathways of the authors. What sources of inspiration and support guided their work? What obstacles have they faced, and how have they dealt with these obstacles? In what ways did their feminist visions influence their thinking about conceptual and methodological issues? The second issue focuses on the impact of feminist perspectives on our understanding of family and close relationships. How has feminist-inspired research reconfigured our knowledge in substantive areas in the field? What unique insights into the dynamics of interpersonal relationships have been provided by the work of these authors? The third issue is where we go from here. What issues and topics are yet to be explored from a feminist perspective?

Feminist Pathways

Caught Between Two Worlds

As we reflected on the journeys described in this book, three themes emerged in the experience of all these feminist researchers: (a) experiencing tension in the dual worlds of an academic discipline and feminism, (b) struggling over the "right" research methods to use, and (c) contemplating the ethical implications of their work. A striking point voiced by many of the contributors was the dissonance they experienced as their scholarly journeys necessitated balancing between two worlds. This dissonance reflects the theme of opposition and tension identified by Westkott (1979), whose words provided the opening lines for our first chapter. Westkott believes that feminist scholars are both insiders and outsiders and that this personal tension informs their experience and their work. This theme of opposition and tension has been identified by other feminist scholars as well. Cook and Fonow (1990), for example, note the "double vision" or "double consciousness" that is characteristic of being a feminist scholar. Similarly, in Chapter 2, Anne Peplau, a noted social psychologist, emphasizes that feminist social scientists are working at the intersection of two different worlds: the world of their discipline and the world of feminist scholarship. Each world has its own values and conventions, which quite often are discordant. Feminist scholars often find themselves doing a balancing act as they move between these two worlds, and they may feel a sense of being marginalized in both—not totally a part of either one.

In Chapter 10 Kersti Yllö describes this situation as a typical one for women scholars who found themselves at odds with their own training. She writes:

> Family studies (specifically family sociology) is the field in which I am trained and that houses my scholarly work. However, I do not feel that it is my home. My passion (in research and in life) is feminism. When I present or publish my work in family studies, I often think I must proceed carefully, lest my feminist consciousness be seen as just a political bias (as if other perspectives are non-political). In contrast, I feel at home at feminist conferences and with feminist publications. I have more in common with feminist scholars studying a wide array of topics than I do with many family scholars focusing on the same issues of violence by intimates. So although I am in family studies, I am also outside it, and the debates in the area of wife abuse are often a dialogue I carry on with myself. (this volume, p. 214)

Katherine Allen (Chapter 5) uses the image of double vision to describe the experience of living in two worlds. Her experiences as an insider to the academy as a professor, and as an outsider as a woman and a lesbian, fostered a struggle between certain freedoms and restraints. For Allen, her individual experience and her scholarly path are inextricably entwined. She states that "distinguishing between one's personal and professional identity seems dishonest to me now, as if anyone could really believe that the private life of the inquirer does not matter in the conduct of her research" (this volume, p. 114).

Not infrequently, the contributors reflected on a sense of failing to live up to the expectations of these two worlds. Maureen Perry-Jenkins

(Chapter 8) identifies the struggles she has felt between her graduate school training in quantitative research methods and her belief that a more qualitative approach offers insights that cannot be obtained through more traditional methodologies. She often feels caught in the middle, on the one hand worried that she is losing "objectivity" in the research she is doing, while on the other hand concerned about whether she is doing justice to her feminist ideology. Kristine Baber (Chapter 3) identifies similar concerns as she talks about the tensions of being both in a discipline-oriented department and in women's studies. Is she "too feminist" for her department but "not feminist enough" for her women's studies colleagues? Sharon Harley (Chapter 9) writes eloquently of the trepidation experienced by many feminist scholars as they tread the academic waters. She "learned to place a veil of silence over my personal feelings and my humanity in nearly all of my intellectual discourse, especially my written work" (this volume, p. 190). The very real need for acceptance within one's discipline may conflict with feminist convictions, and all too often beginning scholars are placed in the position of having to conform to the positivist tradition in order to survive in the academic arena.

Stephen Marks (Chapter 7) traces a different kind of struggle in being caught between two worlds: his awareness of being a man entering the world of the women he is studying. He poses this question: "Who am I to 'let' them speak?" Marks was aware that the women who were studied originally at the Hawthorne plant in the 1920s sometimes resented the fact that their conversations were being recorded (this volume, p. 161). He wrestled with the ethical dilemma of whether his current analysis of the conversations of these women was creating new invasions.

Thus far, most of the remarks focus on how the disciplinary field, whether family studies, psychology, or history, places constraints on the feminist perspectives of these authors. It is important to acknowledge, however, that the feelings of constraint may come from feminism as well. As Peplau notes, "After 20 years as a feminist academic . . . I am concerned that students and researchers sometimes perceive feminism not as a source of inspiration, but as a set of rules" (this volume, p. 44). Several contributors reflected on this message as they questioned whether their work is "feminist enough." In fact, the struggle sometimes may be more internal than external. Although all of the contributors to this volume identify themselves as feminists, when we contacted them about writing a chapter for this book, many questioned whether their work was appropriate for an edited volume on models of feminist research. Many factors may contribute to such a response. However, we believe our experience as editors in making decisions about including our own work provides one explanation. We had chosen not to include our own work in this volume even though the substantive areas—social support, relationship dynamics, and division of labor—were certainly appropriate. Although very comfortable with our identity as feminists and with acknowledging an activist orientation as teachers and scholars, we, too, would have hesitated if someone had asked us to include our work in a book on feminist research, wondering whether our work lived up to feminist guidelines. Perhaps some of the contributors were plagued similarly by the myth that there is some objective feminist standard to which their work does not measure up. As Westkott (1979) points out, one of the outcomes of being both an insider and an outsider is self-criticism, feeling that we never quite make all of the pieces fit. Whatever the contributing factors, these collective experiences have made us uncomfortably aware of the rigidity that often may be equated with feminist research.

As many of the contributors note, there are no easy answers to the struggle of incorporating feminist perspectives into the more traditional viewpoints and expectations of one's discipline. We believe that the ubiquity of this issue as reflected in the struggles depicted highlights the very real need to value diversity in feminist research and to ensure that these issues are not allowed to inhibit future research. As we continue to work toward incorporating feminism into our understanding of the dynamics of family and close relationships, we need to acknowledge the importance of recognizing not only the diversity of feminist perspectives, but also the multiple paths that scholars may take in incorporating feminist perspectives into their work.

Conquering the Great Qualitative/Quantitative Divide

An ongoing debate among feminist scholars has centered on the correctness of the methodological procedure selected, with the major disagreement being over the appropriateness of qualitative versus quantitative methods. The most poignant example of this is Yllö's experience early in her research career. Yllö's study on how women's status in society affects levels of violence within the family relied on census and other secondary data to construct a Status of Women Index. She submitted a manuscript based on this study to a well-respected feminist journal, where it was rejected because the methodology was "inherently patriarchal." According to the editor, quantitative studies could contribute no feminist insights. Although it is likely that such an event would not occur today, feminist researchers still grapple with questions about the appropriateness of the methodology they select.

Peplau states that feminism urges us to be critical of traditional theories and research methods, but she emphasizes that it should not dictate "proper" thinking or methods. In an earlier paper (Peplau & Conrad, 1989), she argued that all methods, both qualitative and quantitative, are potentially appropriate for feminist research. In this volume, she notes that the unproductive feminist debate over methods appears to be ending and that a consensus appears to be emerging that feminists should encourage the widest possible variety of research methods. Perhaps Peplau is correct about the debate waning among feminist scholars, but most of the contributors still struggle with the unwritten standard within the family studies discipline that views quantitative methods as more stringent and rational and more highly regarded.

Therefore, as most of the contributors in this volume embarked on their research journeys, they found themselves at some point facing the issue of qualitative versus quantitative methods. After years of intensive training with an emphasis on quantitative approaches, a reliance on quantification, and the requirement of objectivity, feminist scholars find themselves grappling with the sometimes unsettling question of whether this approach can address adequately women's experiences. At the same time, they are facing the very real issue of survival in an academic world that values "hard science." Sally Lloyd (Chapter 11) reflects on how her quantitative training and love of statistics and methods courses led to smugness about the "soundness" of the scientific approach. She never thought about the political and philosophical implications of choice of method; rather, she believed wholeheartedly in the "right" way. For much of her research career, then, she did research the right way and published in respected journals in the field. Through her own activism with abused women and her exposure to feminist readings, she began to question her research agenda and became convinced that qualitative methods that would allow women to speak in their own voices were critical for understanding the dynamics of aggression in relationships. From a somewhat different perspective, Harley depicts her movement toward accepting the validity of oral interviews and life histories as ways of understanding the work lives of African American women. She has moved from traditional historical methodologies that emphasize manuscript and textual analysis, to examining African American women's material culture, literary and nonliterary texts, and "good talk." This transition, however, was not an easy one, as the discipline of history traditionally has had fairly rigid expectations about acceptable sources of information.

As noted above, most of the contributors have used both qualitative and quantitative methods, although the tendency is to rely mainly on quantitative approaches and to incorporate some elements of qualitative approaches into their dominant research focus. Although the limits of quantitative methods are well articulated in the feminist literature, several contributors reflect on how using both approaches enabled them to see strengths and weaknesses of each.

Marks notes that traditional surveys do not allow us to "hear women's voices" because researchers supply the focus, topics, languages, and choices. In contrast, qualitative data such as that from the women in the Hawthorne study allow the researcher "to participate in their constant dramas, their continual flow of humor, their stories, their worries, their frivolity, their omnipresent planning for the next grand event, and above all, their intimacy" (this volume, pp. 159-160). Such data allowed him to explore coworker interaction processes in much greater depth and to come closer to the actual experiences of these coworkers. The capacity to generalize to other groups of coworkers, however, is lost.

For Allen, qualitative methods hold the appeal of providing "the opportunity to be an active participant in the research process without assuming the illusion of objectivity that undergirds the positivist traditions" (this volume, p. 105). And although qualitative methods allow us to hear more fully the voices of research participants, Allen points out that qualitative approaches can be subject to the same limitations as quantitative approaches. In this volume she provides a reflection on how our unquestioning adherence to research guidelines may prevent us from fully understanding the dynamics of the phenomena we are studying, even when the methods used are qualitative. For example, she notes that she now is able to question the neat transitions she made from theory to data and back to theory. She also notes the critical importance of recognizing issues or questions that are avoided, either because as researchers we simply do not think to ask about them or because they make us uncomfortable. The end result is a "hygienic" product that ignores touchy subjects and inconsistencies in the data.

A number of writers have emphasized that we should be more inclusive in our views about research methodologies—that how we know what we know is more important than methodology. Linda Thompson advocates such an inclusive approach to methods, in addition to questioning the "authority and glorification of quantitative methods" (Thompson, 1992, p. 3). In her article on feminist methodology and family studies, she emphasizes the importance of moving beyond a debate on methodology. She argues that the more important aspects of research methodology encompass three broad areas: (a) agenda, or the focus of our work, (b) epistemology, or how we know what we know, and (c) ethics, or how subjects are viewed and treated.

Even though much of the feminist literature has called for a move beyond such debates over what constitutes feminist research, the fact that so many of the contributors still are grappling with issues related to defining feminist research and defending their choices of methods indicates that these issues are not yet resolved. We hope these debates over methodology will wane and that greater attention will be directed toward what we know about women's lives and about close relationships.

Feminist Ethics

In addition to grappling with methodological issues, a number of the contributors describe their efforts to deal with ethical issues in the research process. According to Thompson (1992), feminist scholars face two prevailing ethical concerns. The first of these centers on the impact of the research process on the respondents and others who may be involved in the project; the second focuses on the objectification of respondents. These issues, as well as others, were of concern to the contributors as they designed and implemented their research projects.

For example, Alexis Walker (Chapter 4) was concerned about breaking down the hierarchies in the research process and involving graduate students and members of the research staff more fully in the research process. She faced the issues of power hierarchies between faculty members and graduate students, authorship, and the extent of investigator involvement with research participants. Peplau, like Walker, emphasizes the importance of graduate student involvement in all aspects of the research process, particularly in conceptualizing the focus of the study and dealing with the political issues that may surround the choice of research topics.

Of overriding concern to most of the contributors was the ethical issue of treating respondents with respect. In her research on lesbian relationships, Peplau became actively involved in recruiting participants. She met with them personally to explain the focus of the study and potential benefits of participating in the research process and to address their concerns about how lesbians typically were treated in the psychological literature. Walker, too, was actively involved with research participants. Rather than relegate all of the data collection to graduate assistants, Walker interviewed many of the participants in her project, coming to know several of them quite well during the process. An additional benefit of talking with the respondents was the realization that the interview schedule did not adequately capture the richness of the mother-daughter relationship. The "discovery" that care-receiving mothers were active relationship participants would not have occurred if Walker had not conducted interviews herself. As she notes, the insights she gained from her involvement in the interview process reflect the benefits of the feminist process.

Allen and Marks, too, addressed the issue of how respondents are treated, emphasizing the importance of nonoppressive research that empowers, not exploits, women. Allen writes movingly of the importance of "not pushing respondents to tell more or probe in ways that are not exquisitely close to their own words" (this volume, p. 107). Yet she notes that researchers also can silence respondents by not taking proactive approaches in asking about subjects that may be touchy. Marks emphasizes the importance of (unconditionally) caring about participants as a way of increasing the likelihood that we will understand them more completely.

Another ethical dilemma faced by contributors was the question of how the data would be used and interpreted and by whom. Peplau emphasizes that serious attention was given to the choice of publication outlets for her research on gay and lesbian relationships. She and her colleagues realized the importance of not publishing their research on gay and lesbian relationships in sexuality journals in order to avoid presenting these relationships solely in the context of their sexual components. Seeking other publication outlets leads to the recognition that, as for heterosexuals, sexuality is only one component of intimate relationships. Yllö dealt with a similar dilemma when looking for funding for her study of marital rape. Although Playboy Press offered to fund this research, there were clear ethical issues in having research on violence against women supported by a foundation whose philosophy objectified women. Beth Emery and Sally Lloyd (Chapter 11) questioned whether their research on why women hit could potentially be taken out of context and used in ways that would misrepresent female violence.

Up to this point our discussion has centered on the impact that taking a feminist perspective has had on the scholarly pathways of the contributors. Several themes emerged in the descriptions of these research journeys: feeling caught between feminist approaches and more traditional disciplinary approaches to studying families and close relationships, grappling with issues relating to the use of qualitative or quantitative methodologies, and awareness of the importance of recognizing and sensitively addressing ethical issues in the process of doing research on women's lives. Next we examine the impact that the choices these researchers made have had on our understanding of families and close relationships.

Feminist Perspectives on Close Relationships

What do the feminist research journeys detailed in this book tell us about women's and men's lives and relationships? What do we know that we did not know before or would not have known without feminist research questions and perspectives? Certainly as a result of the research conducted by the contributors, we know more about women—about their experiences, their relationships, and the difficulties they face. And this knowledge is rich because it comes from listening to women in more direct ways and from asking questions that had been largely ignored or previously overlooked. We also know more about the central roles that both autonomy and connection play in their lives. We know more about the diversity of pathways and lifestyles that women's lives follow, and the dynamic of relationships that influence men's and women's lives.

The chapters in this book reflect three major themes in relationships, and in women's lives in particular: intimacy, work, and violence. The separation of these themes into three distinct parts is somewhat artificial because these themes often are interwoven in women's lives. Similarly they are interwoven in much of the work presented in this volume. For clarity, however, we grouped chapters by the primary theme addressed by contributors, recognizing that often elements of the other themes were incorporated into the work of these authors.

Intimacy in Close Relationships

The chapters in Part 1 of this book focus on the experiences of intimacy in close relationships. In these chapters we see an emphasis placed on the importance of intimacy experienced in a diversity of relationships. Within the field of close relationships, most research on intimacy focuses on male-female relationships, with a preponderance of this research focused on young adult relationships. In general, then, this body of research has tended toward heterosexist bias, as well as age bias. As the topics explored in this part indicate, however, intimacy is an important element of other types of relationships, including same-sex love relationships, mother-daughter relationships, friendships, and coworker relationships. Intimacy may appear at unexpected times in the life course, such as in the relationships of single older women, and may change over the life course.

The research described in Chapter 2, by Peplau, focuses on romantic relationships, both heterosexual and homosexual, in addition to delineating changes in relationships over time. Peplau's work spans the longest time frame and thus provides an excellent example of how feminist perspectives have changed. Her earliest research project, the well-known Boston Couples Study that she and her colleagues conducted in the 1970s, had a major influence on views about appropriate roles in dating relationships. By examining the kinds of issues that couples were facing during a time of societal change, Peplau and her colleagues acknowledged the impact of societal expectations and larger cultural constraints on issues within intimate relationships. And by moving beyond the traditional research format of relying on one partner to provide information about an intimate relationship to seeking information from both members of the dating couples, these researchers highlighted the importance of using both men's and women's experiences to understand intimate relationships. Their focus on attitudes about male-female sex roles, cultural stereotypes about love and self-disclosure, power, sexuality, and intellectual competition offered an in-depth look at the dynamics influencing dating relationships. This study, which is a seminal work in the field of close relationships, still is used frequently to describe patterns of interaction in dating relationships.

Peplau's research on lesbian relationships was directed toward countering the stereotype that lesbians have difficulty establishing stable and satisfying relationships, as well as acknowledging the diversity of these relationships. Historically the focus of research on homosexuality had been on gay men, with an emphasis on etiology and personal adjustment. As Peplau notes, she and her colleagues wanted to explore different aspects of lesbian relationships. In their initial research, they consciously avoided comparing lesbian relationships to heterosexual relationships. By examining various dimensions that characterize intimate relationships, such as attachment and autonomy, and moving away from a focus on the sexual dimension of the relationships, Peplau's research challenges us to rethink our assumptions about lesbian relationships and about "typical" family relationships.

An important dimension of many intimate relationships is sexuality. A common theme unifying Baber's research on various dimensions of female sexuality centers around agency and control. Her early research on factors influencing the decision-making process about childbearing resulted from an interest in what influenced women to resist the normative expectations of motherhood. Results from her research indicated that women who have delayed childbearing are quite conscious of the very real impact of motherhood on other life choices and take active steps to control their reproductive lives. Interestingly, younger women seemed to have idealistic beliefs about their abilities to balance having children and maintaining demanding careers, with most expecting that their partner will assume equal responsibility for child care and housework. As Baber notes, however, these young women may underestimate the power of social norms and gender arrangements that may present obstacles to their plans.

Baber's more recent research program of research on women's constructions of their sexuality and concerns about reproductive issues focuses on how women think about and experience their sexuality. By providing a format in which young women are encouraged to talk about their experiences, share information, and discuss the influence of societal norms and messages on female sexuality, these young women's sexual experiences and views are validated. Additionally, as Baber notes, the group setting, combined with educational materials, should result in these young women making "assertive, responsible, and self-aware decisions about their sexual and reproductive lives" (this volume, p. 68). Baber's research on women's sexualities provides a context for young women to challenge sexual scripts that may prevent them from acting assertively and developing sexual agency. Recognizing the diversity of women's sexual experiences and acknowledging the positive aspects of female sexuality support female sexual agency.

Walker (Chapter 4) deals with the fundamental issues of both connection and autonomy in relationships between mothers and daughters. Her research focuses on the dynamics of the relationships between adult daughters performing caretaking roles for their mothers. Walker's research on the relationships between caregiving daughters and their mothers brings to light an unrecognized dimension of these relationships; her descriptions of the reciprocity and caring in these relationships vitalize what too often has been regarded as a tedious task-focused burden that daughters shoulder. From her research we see and rejoice in the vitality of these relationships. We also see the recognition that both generations give to the importance of autonomy, with respect for each other and each other's autonomy being paramount in most cases. Walker's research, then, shows us very positive dimensions of a caregiving relationship that typically has been viewed as stressful and not particularly rewarding.

Allen's research on single older women brought to light the experiences of women who did not follow the normative course of marriage and motherhood. She asks: Why are these women so invisible, and why are they characterized by what they are *not*—"never-married, childless women"—rather than by what they are? Women who have followed this pathway have typically been ignored, and Allen's exploration of the richness and diversity of their lives gives insights into this pathway. This groundbreaking research has depicted the experiences of lifelong single women in an encompassing and positive way. We see the richness of the intimacy they experienced in a diversity of relationships, with both children and other adults, and the importance of their caretaking roles. We also see the value they placed on their autonomy and independence. Allen's research highlights the importance of moving beyond static conceptualizations of normative life course patterns to a recognition of the diversity of experiences and pathways in women's lives. Allen further notes that, to understand women's lives and family experiences more completely, we must question why certain topics—notably abuse and lesbianism—have, for the most part, been ignored in the field of family studies.

Rosemary Blieszner's (Chapter 6) research also is characterized by an interest in older women and men and their relationships, with a focus on friendships and other factors that influence well-being. Her own collaboration with a friend and colleague, Rebecca Adams, resulted in conceptualizations and research on friendship that benefitted from the blend of their sociological and developmental focus. As Blieszner notes, feminist perspectives have been applied only recently to the study of friendships, perhaps because friendship is likely to be viewed as a relationship between equals. Blieszner's body of research has resulted in the recognition of changes that may occur in friendships during the later stages of the life cycle, and the implications of these changes. Additionally her research points to the positive and unique aspects of friendship in later life, such as role continuity that friendships can provide during periods when other roles, such as spouse or worker, are being lost. Friendships play a very important role in providing a sense of connection to others.

The Role of Work in Close Relationships

The chapters in Part 2 focus on the effect of various aspects of work on close relationships, from the work done for pay to the work of maintaining a family. Marks's research on intimacy in the workplace provides glimpses into a fascinating dimension of women's lives. Research on people's employment typically has overlooked the day-to-day interactions between workers and the relationships that develop in the workplace environment. By delving into the intricacies of workplace intimacy, Marks provides an avenue for the voices of women workers to be heard. His explorations of the daily lives of these women provide glimpses into the mundane realities and supportiveness of women's wage work environments and the depth and complexities of their relationships with each other. Marks's research details a type of relationship that is an important source of support for many women: Workplaces, as he notes, often provide havens for women.

Marks's early research on workplace intimacy focused on dental offices, and the results indicated that self-disclosure on fairly intimate topics characterized relationships between coworkers; further, these coworker relationships appear to serve a restorative function in that individuals use these relationships to process and evaluate other significant occurrences in their lives. Marks concludes that producing intimacy is "part of the work that women do, part of the emotional service that women provide," (this volume, p. 158), and he emphasizes that we should acknowledge the significance of this emotional work for the lives of these women. Marks also studied women workers from an earlier time period, using data from the Hawthorne studies that were conducted between 1927 and 1932. Again focusing on the daily interactions between women coworkers, Marks found evidence of intimate disclosure, companionship, and caring among the Hawthorne women. It is truly amazing that no attention has been paid to this wealth of data for more than 50 years. Marks has reclaimed the lives of these women and, in doing so, has highlighted the havens at work that they experienced.

Perry-Jenkins's (Chapter 8) research on the division of household labor in families moves us from a focus on tallying how many tasks each person performs or how much time each person spends in household labor to the issue of the meanings and value that work holds for family members. Her research has focused on the meaning of the provider role and the implications of the meanings attached to this role for the amount of housework that husbands perform. Results from her studies suggest that the symbolic meanings attached to provider and homemaker roles have implications not only for the division of household labor, but also for the well-being of spouses. And the findings that young sons and their fathers have similar patterns of participation in household chores, as well as similar beliefs about appropriate gender roles, point to the importance of examining how children learn to construct gender. A common criticism of the family studies field and of much feminist research is the overreliance on traditional white, middle-class families. Perry-Jenkins's current research on women, children, and men in single-parent and two-parent working-class families adds a much-needed focus on other family contexts; the inclusion of children allows an examination of the realities of paid and nonpaid work for all family members.

Harley's research brings to light the interweaving of wage work and family work for African American women. Harley's approach as an historian provides a focus different from that of most of the other contributors. In her examination of African American women's wage and domestic work from the late 19th century through the 20th century, she emphasizes the dual impacts of white social and cultural expectations and black cultural values. Within the African American community, views about appropriate class and gender behaviors often conflicted with the economic realities of African American families. Harley depicts the stresses and strains of African American women during this time period as they tried to find an acceptable balance among the racist attitudes of the larger society, the gendered expectations and values within their own culture, and the economic needs of their families. One solution to these competing demands for many educated African American women was to view their employment in a caretaking framework, identifying themselves as mothers to the race.

The Experience of Violence in Close Relationships

The two chapters in Part 3 on physical abuse are clear examples of research for women that delves into the grim realities of violence against women in our society. Feminist critiques of the violence literature have emphasized the importance of examining the context and outcome of violent behaviors, highlighting the facts that women's aggressive acts are typically self-defense responses to male violence and that women's aggressive acts are much less likely to be lethal. Yllö and Emery and Lloyd in their chapters recognize and respond to the heated debates that have characterized research on family violence.

Probably the major controversy within the field centers on the extent and meaning of violence by women. Feminists are justifiably concerned that survey research findings that suggest women are just as violent as men have been taken out of context and misused. For this reason many feminists are wary of any attention given to violence by women, and research on this topic often is viewed as suspect. By focusing directly on violence by women, then, Emery and Lloyd took quite a risk as they tried to understand why women hit. As they note, however, their interest stemmed from their desire to examine the influence of the larger social context on violence in dating relationships. In particular they note the problems of viewing women as passive victims and argue that we must consider whether women's use of aggression may reflect an active response through efforts to regain a sense of control and balance in relationships. Asking young women why they hit had a very real impact on the respondents themselves. For most of these young women, talking with the researchers about the violence in their relationships was their first experience in talking openly about the abuse they had experienced. Participating in the research project was an empowering experience and resulted in pride that by telling their stories, these young women might be able to help others in abusive relationships.

Yllö points to the importance of recognizing both the societal and the academic contexts that tacitly condone the status quo by ignoring or downplaying women's lack of power, a major factor that allows violence against women to continue virtually unchecked. Yllö's groundbreaking research on violence against women has made major contributions in a number of respects. As noted earlier, Yllö's initial research on family violence was criticized because the quantitative methodology was viewed by some feminists as inherently patriarchal. However, by constructing an index that assessed the status of women and then ranking states based on the economic, political, educational, and legal status of women, Yllö was able to demonstrate that wife battering was high not only in states where women had low status but also in states where women's status was high relative to men's; this finding suggests that a backlash against women's achievements is played out in violence against women. She was one of the first researchers to examine marital rape, and the in-depth interviews with women who had been raped by their husbands showed the profound and long-lasting consequences of marital rape on the lives of women. Yllö's research career reflects her commitment to expanding our understanding of factors relating to violence against women and the very real implications of this violence for women's lives. Yllö also emphasizes the importance of recognizing the contributions of both researchers and activists for battered women to our understanding of violence against women and the need to integrate these perspectives in designing and providing services for abused women. Yllö's research journey, which is characterized consistently by her willingness to face controversial issues and her insistence that research on violence against women should be geared toward making a difference, demonstrates the impact that feminist perspectives can have on women's lives.

Future Directions

The feminist research perspectives of the contributors in this volume clearly have enhanced our knowledge about women and their experiences and about women and men and their close relationships. In pulling together this volume, however, we have become more clearly aware of important aspects of close relationships to which feminists have given little attention. We originally assumed we would include a chapter on children in families, although in all honesty neither of us knew of a particular body of work in this area. After extensive literature searches and contacts with our network of feminist researchers, we became convinced that gendered aspects of children's experiences in families have been glaringly overlooked by feminist researchers. Barrie Thorne (1987) notes that feminist perspectives have remained centered on adults and adult perspectives. She calls for feminist scholars to "re-vision children," focusing on issues of gender, autonomy, and relatedness. As changes occur in women's roles, in the relationships between women and men, and in parenting roles, we must not lose sight of the implications of these changes for children's lives, not only in terms of the messages they learn about being male and female in our society, but also in terms of children's needs and interests.

A second aspect we believe needs more serious attention in future feminist research is race, class, age, and sexual preference variations and the impact of the variations on experiences within families and close relationships. The many clarion calls by feminists and scholars in family studies for researchers to move beyond a narrow focus on white, middle-class samples and to broaden conceptualizations of what constitutes a family continue to be recognized more in theory than in fact. It is imperative that we study these variations. Certainly a number of researchers, including several whose work is described in this volume, have heeded the call for attention to diversity, but our knowledge is still sketchy.

A third aspect is that we must not lose sight of the reality that gender is constructed for *both* men and women. As feminists we must deal with the tension of believing it is disloyal to be concerned about men. The lives of women and men are intertwined in a number of ways and in many types of relationships—as lovers, friends, coworkers, and parents. Not all relationships between men and women are unequal. For many women their relationships with men are the most rewarding and important aspects of their lives. Because so many intimate relationships are between men and women, we must recognize the importance of viewing men's experiences of close relationships from a feminist vantage point. We must recognize that studying men's experiences does not necessarily invalidate women's experiences. And, finally, we must recognize the necessity of confronting this issue *now* and conveying the message that feminists do value all people.

Fourth, and perhaps most importantly, we believe that feminist research in family and close relationships must recognize and celebrate women's agency in their lives. We are concerned that far too often women are portrayed primarily as victims. Such a one-sided perspective clouds the reality that women are often active in constructing their lives. Certainly many of the contributors in this volume recognize the sense of agency in women's lives and use that frame to structure their research. The picture we get of women's lives, as revealed in this volume, shows movement toward synthesis in their various roles as they try new balances and compositions throughout their lives. And, most importantly, we get a sense of women who are not passive responders to life, but who are actively composing their lives. Further explorations of agency in women's lives will help move us beyond the view that women are responders to life, rather than active agents in creating their lives. We hope the lens of agency continues to gain status in research on women.

Continuing Journeys

As we conceptualized this book, one of the questions of most interest to us centered on the personal journeys of the authors through the research process. We specifically asked the contributors to provide a reflective view of their own process as they modified and built their programs of research to reflect feminist principles. For most of them, this was a challenging and difficult endeavor. At the same time, most described it as one of their most enriching and rewarding writing experiences. Too often, we find ourselves removed from our research as we try to maintain objectivity. Perhaps the most important lesson we can learn from these contributors who have shared their questions, their struggles, and their triumphs with us is the importance of integration in our lives. Being able to integrate our personal beliefs with the creation of knowledge and the recognition that our research can have real and positive impacts on the lives of women, men, and children helps sustain us as we continue to experience transformations as feminist scholars.

Drawing this book to a conclusion leads to reflections about our experiences in editing this volume. Keeping the journey image intact, what a long but enlightening and enriching trip it has been! Before embarking on this project, we had known each other for several years, having met at one of the annual conferences of the National Council on Family Relations. (We cannot remember if we first met at a session where we both were presenting papers or on a dance floor!) We continued to see each other at conferences, discovering similar research interests that centered on the impact of gender on various dimensions of relationships, including social support, the division of household labor, and self-disclosure and satisfaction in different types of intimate relationships. In addition to these commonalities, we simply clicked and had talked in general terms about collaborating on a project some day because we really wanted to work together. This was a case of a scholarly pursuit being inspired not only by scholarly aims but also by interpersonal motivations.

As we noted earlier, the idea for this book originated on a long train ride from Oxford to York. As we talked about our reactions to the papers presented at the conference on personal relationships, we noted the lack of feminist perspectives on close relationships, and so we discussed the idea of collaborating on a paper to be presented at the next conference. But as our discussion continued and we thought about the research being done by some of our colleagues as they incorporated feminist views into their perspectives on relationships, we became more excited about the idea of bringing together this work in a book. Not only would such a project allow us to work together on a topic dear to our hearts, but it also would provide a much-needed contribution to the fields of family studies and close relationships.

So we were excited about the book and looking forward to working together. At the same time, we experienced moments of doubt about this project that centered on our "correctness" as feminists. Did we have the appropriate feminist credentials to undertake such a project? We already have noted that we decided not to include our own work in the book because of our fears that we had not lived up to feminist standards in asking appropriate questions or in using appropriate methodology. We felt more confident that we could perform adequately as editors of a feminist volume, but not as contributors. Facing these doubts and talking about them together has made us very aware and appreciative of the courage demonstrated by the contributors in this volume as they evaluated their own work from feminist perspectives. We are all part of our texts, but as editors we were not forced to experience the difficulty and exhilaration of "reading ourselves into the text" (to use Katherine Allen's words) to the extent that the contributors were.

Another factor that contributed to our interest in bringing together feminist perspectives on families and close relationships centers on our concern about the discipline of family studies. As scholars in this field, we began our academic careers with idealistic views and a commitment to doing research that would make a difference in people's lives. We are convinced that only by recognizing the pervasive impact of gender on relationships, families, and the larger society can such differences be realized. Feminism clearly is influencing academic disciplines and the study of families and close relationships. But we continue to question and evaluate whether and how we are making a difference. It is easy to get comfortable in academic careers. Editing this volume, along with other life circumstances, has re-energized us for the vitally important work of application and activism.

One other life circumstance for us is that during the course of editing this book we each gave birth to our first child. Becoming mothers influenced the ways we thought about the questions that are important to ask and the imperativeness of an applied focus in research on families and close relationships. Obviously our lives have become more complex, and we are now much more conscious of how our time is spent and whether our efforts are worthwhile. As mothers of young children, our work, although an important part of our identities, is now competing with a new identity and with different responsibilities and demands. The questions we ask about our work and our lives have a different tenor; whether the work we do makes a difference has become more personal and more important. We both had sons, and thus we also are faced with the question of what it means as a feminist to raise a son. Perhaps Bateson (1989) best captures this complexity as she notes, "Women today, trying to compose lives that will honor all their commitments and still express all their potentials with a certain unitary grace, do not have an easy task" (p. 232).

In the concluding chapter of *Composing a Life,* however, Bateson states:

Perhaps what women have to offer in the world today, in which men and women both must learn to deal with a new order of complexity and rapid change, lies in the very rejection of forced choices: work or home, strength or vulnerability, caring or competition, trust or questioning. Truth may not be so simple. (p. 232)

We hope the various truths of women's and men's lives today and in the future will reflect, and more importantly, accept, this complexity. Challenging the existing order undoubtedly will guide the continuing journeys of feminist scholars.

References

Bateson, M. C. (1989). *Composing a life.* New York: Atlantic Monthly Press.

Cook, J. A., & Fonow, M. M. (1990). Knowledge and women's interests: Issues of epistemology and methodology in feminist sociological research. In J. M. Nielson (Ed.), *Feminist research methods* (pp. 69-93). Boulder, CO: Westview.

Peplau, L. A., & Conrad, E. (1989). Beyond nonsexist research: The perils of feminist methods in psychology. *Psychology of Women Quarterly, 13,* 379-400.

Thompson, L. (1992). Feminist methodology for family studies. *Journal of Marriage and the Family, 54,* 3-18.

Thorne, B. (1987). Re-visioning children. *Gender and Society, 1*(1), 85-109.

Westkott, M. (1979). Feminist criticism of the social sciences. *Harvard Educational Review, 49*(4), 422-430.

Author Index

Subject Index

About the Contributors

Katherine R. Allen is an Associate Professor of Family and Child Development at Virginia Polytechnic Institute and State University, Blacksburg. She is also a member of the Virginia Tech Women's Studies Advisory Board and teaching faculty. She received her Ph.D. in child and family studies, with a certificate in gerontology, from Syracuse University. She is active in the National Council on Family Relations and is writing a book about marriage and family diversity over the life course. She and her partner, Tamara Stone, are raising their two sons, Matthew and Zachary, in Blacksburg, Virginia.

Kristine M. Baber is a Professor in the Department of Family Studies at the University of New Hampshire, Durham, and a core faculty member in the Women's Studies Program. She received her Ph.D. in family studies from the University of Connecticut, Storrs. Her research and writing focus on issues related to fertility and reproduction, sexuality education, and the status of women. She is the author of a number of articles on these topics and the coauthor (with Katherine Allen) of *Women & Families: Feminist Reconstructions*. She and her husband, Bill, spend their leisure time hiking in the White Mountains and exploring the coast of Maine. She also enjoys gardening and reading mystery novels and poetry.

Rosemary Blieszner is a Professor in the Department of Family and Child Development and Associate Director of the Center for Gerontology at Virginia Polytechnic Institute and State University, Blacksburg. She received her Ph.D. from Pennsylvania State University, University Park, in human development and family studies. Her research focuses on friend and family relationships and life events in adulthood and old age, with an emphasis on the contributions of close relationships to personal development and psychological well-being. She is coauthor (with Rebecca Adams) of *Adult Friendship,* coeditor (with Victoria Bedford) of *Handbook of Aging and the Family,* and has published numerous articles in gerontology, family studies, and social psychology journals. With her husband, Steve Gerus, and children, Suzanne and Mark, she watches the changing tapestry of the seasons as reflected in the surrounding mountains of southwestern Virginia.

Beth C. Emery is an Associate Professor in the Department of Human Sciences at Middle Tennessee State University, Murfreesboro. She received her Ph.D. from Oregon State University, Corvallis, in family studies. Her research interests focus on physical and sexual aggression in dating relationships, interpersonal communication, conflict, and feminist methodology. She and her husband, Chuck, enjoy gardening, blues, and jazz.

Sharon Harley is Director and Associate Professor of the Afro-American Studies Program at the University of Maryland, College Park. She received her Ph.D. in United States history from Howard University, Washington, DC. She is the coeditor (with Rosalyn Terborg-Penn) of *Women in Africa and the African Diaspora* and of *Afro-American Women: Struggles and Images.* Her research focuses on the history of Black wage-earning women and Black women's organizational activities in the District of Columbia. She has received numerous scholarships and fellowships, including the Smithsonian Postdoctoral Fellowship and the Rockefeller Fellowship for Minority Group Scholars. She is a divorced mother raising an 8-year-old daughter with her ex-husband, her twin sister and her co-resident graduate students. She spends her leisure time playing tennis and skiing.

Leigh A. Leslie is an Associate Professor in the Department of Family Studies at the University of Maryland, College Park. She is also an Adjunct Faculty in women's studies. She received her Ph.D. from Pennsylvania State University, University Park, in individual and family studies.

She is a clinical member and approved supervisor of the American Association of Marriage and Family Therapists. Her research interests are in the areas of social support, division of labor, and the impact of gender and ethnicity on service delivery. She and her husband, Fred Curdts, find most of their free time consumed by their young son, Evan.

Sally A. Lloyd is a Professor in the Department of Family and Consumer Sciences and Associate Dean of Education and Allied Professions at Miami University, Oxford, OH. Her work has concentrated on the study of conflict and aggression in courtship and marriage. She is the coauthor (with Rodney Cate) of *Courtship.* Her husband, Andrew, is a chemist, and they have one son, Alexander.

Stephen R. Marks is a Professor in the Department of Sociology at the University of Maine, Orono, where he has taught since 1972. He received his Ph.D. from Boston University in 1971. He is the author of *Three Corners: Exploring Marriage and the Self.* His articles have appeared in the *American Journal of Sociology, American Sociological Review, Journal of Marriage and the Family,* and *Social Forces.* He remains most interested in the relationship between cultural frameworks and optimal human development. He and his wife, Joan, enjoy the Maine coast and cherish visits with their grown sons, Peter and Andrew.

Letitia Anne Peplau is a Professor in the Department of Psychology at the University of California, Los Angeles. where she has taught since 1973. After receiving her Ph.D. in Social Relations from Harvard University in 1973, she moved to UCLA as an Assistant Professor of Social Psychology. She has been active in the development of UCLA's Women's Studies Program and the Center for the Study of Women. She has coauthored (with Harold Kelley et al.) *Close Relationships,* (with Shelley Taylor and David Sears) *Social Psychology,* and (with Zick Rubin and Peter Salovey) *Psychology* and has coedited (with Dan Perlman) *Loneliness.* Anne shares her life with husband Steven Gordon, a sociologist, and son David Gordon, a soccer enthusiast.

Maureen Perry-Jenkins is an Assistant Professor of Family Studies in the Division of Human Development and Family Studies at the University of Illinois, Urbana-Champaign. She received her Ph.D. from Pennsylvania State University, University Park, in individual and family studies. Her current research interests focus on the division of labor and the way gender ideology affects the ways women and men assign value to family work and paid employment. She also continually explores these issues in her own family as she struggles to maintain a balance between work, her relationship with her husband Michael, and being a mother to her two sons, Chris and Scott.

Donna L. Sollie is a Professor in the Department of Family and Child Development at Auburn University, Auburn, AL, and the Director of the Women's Studies Program. She received her Ph.D. from the University of Tennessee in family studies. Her research interests focus on the influences of gender on close relationships, transitions during young adulthood, and friendships and social networks. She and her husband, Chuck, delight in sharing their lives with their young son, Ethan.

Alexis J. Walker is a Professor in the Department of Human Development and Family Sciences at Oregon State University, Corvallis, where she teaches Applied Research Methods; Gender and Family Relationships; U.S. Families: Gender, Race, and Class; and a writing-intensive, entry-level family studies course for graduate students. She received her Ph.D. from Pennsylvania State University, University Park, in family studies. She is writing a book about her research on the relationships between aging mothers and their caregiving daughters. Alexis lives in Portland, Oregon with her partner, Cindy Noble, a physician; their cats, Tom and Cora; and an expanding collection of feminist crime novels.

Kersti Yllö is the Dorothy Reed Williams Chair of Sociology and Department Chair at Wheaton College, Norton, MA. She received her Ph.D. from the University of New Hampshire, Durham, and has held Research Fellowships at UNH's Family Violence Research Program and at the Family Development Clinic at Boston Children's Hospital. Her publications on domestic violence include (with David Finkelhor) *License to Rape* and (with M. Bograd) *Feminist Perspectives on Wife Abuse*. She also works with her husband, Rich Schwertner, at an alternative school which they started a decade ago. Their son and daughter are grade school students there.